T0348069

# Gender, Race and Religion

*Gender, Race and Religion* brings together a selection of original papers published in *Ethnic and Racial Studies* that address the intersections between gender relations, race and religion in our contemporary environment. Chapters address both theoretical and empirical aspects of this phenomenon, and although written from the perspective of quite different national, social and political situations, they are linked by a common concern to analyse the interface between gender and other situated social relationships, from both a conceptual and a policy angle. These are issues that have been the subject of intense scholarly research and analysis in recent years, as well as forming part of public debates about the significance of gender, race and religion as sites of identity formation and mobilisation in our changing global environment. The substantive chapters bring together insights from both theoretical reflection and empirical research in order to investigate particular facets of these questions. *Gender, Race and Religion* addresses issues that are at the heart of contemporary scholarly debates in the field of race and ethnic studies, and engages with important questions in policy and public debates.

This book was originally published as a special issue of *Ethnic and Racial Studies*.

**Martin Bulmer** is Emeritus Professor of Sociology at the University of Surrey, UK. He retired in 2008, prior to which he was also Director of the ESRC Question Bank. He has edited the journal *Ethnic and Racial Studies* since 1993.

**John Solomos** is Professor of Sociology at City University London, UK. He has carried out extensive research on race, politics and social change and on theories of race and ethnicity. He is co-editor of *Ethnic and Racial Studies*.

## Ethnic and Racial Studies

Series editors: Martin Bulmer, *University of Surrey, UK*, and John Solomos, *City University London, UK*

The journal *Ethnic and Racial Studies* was founded in 1978 by John Stone to provide an international forum for high quality research on race, ethnicity, nationalism and ethnic conflict. At the time the study of race and ethnicity was still a relatively marginal sub-field of sociology, anthropology and political science. In the intervening period the journal has provided a space for the discussion of core theoretical issues, key developments and trends, and for the dissemination of the latest empirical research.

It is now the leading journal in its field and has helped to shape the development of scholarly research agendas. *Ethnic and Racial Studies* attracts submissions from scholars in a diverse range of countries, fields of scholarship and crosses disciplinary boundaries. It has moved from being a quarterly to being published monthly and it is now available in both printed and electronic form.

The Ethnic and Racial Studies book series contains a wide range of the journal's special issues. These special issues are an important contribution to the work of the journal, where leading social science academics bring together articles on specific themes and issues that are linked to the broad intellectual concerns of *Ethnic and Racial Studies*. The series editors work closely with the guest editors of the special issues to ensure that they meet the highest quality standards possible. Through publishing these special issues as a series of books, we hope to allow a wider audience of both scholars and students from across the social sciences to engage with the work of *Ethnic and Racial Studies*.

## Other titles in the series include:

**The Transnational Political Participation of Immigrants**
*Edited by Jean-Michel Lafleur and Marco Martiniello*

**Anthropology of Migration and Multiculturalism**
*Edited by Steven Vertovec*

# Gender, Race and Religion
## Intersections and Challenges

*Edited by*
## Martin Bulmer and John Solomos

Routledge
Taylor & Francis Group

LONDON AND NEW YORK

ETHNIC
◄ AND ►
RACIAL
STUDIES

First published 2012
by Routledge
2 Park Square, Milton Park, Abingdon, Oxon, OX14 4RN

Simultaneously published in the USA and Canada
by Routledge
711 Third Avenue, New York, NY 10017

*Routledge is an imprint of the Taylor & Francis Group, an informa business*

ISBN13: 978-0-415-68632-7

Typeset in Times New Roman
by Taylor & Francis Books

**Disclaimer**
The publisher would like to make readers aware that the chapters in this book are referred to as
articles as they had been in the special issue. The publisher accepts responsibility for any
inconsistencies that may have arisen in the course of preparing this volume for print.

# Contents

# CONTENTS

# Notes on contributors

**Stephanie Crist** is a doctoral student in the Sociology Department at Syracuse University, USA.

**Cileine de Lourenço** is Associate Professor in the Department of Literary and Cultural Studies, Bryant University, USA.

**Claudia Diehl** is Junior Professor of Migration and Ethnicity in the Department of Sociology at University of Göttingen, Germany.

**Zareena A. Grewal** is Assistant Professor in American Studies and Religious Studies at Yale University, USA. She is an historical anthropologist who works on the intersections of race and religion for Muslim Americans. She also directed By the Dawn's Early Light: Chris Jackson's Journey to Islam, a film featured on the Documentary Channel which examines the hyper-scrutiny of Muslim patriotism.

**Matthias Koenig** is Professor of Sociology of Religion in the Department of Sociology at University of Göttingen, Germany.

**Anna Korteweg** is Assistant Professor of Sociology at the University of Toronto, Canada.

**Amy Lutz** is an Assistant Professor of Sociology at Syracuse University, USA.

**Uvanney Maylor** is Senior Research Fellow at the Institute for Policy Studies in Education at London Metropolitan University, UK.

**Judith McDonnell** is Associate Professor in the Department of History and Social Science, Bryant University, USA.

**Kerstin Ruckdeschel** is a Researcher at the Federal Institute for Population Research, Wiesbaden, Germany.

**Sawitri Suharso** is Professor of Intercultural Management in the School of Management and Governance at the University of Twente and in the Department of Sociology at VU University, The Netherlands.

**Gabriela Sandoval** is Assistant Professor of Sociology at the University of California Santa Cruz, USA.

**Johannes M. Smit** is a Professor in Survey Methodology in the Department of Sociology at VU University Amsterdam and in the Department of Psychiatry at VU Medical Center in Amsterdam, The Netherlands.

**Anton J.L.M. van Balkom** is a Professor in the Department of Psychiatry at VU University and works as a Clinician at VU Medical Center in Amsterdam, The Netherlands.

**Diana van Bergen** is a PhD candidate in the Department of Sociology at VU University Amsterdam, The Netherlands.

**Gökçe Yurdakul** is Lecturer in Sociology at Trinity College, Dublin. She was Post-Doctoral Fellow in the Berlin Program for Advanced German and European Studies at the Freie Universität in 2008-2009.

# Introduction

# Gender, race and religion: intersections and challenges

Martin Bulmer and John Solomos

In this edited collection we have brought together a selection of research based chapters that address the intersections between gender relations, race and religion in our contemporary environment. All the chapters were included in a themed issue of *Ethnic and Racial Studies* and they reflect trends in contemporary scholarship and research on these issues. Although written from the perspective of quite different national social and political situations, they are linked by a common concern to analyse from both a conceptual and a policy angle the interface between gender and other situated social relationships.

## Intersections of race, gender and religion

Over the past two decades we have seen a growing and diverse range of scholarship and research on the role of gender in the shaping of race and ethnic relations in contemporary societies. Much of this has been reflected in the pages of *Ethnic and Racial Studies*, where we have been able to highlight some of the most important trends on these issues over the years. In particular we have been able to publish both theoretical and empirical contributions on the intersections between gender and whiteness, nation and gender and related issues (Ferber, 1998; Yuval-Davis, 1993; Twine, 2006; Collins, 2001). Indeed over the past two decades or so the journal has done much to foster more debate on the intersections between race and gender, and to publish articles that address these issues together. More recently there has also been a more sustained scholarly debate about the intersections between gender and religion in complex multicultural societies.

As with all edited collections there is no assumption that the various authors included here speak with one voice. Rather we bring them together as a way to highlight the diverse conceptual and methodological challenges that need to be addressed when we explore the complexities of how race and ethnicity intersect with other social relations.

## Structure of the book

The issue of the intersectionalies between gender, race and religion is highlighted in the first chapter by Anna Korteweg and Gökçe Yurdakul, which takes up the issue of how we can make sense of the phenomenon of honour killing in the Netherlands and Germany. This is a phenomenon that has attracted attention in academic and public discourses in both countries and has led to intense debate within academic and public policy circles (Buruma, 2006; Wikan, 2008). Korteweg and Yurdakul's account represents a critical attempt to provide some insight into the complex range of processes that shape the question of honour killing and the social and political responses to this phenomenon.

The following two chapters look at the intersections of race, racialization and gender in two rather different social environments. The chapter by Judith McDonnell and Cileine de Lourenço draws on interviews with immigrant women from Brazil living in the Boston area to explore their experiences of race, gender and ethnicity. The thirty face-to-face interviews on which this chapter draws are a valuable empirically focused account of the interplay between race, ethnicity and gender in the construction of racialized and national identities. They also help to highlight the often complicated ways in which ideas of race and gender intersect in shaping patterns of racialization. The chapter by Gabriela Sandoval concerns itself with the ways in which tobacco production in the Dominican Republic is deeply imbued by the racialized and gendered structures that have developed over the history of the republic. Sandoval's chapter is concerned on the surface with the production of cigars to be consumed as a commodity: an industry with a long history in the Dominican Republic. She argues forcefully, however, that it is important to move beyond appearances and explore the 'significance of racial, political and gendered symbolism that is inscribed into tobacco'.

The interplay between religion and discourses of gender equality is the focus of the next chapter by Claudia Diehl, Matthias Koenig and Kerstin Ruckdeschel. Utilizing research in Germany among Turkish migrants and majority Germans, the authors seek to explore the ways in which religiosity both shapes and is in turn shaped by questions of gender and ethnicity. Diehl et al.'s account suggests that attitudes to gender equality among both immigrant minorities and majority populations cannot be read through the lens of religion in any simple fashion. Rather they suggest that attitudes to gender equality need to be seen as the product of intersections between individual religiosity and wider social and cultural transformations.

Following on from this account is the chapter by Diana van Bergen et al. on the role of suicidal behaviour among young immigrant women in the Netherlands. This is an issue that has attracted some attention in public policy debates and in the popular media over the years in a number of European countries. Drawing on detailed research involving 115 case studies of South Asian, Turkish and Moroccan young women, the authors explore the ways in which questions of family, religion and culture are interlinked with wider social processes in shaping patterns of suicidal behaviour. In exploring this issue the chapter also goes on to suggest that there is a need to rethink Durkheim's classic account of 'fatalistic suicide' in today's social and cultural environment.

The next chapter by Zareena A. Grewal focuses on research in North American mosques that serve communities from Arab and South Asian backgrounds. Grewal's account provides a nuanced insight into the ways in which colour, race and class play an important role in choice of marriage partner among Muslim Americans. Contrasting the attitudes of parents and their children, the chapter suggests that questions of colour and race are experienced differently across the generations and that in specific contexts religion may provide a space for negotiating conflicting visions of the ideal marriage partner.

The chapter by Amy Lutz and Stephanie Crist has a somewhat different focus, analysing the issue of bilingualism among the children of Latino/a immigrants to the United States. Drawing on detailed empirical research about both boys and girls, Lutz and Crist set out to explore the ways in which family relations, gender and language intersect to shape the differential educational performance of Latino/a children.

The final chapter in this volume is by Uvanney Maylor and it focuses specifically on the ways in which constructions of the idea of blackness are made and re-made in specific work and social environments. Maylor's account draws on original research in an educational environment to explore how black is a social construction that is imbued with specific meanings as a result of the ways in which racial identities and politics are inscribed with meaning through both individual and collective experiences.

Taken together the eight chapters we have included in this volume provide important insights into the complex intersections of gender, race and religion in contemporary multicultural societies. They also suggest that there is a need for more sustained conceptual and empirical research in this field.

## References

BURMA, I. 2006 *Murder in Amsterdam: The Death of Theo Van Gogh and the Limits of Tolerance.* London: Atlantic Books.

COLLINS, P.H. 2001 'Like One of the Family: Race, Ethnicity and the Paradox of US National Identity', *Ethnic and Racial Studies*, vol. 24, no. 1, pp. 3–28.

FERBER, A.L. 1998 'Constructing Whiteness: The Intersections of Race and Gender in US White Supremacist Discourse', *Ethnic and Racial Studies*, vol. 21, no. 1, pp. 48–43.

TWINE, F.W. 2006 'Visual Ethnography and Racial Theory: Family Photographs as Archives of Interracial Intimacies', *Ethnic and Racial Studies*, vol. 29, no. 3, pp. 487–511.

WIKAN, U. 2008 *In Honor of Fadime: Murder and Shame*. Chicago: University of Chicago Press

YUVAL-DAVIS, N. 1993 'Gender and Nation', *Ethnic and Racial Studies*, vol. 16, no. 4, pp. 621–32.

# Islam, gender, and immigrant integration: boundary drawing in discourses on honour killing in the Netherlands and Germany

Anna Korteweg and Gökçe Yurdakul

**Abstract**

Public discourse on Muslim immigrant integration in Europe is increasingly framed around the presumed incompatibility of Islam and Western values. To understand how such framing constructs boundaries between immigrants and majority society in the media, we analyse newspaper discussions of honour killing in the Netherlands and Germany. These debates reinforce existing bright boundaries, or a strong sense of us versus them, between immigrants from Muslim and/or Turkish backgrounds and the majority population. Limited elements of boundary blurring are also present. We extend existing theory by showing that these boundaries are inscribed in the intersection of ethnicity, national origin, religion and gender.

In 2005, public debate on family violence among Muslim immigrants, especially honour killing, intensified in the Netherlands and Germany. In the Netherlands, such debates ignited after the murder of Theo van Gogh, whose film *Submission* criticized violence against women in Muslim societies. After his murder, an ongoing political debate on the incidence of domestic violence in the Netherlands came to intersect with a debate on the position of Muslims in Dutch society. In Germany, a similar set of questions came to focus on the issue of honour killing after the brutal murder of 23-year-old Hatun Sürücü by her brother at a Berlin bus stop (Ewing 2008).

In this article, we treat newspaper discussions of honour killing as a site in which boundaries between immigrants and majority society in the Netherlands and Germany are drawn. Boundaries create a sense of 'they are not like us because ... ', or a strong sense of us versus 'not us', capturing the social or cultural distance between immigrant and majority society (Zolberg and Long 1999, p. 8; Alba 2005, p. 22–3). Whether boundaries are 'bright' or 'blurred' has implications for the kinds of immigrant integration that are possible. Bright boundaries imply that society is structured around a sharp 'distinction between insiders and outsiders' so that individual members of minority groups (but not groups in their entirety) can cross into majority society only if they give up part of their group identity and adopt some of the practices of majority society (Zolberg and Long 1999, p. 8; Alba 2005). By contrast, blurred boundaries imply tolerance for various forms of difference and for multiple memberships in different groups so that, for example, an immigrant group can be considered Muslim and Dutch. Blurring bright boundaries entails a change in the dominant perception of immigrants as dramatically different from majority society (Alba 2005).

In the literature, boundaries are seen as cultural (Zolberg and Long 1999) or ethnic, rooted in part in Weber's 'subjective belief in common descent' (in Alba 2005, pp. 22–3). Boundaries are analysed in the divergent domains of language, religion, citizenship, and race, tracing how collective identity and notions of difference are shaped through various institutions. We focus on one such institution, the media. In our analysis, we treat boundaries as cultural, defining culture as providing shared meaning through which to articulate belonging to social groups. The boundaries between Muslims and majority society in European immigration countries are generally bright (Zolberg and Long 1999; Alba 2005). An analysis of honour killing, which in media discourse is treated as an extreme example of the differences between Muslims and majority society, allows us to show; a) which *elements* of culture are mobilized in the drawing of boundaries; b) that such boundaries can be blurred; and c) the implications of these processes for immigrant integration. We find that in this case cultural differences are articulated in reference to ethnicity, national origin, religion, and gender, requiring an intersectional analysis to illustrate how these elements interact in drawing bright or blurred boundaries.

## Extending theories of boundary formation

The focus on boundaries between immigrants and majority society comes out of a renewed interest in the concept of assimilation (Alba and Nee 1997, 2003; deWind and Kasinitz 1997; Brubaker 2001; Joppke and Morawska 2003). In the contemporary era many immigrants eventually integrate into their host societies while retaining some aspect of their (group) identity. This empirical reality has generated a shift in the definition of assimilation from the old-school assumption and even normative goal of complete absorption into majority society to one in which assimilation is achieved when (perceived) differences no longer have an impact on life chances (Alba and Nee 2003; Alba 2005; see also Brubaker 2001).

In theories of boundary formation different integration or assimilation trajectories are associated with three 'distinct patterns of negotiation between newcomers and hosts': crossing, blurring, and shifting (Zolberg and Long 1999, p. 8; see also Bauböck 1994; Alba and Nee 2003; Alba 2005). Boundary crossing and boundary blurring are particularly relevant here. *Boundary crossing* coincides with bright boundaries – only individuals can cross such boundaries, and crossing entails the adoption of majority society attributes, practices or values (Zolberg and Long 1999; Alba and Nee 2003; Alba 2005). In addition, crossing does not affect the boundary itself; if anything, crossing affirms the existence of the boundary. In the extreme, bright boundaries do not allow for group incorporation with retention of group identity markers, and assimilation is associated with giving up important aspects of immigrant culture. *Boundary blurring* is indicated by immigrants' ability to cross as a group into majority society without relinquishing distinct aspects of their identity. Simultaneously, the majority society changes its legal, social, and cultural institutions to enable multiple memberships and the participation of immigrants (Zolberg and Long 1999, p. 8).

Boundaries have strong cultural components and it is culture that concerns us here (see also Lamont and Molnar 2002; Alba and Nee 2003). In boundary theory, the term culture refers to everything from ethnic food and leisure activities (Alba and Nee 2003) to 'fundamental beliefs and ideas regarding existence' (Zolberg and Long 1999, p. 8). We use the term to denote shared meaning involving the imputed norms, values and traditions of a perceived group.

In the European context, dominant understandings of Islam inform the drawing of bright boundaries between Muslim immigrants and majority society (Zolberg and Long 1999; Alba 2005). Yet, oftentimes it is not Islam in general but gender inequalities attributed to Islam that are the basis for drawing these bright boundaries (see Norris and Inglehart 2002; Razack 2004). Hence we argue that we need to unpack which sources of meaning are mobilized in processes of boundary formation.

To understand the linkages between cultural elements deployed in boundary formation, we use intersectional theory, which sees markers of difference that inform the production of meaning, such as race, class, or gender as mutually constituted, with each given meaning through the others (Yuval-Davis 1997; Glenn 1999). We argue below that in discussions of honour killing ethnicity, national origin, religion, and gender are the relevant differences and that the ways they intersect to exclude immigrants from majority society is understudied.

Making these cultural sources of meaning and their intersections explicit advances the concept of boundaries in two ways. First, it brings the interacting effects of ethnicity, national origin, religion, and gender's cultural dimensions to the foreground in the process of boundary formation. Here, we build on work arguing that ethnicity and national origin intersect to create ethnonational identities but find that religion and gender play a similar role (Fenton and May 2002; see also Brubaker 2004). Second, this analysis lets us draw some tentative empirical conclusions about the kind of integration (or assimilation) that is possible for immigrants from predominantly Muslim countries in Western European countries.

**Immigrant integration in the Netherlands and Germany**

Immigrants from predominantly Muslim countries entered the Netherlands and Germany as guest workers starting in the 1960s, with current immigration resulting mainly from family reunification and marriage. These immigrants now make up an estimated 4.5 per cent of the total population in the Netherlands and, depending on the source, 3.8 to 4.2 per cent in Germany (Forum 2008). They lag behind majority society socio-economically. For example, between 1996 and 2006, non-Western immigrants were 3.5 times more likely than non-immigrant Dutch to be unemployed (*Jaarrapport Integratie* 2007, p. 139). In 2006, the unemployment rate for Turkish immigrants in Germany was 31.4 per cent and approximately 10 per cent for Germans (Bundesagentur für Arbeit 2007).

Historically, the Netherlands and Germany approached the integration of immigrants in different ways. Starting in the early twentieth century, the Dutch approached confessional political conflict through 'pillarization', or the institutionalized recognition of different forms of Christianity through the establishment of Protestant and Catholic schools, political parties, and social welfare organizations. Large-scale immigration from Muslim countries led the Dutch government to establish a Muslim pillar, thus marking immigrants from predominantly Muslim countries by their religion as well as their national origin (Entzinger 2003; Koopmans et al. 2005). However, in recent years, Dutch multiculturalism has been challenged by a new emphasis on cultural integration through mandatory language classes and integration exams even for long-term immigrants (Entzinger 2003, 2006; Korteweg 2005).

In Germany, religious discourse is often masked by discussions of 'cultural competence' and national differences between Turks and Germans. This also fits with historical understandings of citizenship, which root belonging in an ethnic conceptualization of nationhood (Brubaker 1992; Koopmans *et al.* 2005). At the same time, a more multicultural approach to immigration developed in the 1990s with the rise of the Red–Green coalition of the social-democrats and the Green Party. The implication of these different national trajectories is that boundaries might be drawn differently, with religion more influential in the Netherlands and ethnic understandings more prevalent in Germany.

## Violence against women, honour killing, and boundary formation

Discussions of gender also mark Muslim immigrants as different from majority society in both countries with violence against women in Muslim immigrant families – in its most extreme form honour killing – cast as impeding immigrant women's integration in both societies. In the Netherlands, reports show that domestic violence is even more prevalent in immigrant communities than in non-immigrant ones (*Privé Geweld, Publieke Zaak* 2002; Commissie Blok 2004; TransAct 2005). Similarly, in Germany, recent research has shown that while violence against women is an issue for all women in Germany, immigrant women, particularly Turkish women, suffer disproportionately (*Bundesministerium für Familie, Senioren, Frauen und Jugend* 2004).

In the literature and public debate, honour killing is a particular response to the sense that a woman or girl has violated her family's honour, usually because of perceptions of sexual impropriety (Sev'er and Yurdakul 2001; Van Eck 2003; Mojab 2004). Men are obligated to guard their family honour and honour killings are planned by family councils. Many scholars argue that honour killing is an outcome of patriarchy rather than Islam (Pitt-Rivers 1974; Mojab 2004; Kvinnoforum 2005, p. 16). In this context, patriarchy is a form of rule through kin relations in which family and society closely overlap, and in which family is stratified according to gender and age (Kandiyoti 1988). At the same time, contemporary economic and social forces, including the migration experience, also shape the guarding of women's honour (Maris and Saharso 2001; Abu-Lughod 2002; Kogacioglu 2004; Warrick 2005).

In European debate, discussions of honour killing become sites in which different cultural elements associated with drawing boundaries between immigrants and majority society can be analysed. Discussions of honour killing brighten boundaries insofar as they enable the voicing of concerns about Muslim immigrants that in other contexts might be construed as anti-religious, ethnocentric or racist, while a focus on similarities between immigrant and majority society offers opportunities for boundary blurring (see also Abu-Lughod 2002; Razack 2004).

## Methodology

We analyse newspaper articles that discuss honour killing, including news, background pieces, and op-eds, in three Dutch and three German newspapers. We use newspapers, not because they give an unmediated reflection of general public debate, but because they are one of the loci from which discursive strategies that influence such debate are drawn (Gamson and Modigliani 1989).

In each country, we focus on three nationally distributed quality newspapers that reflect the political spectrum. In the Netherlands, we selected *De Volkskrant, NRC,* and *Trouw.* In the German case, we focus on *die Tageszeitung [TAZ]*, the *Süddeutsche Zeitung [SZ]* and the *Frankfurter Allgemeine Zeitung [FAZ]*. We chose quality newspapers because this is where the discussions of honour killing took place. A search of popular publications netted very few in-depth discussions (see Koopmans *et al.* 2005, p. 27 for a similar finding). Moreover, by using newspapers that span the political spectrum in both countries, we ensure that our comparative conclusions are not the result of the political outlook of a given newspaper.

We selected articles that discuss honour killing by searching for the term 'Ehre' or 'Ehrenmorde' (honour and honour killing) or 'eerwraak' (literally 'honour revenge', which covers both honour killing and honour-related violence) in either the title or the body of the text. From these, we selected those dealing with honour killing as it occurs in the Netherlands or Germany (see Table 1).

Our qualitative analysis looked at which underlying ideas about differences are mobilized in dominant discourses about immigrants in the reporting on honour killing. In our initial coding of the newspapers, we asked how honour killing was defined. Guided by the literature on boundaries and the categories that emerged after multiple

**Table 1.** *Distribution of articles dealing with honour killing for three Dutch and three German newspapers in the year 2005*

| Dutch newspapers | | German newspapers | |
|---|---|---|---|
| *Volkskrant* | 33 | *TAZ* | 36 |
| *NRC* | 30 | *SZ* | 17 |
| *Trouw* | 38 | *FAZ* | 15 |
| Totals | 101 | | 68 |

rounds of coding, we identified a discourse as reinforcing bright boundaries if honour killing is portrayed in ways that highlight differences between immigrant and majority society. We identified discourses as containing elements of boundary blurring when they emphasize similarities between immigrant and majority society. A given article may contain both bright and blurring discourses depending on who it gives voice to.

In presenting our evidence, we use quotes that exemplify the ways in which bright boundaries are established or in which those boundaries show the possibility of blurring. We emphasized quotes by immigrants, cited by others or writing themselves, because their positioning in the discussions further illuminates how boundaries between immigrant and majority society are established.

**Drawing boundaries: honour killing in the Netherlands**

In the Netherlands, we saw evidence for both bright and blurred boundary drawing, though in each of the three newspapers, bright boundaries dominated. Articles containing elements of boundary blurring are a smaller proportion of the articles in each newspaper and in our overall sample (see Table 2).[1] In both cases, we found definitions of honour killing as a Muslim practice, as one informed by ethnicity and national origin, and/or as a form of violence against women. However, these references to religion ethnicity, national origin, and gender intersect differently depending on whether boundaries are bright or blurred, indicating different integration trajectories.

*Drawing bright boundaries*

In 53 out of 86 articles that drew boundaries, honour killing was discussed in ways that solely evoke bright boundaries. Two influential Dutch women of Muslim origin, writer, columnist, and translator Nahed Selim, and writer and politician Ayaan Hirsi Ali, give examples of how such bright boundaries between Muslims and non-immigrant Dutch are drawn in the intersection of ethnicity, national origin, religion and gender.

**Table 2.** *Bright and blurred boundaries in Dutch newspapers*

|  | Bright | Blurred | Both | Totals |
|---|---|---|---|---|
| *Volkskrant* | 16 | 8 | 6 | 30 |
| *NRC* | 18 | 3 | 4 | 25 |
| *Trouw* | 19 | 7 | 5 | 31 |
| Totals | 53 | 18 | 15 | 86 |

Selim, who immigrated to the Netherlands from Egypt in the early 1980s, considers herself religious but not orthodox. She describes the Muslim community in the Netherlands as dramatically different from Dutch society, referring to several forms of gendered violence often cited in the newspaper articles as evidence for this difference:

The largest segment of Muslim youth in the Netherlands receives a traditional education from their illiterate, ignorant parents that combines the worst of Islam (discrimination against women, homosexuals, atheists and Jews) with the traditions from the oppressed and undeveloped regions of origin (forced marriages, abuse of women and children, circumcision, honour killing, etc.). The second and third generation of Muslims regard this mixture of religion and tradition from their parents' countries of origin – where they themselves would of course never want to live – as their identity, something elevated above western norms and values.... Dutch society encourages this "own identity" by facilitating and subsidizing the establishment of mosques, Islamic foundations, organizations, and schools – in effect creating an anti-integration policy. (*Trouw*, 19 February 2005)

Selim attributes gender inequality to Islam and gendered violence to national origin or ethnicity, using honour killing as an example of the particular form violence against women takes. Thus, ethnicity, national origin, religion and gender intersect to segregate Muslims from Dutch society and its 'western norms and values'. Selim then argues that Dutch society is complicit in this segregation because multicultural policies reinforce the ways in which this particular blend of ethnicity, national origin, religion and gender shapes Muslims' identity (see also Okin 1999).

Where Selim situates honour killing in tradition and gender inequality in Islam, Ayaan Hirsi Ali connects both honour killing and gender inequality to Islam:

Honour killing is a component of something bigger. It has to do with sexual morality within Islam, the desire to control women's sexuality.... A woman who does not abide by the rules is allowed to be expelled [from the community], hit, murdered. (*Volkskrant* 2 February 2005)

In this interview, Hirsi Ali recounts her proposal to label honour killings acts of terrorism and to hold entire families, not only individual perpetrators, accountable. She links this to her opposition to Islamic schools because through them, 'We raise a cohort of children who have been born here but who have an understanding of the relationship between men and women between their ears that we in the Netherlands do not condone' (*Volkskrant* 2 February 2005). For Hirsi Ali, honour killing indicates that the relationship between Islam and gender inequality makes it impossible for orthodox Muslims to integrate into Dutch society. These Muslims' values are diametrically opposed to those shared by 'we in the Netherlands', a we that Hirsi Ali places herself amongst.[2]

Such analyses of the link between honour killing as a form of violence against women and Islam lead right-wing politicians like Marco Pastors of Leefbaar Rotterdam (Liveable Rotterdam)[3] to argue that 'change should *not* come from both sides' when it comes to the integration of Muslims into Dutch society (*NRC*, 19 February 2005, emphasis added). Rather, Muslims should adopt the values of Dutch society, which he defines as based in 'Judeo-Christian humanist norms and values ... that's who we are' (ibid.).

In such accounts Islam has few positive attributes and people affiliated with traditional forms of Islam are positioned as sharply different from Dutch society, particularly in the impact that their religion has on gender relations, an impact further reinforced by 'traditional' practices associated with national origin and ethnicity. Such discourses inscribe a divide between immigrants and majority society that can be crossed but not blurred.

## *Elements of boundary blurring*

Eighteen out of 86 articles gave a sense that the bright boundary we describe above could be blurred (with another 15 articles containing elements both of bright and blurred boundary drawing, see Table 2). A number of these articles discuss feminist organizing among secular and religious women from Muslim backgrounds in the Netherlands, presenting an image of immigrant women not as victims of their religion, ethnicity or national origin, but as claiming full membership in their immigrant group while also questioning practices within the group.

For example, columnist Nazmiye Oral, whose parents moved from Turkey to the Netherlands before she was born, describes in her column a gathering she attended where a diverse group of women from Turkish descent discussed the phenomenon of honour killing. 'The room was filled with girls and women, with and without headscarf, who all shared the same desire: "Violence against us women has to stop"' (*Volkskrant*, 21 June 2005). Based on the ensuing discussion, Oral argues:

> The vast majority of Turks do not need to be convinced that murder is no solution for salvaging family honour.... [but] there is no

answer to the question this leaves: what is the definition of *namus* (honour)? The woman plays an important part in this. She has to release the man of the heavy responsibility of being the guardian of her honour by taking that responsibility back. (*Volkskrant*, 21 June 2005)

While Oral acknowledges that honour killing is a severe form of violence against women, she also positions women in the larger Turkish community as capable of addressing this issue, undermining images of immigrant or Muslim women as victimized and in need of rescue, images that reinforce bright boundaries between immigrants and majority society (see also Ahmed 1992; Abu-Lughod 2002). Oral shows that women representing a range of religious observances (i.e. some wearing a headscarf) who also can be identified by their national origin as Turks do not accept that violence against women is inherent in their religion or national identity.

Oral also argues that norms and values often claimed to lie only on the Dutch side of the divide between immigrants and Dutch society are already shared: 'Freedom and the right to self determination are a universal human need that cannot be claimed by anybody. It is not western. It is human' (*Volkskrant*, 21 June 2005). Such discussions offer resources that can change dominant perceptions of immigrants, particularly of immigrant women, a key element of boundary blurring. First, Oral exemplifies the possibility of membership in multiple communities. Second, appeals to universal human rights position immigrant women as different in some but not all respects from women in Dutch society, transcending identification based solely on religion or nationality.

However, this is only one side of the story. Oral argues that the process of addressing violence against women is happening 'organically' in Turkey where there have been dramatic changes to the law pertaining to honour killing since 2004. In the Netherlands such change is 'infected with the label westernization. Every little piece of freedom means ... betraying ones own tradition and abandoning the identity of the group or origin' (*Volkskrant*, 21 June 2005). Here, Oral shows how the possibilities for boundary blurring are limited by the existing bright boundary. The discussions she reports on are weighted down by the negative portrayals of religion (Islam) and nationality (Turkishness) that is reflected in much of the debate on honour killing in the Netherlands and that make any recommendation by members of Turkish communities to alter its traditions suspect.

Another indication of boundary blurring comes from Geert Mak, a social historian whose works are widely read. Mak argues that the parliamentary debate on honour killing instigated by Hirsi Ali is about confirming the superiority of Dutch norms and values while avoiding a true encounter between the new and the old Dutch citizens. In other words, such debates reinscribe existing bright boundaries. In a long piece on the state of integration in the Netherlands, Mak argues,

> Words have enormous power, but how are we doing on action? It's striking how this government ... speaks with two tongues. On the one hand, strong language about honour killing, arranged marriages, violence against women and other excesses that are linked to Islam. On the other hand, the current policy has little to no support for the (women's) groups who form the front line in this battle. (*NRC*, 14 May 2005)

Mak directly critiques the framing of violence against women as a Muslim problem while claiming that a number of women's organizations involving women from Moroccan or Turkish descent have had their subsidies cut. From his perspective, Dutch policy makers actively *prevent* the emancipation of women from an immigrant background. He argues that this shows that these debates serve to create an 'image of the enemy' (ibid.), the enemy being Muslim immigrants.

Such accounts outline how boundary blurring might take place by addressing the need for change on the majority side of the boundary. By positioning Muslim women as capable of altering violence against women within their communities, they also decouple the link between gender inequality and Islam and/or national origin and give less starkly different meanings to immigrant identity. This implies the possibility for integration with retention of a (fluid) immigrant collective identity. However, as Table 2 shows, the elements of boundary blurring represented by Oral and Mak do not dominate in the Dutch debate.

### Drawing boundaries: honour killing in Germany

In Germany bright boundary drawing also dominates, though less than in the Netherlands (see Table 3). This is largely due to the overrepresentation of boundary-blurring articles in the *TAZ*, which represents left-wing discourses influenced by the German Green Party and its multicultural politics. As Table 3 shows, though, the *TAZ*'s approach to immigrant portrayals does not extend to the other newspapers which were less likely than the equivalent Dutch newspapers to contain elements of boundary blurring. As in the Dutch case, ethnicity, national origin, religion and gender are mobilized in both kinds of boundary drawing in ways that also indicate particular integration trajectories.

**Table 3.** *Bright and blurred boundaries in German newspapers*

|        | Bright | Blurred | Both | Totals |
|--------|--------|---------|------|--------|
| *TAZ*  | 5      | 17      | 2    | 24     |
| *SZ*   | 12     | 4       | 1    | 17     |
| *FAZ*  | 12     | 2       | 1    | 15     |
| Totals | 29     | 23      | 4    | 56     |

## Drawing bright boundaries

Twenty-nine out of 56 articles in German newspapers solely drew bright boundaries. In the German context, we would expect that bright boundaries are mostly drawn through references to immigrants' ethnonational origins and traditions, where ethnicity is imputed from membership in a particular national group, rather than their religious affiliation (Kastoryano 2002; Koopmans 2005 *et al.*; Yurdakul 2006). Indeed, *FAZ* writer Mark Siemons explicitly argues that 'Islam cannot be made responsible here ... it is actually the culture, which is so murderous' (*FAZ*, 3 March 2005), something Muslim clerics agree with (*TAZ*, 22 February 2005; *TAZ*, 11 April 2005). Likewise, an article discussing reports that some high school students had cheered Sürücü's murder states: 'Evidently, ... the youth of Turkish or Arab origin had the view: the woman behaved like a German – it was her own fault. Hatun Sürücü was a German woman and wanted to live like a German, namely emancipated, free, Western' (*TAZ*, 22 February 2005). This description inscribes a bright boundary by juxtaposing 'Turkish or Arab origin' with the 'emancipated, free, Western', in short German, life Hatun Sürücü lived. Such discourses call forth a sharp distinction between a German 'us' and an immigrant 'them'. This shows how a bright boundary is constructed in the intersection of ethnicity and nationality, becoming gendered by labelling Hatun Sürücü a 'German woman.'

In newspaper articles that focus on ethnonationality to explain honour killing, religion only shows up to have its impact denied. However, other articles explicitly refer to Islam as the root cause of honour killing: 'These so-called honour killings do not concern individual dramas but are social phenomena in societies that have a modernization deficit and that are disproportionately stamped by Islam' (*TAZ*, 22 February 2005). Contrary to our expectations, then, religion is deployed to explain differences between immigrant and majority society in Germany. Quotes like this show that Islam is mobilized with the same effect as references to ethnonationality to inscribe a bright boundary.

Both ethnonational and religious explanations for violence against women thus reinforce a sharp divide between immigrants as Muslims and German majority society, one that is often captured by the term *'parallelgesellschaften'* (parallel societies). An example of linking these differences comes from a discussion of the new coalition's approach to immigrant integration associated with Chancellor Angela Merkel:

> Merkel, despite wanting to have an open dialogue with Islam, will not tolerate parallel societies in Germany. The coalition agreement is entitled "Jointly Together for Germany." Parallel societies with fundamentally different values about living together would not fit in this way of thinking. Forced marriages and so-called honour killings would not be tolerated. Mastery of the German language is a requirement for integration, emphasized the Chancellor. The dialogue with Islam has great significance, differences however should not be blurred but have to be explicitly named. Germany is a tolerant and open country that at the same time takes care of its culture. (*FAZ*, 30 November 2005)

Here, ending gendered practices like forced marriages and honour killings is linked to successful immigrant integration, which, in turn, is marked by learning German. This connection of gendered forms of violence, Islam, and integration through language shows how the bright boundary between immigrants and German majority society is inscribed in the intersection of ethnicity, national origin, religion and gender. The *FAZ*'s discussion of the new government's proposed treatment of immigrants shows how such discourses foster approaches to integration that focus on change by immigrants while leaving dominant understandings of German national identity and institutions intact.

As we saw in the Dutch case, the ways bright boundaries are drawn in Germany often assume a homogeneous German culture into which immigrants should integrate. In such discourses, immigrants' integration comes to depend on their capacity to adopt the values majority society is said to hold.

### Elements of boundary blurring

German articles, like the Dutch ones, also contain elements of boundary blurring. Twenty-three out of 56 articles fit in this category (17 appearing in the *TAZ*) while 4 out of 56 show elements of both bright boundaries and boundary blurring (see Table 3). Boundary blurring occurs, first, in attempts to offer alternative representations of Turkish immigrant communities than those presented in bright-boundary discourses, and second, in appeals to human rights values as a common ground that already bridges purported differences between German Turks and German majority society. As in the

Dutch case, this means articulating alternative linkages between gender inequality, Islam and ethnonationality.

In the German newspapers, representatives from Muslim and secular Turkish organizations are positioned to create images of Turkish immigrants, Islam, and ethnicity that differ in some important aspects from those that inscribe bright boundaries. These representatives are often actively involved in their communities while simultaneously being part of majority society (Yurdakul 2006). They have crossed the bright boundary without losing their ethnic, national, or religious affiliation and embody the possibility of multiple memberships associated with blurred boundaries. In addition, Turkish women take leading roles in discussions of honour killing, which contradicts the perception that Turkish women are victimized and silenced. Furthermore, we see a description of contemporary Turkish communities in Germany in which Turkish culture is not understood as an 'import' brought wholesale from a distant homeland but rather as continuously developing, though now in a new national context (see also Adelson 2005). This contradicts the view of Turkish ethnonational identity or Islam as not modern that comes to the fore in the drawing of bright boundaries.

Seyran Ateş exemplifies these trends. Ateş, a participant in a fourway interview with representatives of Muslim religious and secular (Turkish) organizations, is a lawyer, a member of the Green Party, and an activist in the gay–lesbian movement in Germany, who also very much claims her Turkish identity, including a sense of religiosity (*TAZ*, 28 February 2005). In terms of how she portrays the Turkish German community, Ateş inhabits a complicated position – on the one hand, she is highly critical of the German left's multiculturalism, stating that 'It seems to me that multikulti is organized irresponsibility' (*TAZ*, 28 February 2005). She sees multiculturalism as leading to segregation much as Selim and Hirsi Ali do in the Netherlands. On the other hand, she also blurs the bright boundary such discourses create. Ateş argues that '[T]he high status of women in Islam is a myth' (*TAZ*, 22 February 2005). But rather than using this indictment of Islam to situate Islam in unchanging tradition, Ateş sees change in gender relations as something that can come from *within* Turkish communities in Germany. The two representatives of religious organizations who participate in this interview assert that definitions of honour are changing within Turkey itself, though seemingly not in the German-Turkish communities, which appear to retain their traditions in the diaspora. In response Ateş contends:

These definitions have been sticking in their [Turkish men's] heads for decades. And to change that, we need the support of your organizations. Female lawyers and female social workers can put out fires, but we have to start a larger process of development. For that, we need models. Youth should not have certain values imposed upon them by the majority society, but our men should tell them: *Those are our values too!* At issue is the position of women. (*TAZ*, 22 February 2005, emphasis added)

In arguing that alternative definitions of honour can be supported within Turkish communities in Germany, Ateş rejects dominant discourses that link violence against women to practices of an explicitly Turkish, i.e. ethnonational, community or to Islam. Ateş portrays a contemporary Turkish community in Germany that does not need to adopt majority values to change, giving alternatives to discourses that inscribe a bright boundary by linking ethnonationality and religion to violence against women.

Another example of alternative representations of both the Turkish communities and honour killing comes up in an interview with Hatice Akyün, a journalist and the writer of a popular book about Turkish women and girls:

I do not deny what is reported in the media. Of course there are forced marriages, honour killings, and women who are not allowed to leave their homes. But that is only a small proportion. By contrast, there are thousands, thousands of Turkish young women in this country who live a completely normal life. I wrote a book that represents the life of a normal German-Turkish woman. At least it represents the many Turkish women that I know. The murder of Hatun Aynur Sürücü in Berlin is a tragedy. For Turks too. The Koran says nothing about honour killings. It is not Islamic and it is also not Turkish. Is a woman, a German mother, who starves her child, a typical German? No, she is inhuman. The people do not differentiate. (*TAZ*, 11 October 2005)

Akyün positions herself both in the Turkish and the German community, using a hyphenated identity in her self-description as a 'German-Turkish woman' to indicate her multiple memberships. Akyün also describes a Turkish immigrant community in which women's existence is not defined by violence against women. At the same time, she argues that issues like honour killing represent neither Islam nor Turkish ethnonationality. Thus, Akyün inserts an image into public discourse that contradicts those that are mobilized in the drawing of bright boundaries. While this, in and of itself, does not blur that boundary, by delinking gender inequality from ethnonational origin and Islam, Akyün, like Ateş, creates discursive avenues for such boundary blurring.

Addressing the issue of honour killing by using a human rights frame creates another opening for boundary blurring. Safter Çınar, the former spokesperson for the immigrant association, Türkische Bund Berlin-Brandenburg [TBB] argues that religious and other Turkish organizations should say:

> We maintain that honour killings, forced marriage, and the oppression of women are not compatible with our religion. But the majority society has to finally stop discussing German values as values that foreigners should adjust to. It is not a matter of German or Turkish values. It is about universal human rights. (*TAZ*, 22 February 2005)

Like the example given by Nazmiye Oral in the Netherlands, Çınar shows how the discourses that are used to draw bright boundaries make it difficult to address both the divide between immigrant and majority society and specific problems like honour killing. He appeals to a shared belief in human rights to bridge this boundary. Similarly, Eren Ünsal, a prominent woman in the TBB, argues that 'We must refrain from saying Turkish or German values, there are universal human rights here' (*TAZ*, 28 February 2005). Rather than categorizing Turks in Germany as trapped in tradition, whether that tradition is informed by Islam or not, these immigrants argue that liberatory values are already shared. Here, human rights are neither indigenously German (or Western) or Turkish, but universal. This framing offers a way out of the dominant dichotomy between German values (gender equality) and Turkish values (family honour) that informs the drawing of bright boundaries.

These alternative discourses share two important characteristics. First, they are mostly initiated by German Turks; there are very few Germans who create framings that could be used to draw a more blurred boundary between immigrant and majority society. Second, these alternative representations appear less often than those that create bright boundaries, therefore they seem 'weaker' voices. They can mostly be found in the left-wing newspaper, *TAZ*. In sum, while these discourses offer alternatives to the dominant representations of what it means to be an immigrant of Turkish descent in Germany, such alternatives are less dominant in German newspapers, specifically in the *FAZ* and *SZ*, than those that draw boundaries brightly.

## Conclusion

These findings show that an analysis of the media is fruitful for understanding how the boundaries between immigrants and majority society can be shaped discursively. In both the Netherlands and

Germany, much of the newspaper reporting reinforced bright boundaries by discussing honour killing in ways that posited stark differences between immigrant and majority society. They did so by describing honour killing as a form of violence against women rooted in Islam, ethnicity or national origin, and portraying religion, ethnicity, and national origin as homogenous, unitary, and/or a-historical forces that by definition lead to gender inequality. Some articles contained possibilities for boundary blurring as they: a) approached honour killing as a violation of women's human rights similar to other forms of violence against women; b) stressed differences *within* immigrant communities and (religious) practices when discussing honour killing; or c) showed how immigrants themselves work to change honour-related violence.

The resulting analysis shows that ethnicity, national origin, religion and gender intersect in giving meaning to the group identities of immigrants, though they do so in importantly different ways in Dutch and German newspapers. We found that in the Netherlands, bright boundaries are produced as violence against women is tied to religion, i.e. to Islam, which reflects how the Dutch institutionalized differences between Christian denominations and tacked Islam onto that framework. In Germany, the discussions link ethnicity to national origin to create ethnonational distinctions which then alternate with religion to explain the occurrence of honour killing. Prior research found a tendency to discuss group differences in terms of national origin, rather than religion. However, we show that in Germany honour killing is presently discussed both in terms of religious and of ethnonational difference.

In both countries, these cultural elements intersect differently in discourses that contain possibilities for boundary blurring. In such discourses, gender equality is positioned as a universal (human rights) value that is congruent with Islam, ethnicity and national identity. Yet, in each country blurring discourses are relatively rare and articulated mostly by immigrants, indicating limited change on the part of majority society.

The ways in which these boundaries are drawn has implications for general processes of assimilation. The dominance of bright boundaries in both countries indicates that absorptive assimilation, which requires giving up ones group identity and adopting the majority society's norms and values, becomes the route towards integration. Indications of boundary blurring in both countries suggest a less assimilative form of integration.

A number of costs are associated with the dominance of bright boundaries, and the accompanying pathways for integration. First, drawing such bright boundaries forecloses the possibility of ending violence against women within immigrant communities. In particular, from a bright boundaries perspective culture appears immutable, and thus change can only come from the outside. Yet, an understanding of the various elements of culture as flexible has enabled people to find solutions do not require dislocating women from their particular communities (Maris and Saharso 2001; Mojab 2004, pp. 20–1). If such an understanding of the link between ethnicity, religion, national origin and gender relations would become widespread, the issue of honour killing might be more effectively addressed. Second, the emphasis on honour killing can lead to a failure to appreciate the extent to which domestic violence is a problem for *all* women. The risk of domestic violence among non-immigrant women is great enough to call into question the implicit assumption that immigrant women would be safer if they lived like Dutch or German women (see also Narayan 1997; Bhabha 1999).

In conclusion, our analysis extends theories of boundary formation by seeing such boundaries as constructed in the intersections between different cultural resources such as ethnicity, national origin, religion and gender. From this perspective, we can begin to identify the discursive forces that retard immigrant integration in the Dutch and German contexts as well as those that might facilitate such integration. Here, we advocate for further research on how these discourses impact the integration process.

## Acknowledgements

An earlier version of this paper was presented at the Seventh Mediterranean Social and Political Research Meeting, Florence and Montecatini Terme, 22–26 March 2006, organized by the Mediterranean Programme of the Robert Schuman Centre for Advanced Studies at the European University Institute and at the European Studies Conference in Chicago, March 2006. We thank Stefano Allievi, Martin van Bruinessen, Randall Hansen, Marcel Maussen, Ruud Peters, Elisabeth Beck-Gernsheim, Bob Brym, Michal Bodemann, Jim Davis, Adam Green, Linn Clark and Nadine Blumer for their feedback.

## Notes

1. We exclude a few articles containing solely factual reporting.
2. Her membership in this 'we' proved tenuous. In the spring of 2006 Hirsi Ali was accused of lying on her refugee application and her Dutch citizenship was (temporarily) revoked. She gave up her seat in parliament and moved to the United States to work for the American Enterprise Institute.
3. In 2005, Leefbaar Rotterdam was the largest party in Rotterdam's city government holding 13 out of 45 seats and supplying 3 of the 7 members on the city governing council (www.rotterdam.nl).

# References

ABU-LUGHOD, LILA 2002 'Do Muslim women really need saving? Anthropological reflections on cultural relativism and its others', *American Anthropologist*, vol. 104, no. 3, pp. 783–90

ADELSON, LESLIE 2005 *The Turkish Turn in Contemporary German Literature: Toward a New Critical Grammar of Migration*, New York: Palgrave-Macmillan

AHMED, LEILA 1992 *Women and Gender in Islam: Historical Roots of a Modern Debate*, New Haven, CT: Yale University Press

ALBA, RICHARD 2005 'Bright vs. blurred boundaries: second-generation assimilation and exclusion in France, Germany, and the United States', *Ethnic and Racial Studies*, vol. 28, no. 1, January, pp. 20–49

ALBA, RICHARD and NEE, VICTOR 1997 'Rethinking assimilation theory for a new era of immigration', *International Migration Review*, vol. 31, no. 4, winter, pp. 826–74

ALBA, RICHARD and NEE, VICTOR 2003 *Remaking the American Mainstream: Assimilation and Contemporary Immigration*, Cambridge, MA: Harvard University Press

BAUBÖCK, RAINER 1994 'The integration of immigrants', Council of Europe, Strasbourg

BHABHA, HOMI 1999 'Liberalism's sacred cow', in Joshua Cohen, Matthew Howard and Martha C. Nussbaum (eds), *Is Multiculturalism Bad for Women?*, Princeton, NJ: Princeton University Press

BRUBAKER, ROGERS 1992 *Citizenship and Nationhood in France and Germany*, Cambridge: Harvard University Press

—— 2001 'Return to assimilation? Changing perspectives on immigration and its sequels in France, Germany, and the United States', *Ethnic and Racial Studies*, vol. 24, no. 4, pp. 531–48

—— 2004 'Ethnicity without groups', in *Ethnicity Without Groups*, Cambridge, MA: Harvard University Press, pp. 7–27

*BUNDESMINISTERIUMS FÜR FAMILIE, SENIOREN, FRAUEN, und JUGEND*, 2004, Berlin, www.bmfsfj.de (accessed 16 August 2006)

COMMISSIE BLOK 2004 Eindrapport Integratiebeleid van de Tijdelijke Commissie Onderzoek Integratiebeleid (Final Report Integration Policy by the Temporary Committee Research Integration Policy), http://www.tweedekamer.nl/organisatie/voorlichting/commis sies/eindrapport_integratiebeleid.jsp (accessed 16 August 2006)

DEWIND, JOSH and KASINITZ, PAUL 1997 'Everything old is new again? Processes and theories of immigrant incorporation', *International Migration Review*, vol. 31, no. 4, pp. 1096–111

ENTZINGER, HAN 2003 'The rise and fall of multiculturalism: the case of the Netherlands', in Christian Joppke and Ewa Morawska (eds), *Toward Assimilation and Citizenship*, New York: Palgrave Macmillan, pp. 59–86

—— 2006 'Changing the rules while the game is on: from multiculturalism to assimilation in the Netherlands', in Y. Michal Bodemann and Gökçe Yurdakul (eds), *Migration, Citizenship, Ethnos*, New York: Palgrave Macmillan, pp. 121–44

EWING, KATHERINE (2008) *Stolen Honor: Stigmatizing Muslim Men in Berlin*, Stanford, CA: Stanford University Press

FENTON, STEVE and MAY, STEPHEN 2002 'Ethnicity, nation and "race": connections and disjunctures', in S. Fenton and S. May (eds), *Ethnonational Identities*, New York: Palgrave Macmillan, pp. 1–20

FORUM, INSTITUUT VOOR MULTICULTURELE ONTWIKKELING 2008 *The Position of Muslims in the Netherlands: Facts and Figures*, http://www.forum.nl/pdf/fact book-islam-en.pdf (accessed 15 March 2008)

GAMSON, WILLIAM and MODIGLIANI, ANDRE 1989 'Media discourses and public opinion on nuclear power: a constructionist approach', *American Journal of Sociology*, vol. 95, no. 1, pp. 1–37

GLENN, EVELYN NAKANO 1999 'The social construction and institutionalization of gender and race', in Myra Marx Ferree, Judith Lorber and Beth B. Hess (eds), *Revisioning Gender*, Thousand Oaks, CA: Sage, pp. 3–43

JAARRAPPORT INTEGRATIE 2007. 'Sociaal en cultureel Plan bureau', November 2007, Den Haag

JOPPKE, CHRISTIAN and MORAWSKA, EWA 2003 'Integrating immigrants in liberal nation-states: policies and practices', in Christian Joppke and Ewa Morawska (eds), *Toward Assimilation and Citizenship: Immigrants in Liberal Nation-States*, New York: Palgrave Macmillan, pp. 1–36

KANDIYOTI, DENIZ 1988 'Bargaining with patriarchy', *Gender & Society*, vol. 2, no. 3, pp. 274–90

KASTORYANO, RIVA 2002 *Negotiating Identities: States and Immigrants in France and Germany*, Princeton, NJ: Princeton University Press

KOGACIOGLU, DICLE 2004 'The tradition effect: framing honour crimes in Turkey', *Differences: a Journal of Feminist Cultural Studies*, vol. 15, no. 2, pp. 118–52

KOOPMANS, RUUD, STATHAM, PAUL, GIUGNI, MARCO, and PASSY, FLORENCE 2005 *Contested Citizenship: Immigration and Cultural Diversity in Europe*, Minneapolis, MN: University of Minnesota Press

KORTEWEG, ANNA C 2006 'The murder of Theo Van Gogh: gender, religion and the struggle over immigrant integration in the Netherlands', in Y. Michal Bodemann and Gökçe Yurdakul (eds), *Migration, Citizenship, Ethnos*, New York: Palgrave Macmillan, pp. 147–66

KVINNOFORUM 2005 *Honour Related Violence: European Resource Book and Good Practice*, based on the European project 'Prevention of violence against women and girls in patriarchal families', Stockholm, http://www.kvinnoforum.se/english/index.html (accessed 28 October 2005)

LAMONT, MICHELE and MOLNAR, VIRAG 2002 'The study of boundaries in the social sciences', *Annual Review of Sociology*, vol. 28, pp. 167–95

MARIS, CEES and SAHARSO, SAWITRI 2001 'Honour killing: a reflection on gender, culture, and violence', *The Netherlands Journal of Social Sciences*, vol. 37, no. 1, pp. 52–73

MOJAB, SHARZAD 2004 'The particularity of "honour" and the universality of "killing": from early warning signs to feminist pedagogy', in Sharzad Mojab and Nahla Abdo (eds), *Violence in the Name of Honour: Theoretical and Political Changes*, Istanbul: Istanbul Bilgi University Press, pp. 15–37

NARAYAN, UMA 1997 *Dislocating Cultures: Identities, Traditions, and Third World Feminism*, New York: Routledge

NORRIS, PIPPA and INGLEHART, RONALD 2002 'Islam and the West: testing the clash of civilizations thesis', http://ksghome.harvard.edu/~pnorris/Acrobat/Clash%20of%20Civilization.pdf (accessed 20 August 2007)

OKIN, SUSAN MOLLER 1999 'Is multiculturalism bad for women?', in Joshua Cohen, Matthew Howard, Martha C. Nussbaum (eds), *Is Multiculturalism Bad for Women?*, Princeton,NJ: Princeton University Press pp. 7–26

PITT-RIVERS, JULIAN 1974 'Honour and social status', in J.G. Peristiany (ed.), *Honour and Shame: The Values of the Mediterrenean Society*, Chicago, IL: University of Chicago Press, pp. 19–77

*PRIVE GEWELD, PUBLIEKE ZAAK: EEN NOTA OVER DE GEZAMENLIJKE AANPAK VAN HUISELIJK GEWELD* 2002, April, http://www.huiselijkgeweld.nl/doc/beleid/BELEID_prive_geweld_publiek_zaak.pdf (accessed 16 August 2006)

RAZACK, SHERENE 2004 'Imperilled Muslim women, dangerous Muslim men, and civilized Europeans: legal and social responses to forced marriages', *Feminist Legal Studies*, vol. 12, pp. 129–74

SEV'ER, AYSAN and YURDAKUL, GÖKÇEÇIÇEK 2001 'Culture of honour, culture of change: a feminist analysis of honour killings in rural Turkey', *Violence against Women*, vol. 7, no. 9, pp. 964–98

STATISTIK DER BUNDESAGENTUR FÜR ARBEIT 2007 'Analitykreport der Statistik, Analyse des Arbeitmarktes für Ausländer'

TRANSACT 2005 *Eergerelateerd Geweld in Nederland: Een Bronnenboek*, http://www.transact.nl/ (accessed 11 July 2007)

VAN ECK, CLEMENTINE 2003 *Purified by Blood: Honour Killings among Turks in the Netherlands*, Amsterdam: Amsterdam University Press

WARRICK, CATHERINE 2005 'The vanishing victim: criminal law and gender in Jordan', *Law and Society Review*, vol. 39, no. 2, pp. 315–48

YURDAKUL, GÖKÇE 2006 'State, political parties and immigrant elites: Turkish immigrant associations in Berlin', *Journal of Ethnic and Migration Studies*, vol. 32, no. 3 pp. 435–53

YUVAL-DAVIS, NIRA 1997 *Gender and Nation*, London: Sage

ZOLBERG, ARISTIDE R. and LONG, LITT WOON 1999 'Why Islam is like Spanish: cultural incorporation in Europe and the United States', *Politics & Society*, vol. 27, no. 1, March, pp. 5–38

# You're Brazilian, right? What kind of Brazilian are you? The racialization of Brazilian immigrant women

Judith McDonnell and Cileine de Lourenço

## Abstract

This article analyses the responses of Brazilian immigrant women who live and work in the greater Boston, Massachusetts, area of the United States to questions about their racial and ethnic identity. Based on thirty face-to-face in-depth interviews conducted between June 2004 and July 2005, we explore the many ways by which the women's identities are racialized and the variety of responses to the process of racialization. In particular, we focus on the degree to which the women's reported race, ethnicity and immigrant status exacerbate or protect women from the exclusionary aspects of the racialization process.

## Introduction

Racialization is the process of attaching racial meaning to individuals, sub-populations and social phenomenon, making what could be subtle and fluid, for example, racial identity, into a relatively fixed category (Silverstein 2005). This process, at least in the United States, 'slots' (Silverstein 2005) social actors, including immigrants, regardless of their time spent in the United States, into the ethno-racial hierarchy, influencing social mobility, access to societal rewards and resources and overall quality of life. Racialization is also problematic when social actors are characterized by others in a way that is inconsistent with their own racial self-identity. For immigrants in the United States, racialization often leads them to identify with a sub-population in which they have no 'organic' membership. As a result, racialization may provoke a response by the people being racialized including resistance, acceptance or, for some people, re-negotiation of their identity to give them greater distance from what may feel like a false identity.

The title of this article, a comment by Sônia, a respondent in this study, suggests a process of wondering where being Brazilians fit in the racialized system. Using Brazilian immigrant women's narratives we explore the vicissitudes of constructed identities, focusing on the responses of women as they claim and 'disclaim' categories in the ethno-racial hierarchy. Our analysis shows that most of the women that participated in our study seem more aware of the *racialization* of their identities, even if they do not articulate it as such, than they are of their racial identity as drawn up in the US ethno-racial system. The women were racialized for a variety of reasons, including skin colour, presumed ethnicity or nationality, language, accent and gender, or a combination of the factors.

## Characteristics of the interview group

This article is based on thirty face-to-face, in-depth interviews with first-generation Brazilian women living in the Boston, Massachusetts, area, mostly in Framingham, a city of about 67,000 located twenty miles west of Boston. Our interview period was June 2004 through July 2005. Each interview, conducted in Portuguese, was scheduled at the time and place most convenient to the woman. Each woman, anonymous and with a fictitious name, signed an informed consent attesting to her understanding of our project and completed a questionnaire about basic demographic information.

The thirty women vary in age, length of time in the United States, income, education and racial identity.[1] The youngest woman is 20 years old, the oldest is 61. Length of time spent in the United States ranges from just a couple of months to twenty-two years, with an average of just under seven years. Fourteen of the women are currently married. Nineteen have children that range in age from the very young to 30 years old. Twenty women live in Framingham. Sixteen of the women are Catholic.

Seven women did not record their family income but reported incomes range from three families at under US$10,000 dollars to one family at $75,000–100,000. The average income category among the women that did respond was just under $30,000. The level of education received in Brazil varied from less than high school to graduate programmes and some respondents are in the US educational system.

Racial identity is not the sole component of racialization but it is an important factor. Many of the respondents articulated a racial self-identity that was inconsistent with the racializaton of their bodies, typically based on phenotypes, the social space they used and occupied, their accents and even their jobs. We asked the women a variety of questions that allowed them to identify racially both while they were still in Brazil and in the United States,[2] elucidating many of the subtle aspects of what it means to be Brazilian in the US. This proved to be a difficult question for many respondents, who were often more aware of the racial meaning attached to their lives and identities than they were certain of their own racial identity. While still in Brazil, nineteen of the women identified as white, two as black, two as Brazilian, one as brown, four as mixed and two said they did not know. While in the United States, twelve said they are white, two black, five non-white, five asserted Brazilian, three mixed and three did not know. Seven fewer women identified as white in the United States than they did while still in Brazil. Five women claimed a non-white identity, which may reflect their basic understanding of the United States black-white dichotomy. Women know they are not white, but they are also not black so they become the negation of one of the identities. In summary, the stories they tell about themselves reveal that they understand the protean nature of their identity, having dealt with mixed messages about what kind of Brazilians they are.

## Brazilians in Massachusetts

Despite the considerable migrant stream of Brazilians to Massachusetts, New Englanders are often surprised that there are enough Brazilians there to be worthy of a full study. On the other hand, the symbols of Brazilian presence, in, for example, Framingham, MA, just west of Boston, influence the views of others to such an extent that many problems of the local economy are blamed on Brazilians. This form of invisibility/hypervisibility adds to a misunderstanding of Brazilians. To some, the Portuguese heard on the street sounds like Spanish and the green and yellow flags are not the familiar red, white and blue, so *ipso facto* through the racialization process Brazilians become Hispanic. To some, Brazilian's public identity reinforces the stereotypes about people from 'south of the border', including that of the essentialized exotic Brazilian woman. Furthermore, they are the suspicious foreigner, a central tenet of the US American story. Anyone not obviously white American is subject to scrutiny, being compared to a reference point at or near the bottom of the ethno-racial hierarchy: US American blacks. Oboler points out that everyone, and here she is referring to people from Latin America, 'everyone "knows his (or her) place" in US society' (2006, p. 196). Thus, it is within this context that Brazilians in Massachusetts must decide whether to accept their so-called place.

The significant presence of Brazilians in Massachusetts dates back to the 1980s. Because a considerable number of Brazilians living in the

US are not yet documented, it is difficult to know the actual size of the population. Some sources suggest that there are close to 750,000 Brazilians in the United States and could be as many as 150,000 in Massachusetts. However, according to the Census 2000, there are officially only 30,653 in Massachusetts. The residential location of most of the women we interviewed, Framingham, had an unofficial estimate in 2000 of 4,408 people who claim Brazil as the country of their birth. However, the census reports the Brazilian population at 3,500. The discrepancy in numbers is mostly due to the reluctance of even legal immigrants to come forward and be counted. Regardless of the exact number, there had been unprecedented growth of the Brazilian population, prompting political, cultural and social tensions in the area.

## Racialization and Brazilians in the United States

Any social system hierarchy requires methods to reproduce itself and to place social actors within it. Racialization is one such method. Racialization effects and racial identity may be consistent but, as we find in our work, may also be contradictory, which is what seems most vexing to the women we interviewed. As noted above, our work shows that many women are much more aware that they have been racialized than they are aware of their racial identity.

The negative attitudes in areas with relatively high concentrations of Brazilians are exacerbated as local residents opine that their own difficulties are due to the Brazilian invasion. This is one stage in the racialization process: creating and demonizing the 'other'. Although this is an old story about immigrants, the underbelly of the master narrative, it matters little to the people that the stories told about them are the same stories told about the people that came before them.

Our study of Brazilian immigrant women follows a twelve-year research run on Brazilians in the United States, including Sales (1999, 2003), Braga Martes (2000), Margolis (1994, 1998a, 1998b, 2001), Messias (2002), Beserra (2003, 2005), Braga Martes and Resende Fleischer (2004). There are several good studies by Levitt (2001, 2003), and Levitt and some of her colleagues, that examine Brazilians in a variety of theoretical contexts. Margolis's publication in 1994 of *Little Brazil: An Ethnography of Brazilian Immigrants in New York City* and in 1998 of *An Invisible Minority: Brazilians in New York City* spurred an interest in Brazilian immigration to the United States. At the time of the 1998 publication, Margolis had coined the term 'invisibility' regarding Brazilian presence in New York. Although the invisibility phenomenon is not unique to Brazilians, it was and is one of the dilemmas of Brazilian identity construction. Beserra's (2003) study, the most comprehensive and theoretically based study of Brazilian immigrants so far, analysed the influence of capitalism on Brazilians' decisions to come to the United States and Brazilian integration into US society – the nature of 'Americanization'. To this end, Beserra was concerned with some of the same issues that we explore in this paper, especially racial identity and the degree of 'Latinidad' among Brazilians.

With the exception of Beserra (2003, 2005) none of the other studies focuses on the complexities of racialization in the configuration and negotiation of racial identity. They do not address the possibility that identity is not fixed in time or place. Studying Brazilian immigrants in the US provides an opportunity to explore the racialization process during a time when nation-state boundaries are undergoing transformation and globalization continues apace. Boundaries in the United States are both more and less porous. With immigration at an all-time high, we might argue that the boundaries are more porous. However, with suspicion of and retribution against immigrants also high, there is disdain for some national groups that are part of global migration to the US. Some of the research on globalization suggests that immigrants who have come to the United States in the last twenty or so years have entered a highly charged environment of racial, ethnic and gender politics (Barlow 2003).[3] The US has historically rooted, specific yet dynamic racial, ethnic and gender hierarchies, where identities are formed, negotiated, re-formed, discarded and imposed. These identity politics are exacerbated by globalization's feeding new groups at an unprecedented rate into this dynamic yet *a priori* racialized and gendered hierarchy. Brazilians risk having an identity imposed on them on the basis of what are otherwise superficial categories, e.g., skin colour, accent, which is especially relevant to many of the women we interviewed. Individuals may attempt to create and negotiate all aspects, including accepting the bureaucratic category of 'other' where no other logical 'check box' exists to reflect their sense of self and to resist the ineluctable process of racialization.

Three aspects of Brazilian society lead to the dilemma faced by our respondents as they confront racialization and slotting. First, the influence of class identity relative to race has a long history in Brazil, and it is a normative class-based framework for explaining inequality that Brazilians bring with them. A lingering aspect of race construction that remains in Brazil, and that contributes to the dismissal of racial discrimination or even racial acknowledgement, has to do with class reductionism. Second, most Brazilians have rejected the possibility of racism existing in Brazil, investing instead in the discourse of racial democracy (Guimarães 2001, p. 38). Because class reductionism is pervasive, it has become a core element of the second aspect, the myth of racial democracy. If racism is rarely used to explain inequality, and in the Brazilian imaginary, racial democracy precludes racism, something equally compelling must absorb even more explanatory power; thus, class has become the prevailing analytical factor for explaining the mistreatment of sectors of Brazilian society. The portability of the racial democracy discourse is a powerful force in our respondents' response to racialization. The discourse is not discarded at nation-state boundaries and, in fact, may be renewed with vigour as a laudatory aspect of being Brazilian and exacerbated by processes of globalization. Dos Santos and Silva (2006) analysed Brazilians' 'indifference' to racism in Brazil. They note that the myth of racial democracy was still alive in Brazil and splattered across the media in both text and sub-text, rendering Afro-Brazilians barely visible. The media socialize Brazilians into the disregard for racism. We argue that those lessons have come with Brazilian immigrants during the migration process, reinforced by the media including international television and the internet.

Third, racial identity in Brazil, and in all of Latin America, is more nuanced than it is in the US (Sansone 2003). Winant (2004) refers to Brazil's racial system as more of a colour continuum compared to the US's firmer colour lines. Sansone described Brazil's racial and ethnic conceptualization as one of 'immense fluidity'. Thus, as relative newcomers, first-generation Brazilians bring with them a dominant way of thinking about race, informed by the prominence of social class, the idea of racial democracy and the fluidity of racial identities. They are immediately met with a different, equally powerful way of thinking about it. This tension occurs to such an extent that several of the women we talked to became silent, even confused, when asked about their self-defined racial identification but could and did talk more easily about their perceived class position.

Understanding the contingent historical obsession to assign everyone to a racial schema and the punitive aspects that might occur becomes necessary for newer immigrants, especially if they are from south of the border. As Lewis (2003) notes, 'border' skirmishes take place on many levels including around racial categories. 'People experience not merely being identified or labeled, but, as boundaries are drawn, being simultaneously included or excluded; these are the moments when they are treated in a particular way because someone has identified them as a member of a particular racial group' (Lewis 2003, p. 8). Racialization, as a lived experience, is about the tension between inclusion and exclusion as all ethnic and racial groups are positioned on a continuum from white to black. Newcomers especially are confronted with this overly deterministic orthodoxy that includes a greater level of potential social exclusion the closer they are positioned to black. Yet our respondents suggest that racialization occurs even to those that have been in the United States for twenty years. However, despite the tenaciousness of the racial identification process and consequent racialization, individuals do have room to negotiate and manoeuvre. The ability of individuals to position themselves close to their perceived place in the continuum is affected by many factors, including skin colour, accent, English language skills and control of societal resources. Most certainly, racialization and (not) belonging are related. Croucher says that 'the politics of belonging refer to the process of individuals, groups, societies, polities defining, negotiating, promoting, rejecting, violating, and transcending the boundaries of identities and belonging' (2004, p. 41).

## Being an immigrant

For newcomers and anyone with an accent, the first boundary to belonging that they must negotiate is the imposition of immigrant status and a foreigner identity. Acceptance or disavowal of the label 'immigrant' and the more pejorative 'foreigner' is linked to the process of racialization. Both labels are problematic for Brazilians and convey the breadth of racialization. Rejection of the ascription 'immigrant' is also resistance to the process of racialization, which sometimes provokes a counter-assertion of 'Brazilian' identity. To some identifying as Brazilian may be a way of distancing themselves from a racial identity. To say one is Brazilian is to invoke the belief/myth of racial democracy, implying almost a moral claim to being above the need for racial identity and certainly above the lowest of statuses.

Although this article examines the lives of women as our respondents, it does not unpack the relationship between gender and racialization. However, not analysing gender is not to say that we do not recognize that women's racialization is doubly embodied, in their status as immigrants and as women. It goes without saying that women have lower levels of power, occupy a gender-segmented labour force, often have transnational responsibilities and a shifting household division of labour as they are often one of two income earners or sole income earners. Thus the slotting/racialization of women is embodied in their race/ethnicity and by gender. Golash-Boza (2006) has examined women in the context of racialized assimilation, finding that more women than men, when asked about their identity, use their national origin. She asserts that Latinos(as) who hold more tightly to their national origin are also less likely to self-identify as American. We find that a significant number of people insert their Brazilian identity in response to a number of questions about race and ethnicity.

In the majority of our thirty interviews, almost all women acknowledged that they were immigrants. Although some women rejected its relevance to their day-to-day identities, very few disavowed an immigrant identity completely. Most of the excerpts that follow show rather starkly that, although experience in the United States allows some women greater access to scarce resources, it is not similarly a protection from the processes of racialization and marginalization. The following excerpts illustrate the more typical responses to the questions about their immigrant status.

Elza (41, here fourteen years), who did not plan to stay permanently, says: 'Yes, of course [she feels like an immigrant here]. Even though I'm an American citizen and I've been here awhile, I will always feel like an immigrant . . . .I like how I can live here. But I would never say "I'm American".' Elza, who in her heart feels closer to blacks but thinks most people would say she is white, acknowledges that 'immigrant' is part of how she sees herself. Elza seems to illustrate the crux contention of this analysis: her racial identity is contested but is not necessarily a factor that leads to her racialization. Her immigrant status combined with how Americans see her, however, leads her to feel like a 'strange class'. Marta's experience represents a consciousness about racialization that some women share regardless of their time in the United States. Marta was quite emphatic in her assertion that as an immigrant: 'If I don't open my mouth, perhaps I pass as white.'

Lúcia, an interesting contrast in terms of length of experience in the United States, provides another comment on the links between racialization and immigrant status. At the time of the interview, Lúcia, who viewed herself as white in Brazil, is in her late twenties, had been in the US for about only a year and a half. She comments several times about being an immigrant:

> just an immigrant who arrived in this country and feels like an alien. . . . They look at me like if I were black. It's prejudice against immigrants . . . .All immigrants came here searching for something better, but it wasn't what Americans wanted. You are here kind of occupying their space in the job market.

Lúcia juxtaposes the classic anti-immigrant narrative that has long existed with racial prejudice. Immigrant status and race are inextricable; together they lead to Lúcia's juxtaposition of her own racial identity in Brazil with how US Americans see her race. Her identity feels alien to her in the context of the ethno-racial hierarchy.

The aspects of the Brazilian people or experiences that are 'seen' and presumed by others to be authentic are typically just a set of stereotypes and myths. This form of exaggeration means hypervisibility (Guinier and Torres 2002). Yet some Brazilians are often not really seen at all – only their motifs or their superficial representations – thus the invisibility. One of Vilma's experiences best exemplifies this tension. She is 39 years old and has been in the US for seven years.

Vilma, who identified as white both in Brazil and the US, talks about being seen through an anti-immigrant/anti-Brazilian lens.

> They make fun of your accent. They tell us to go back to our country .... I know that discrimination was not because I was a woman but because I am Brazilian ....They would ask me "why don't I go back to Brazil? What was I doing here? Who did I think I was to make my money here and send everything to Brazil?"

Although few women described invisibility/hypervisibility in quite this way, almost all of the women had a story to tell about the negative attention paid to them for their presumed immigrant status.

Sônia (40, here less than a year, but has been in the USA before) voices a connection to being an immigrant several times as she responds mostly with rhetorical remarks about her self-concept relative to being a Brazilian, whom she constructs as someone 'Indian and the negro'.[4] Sônia proclaims she is neither, so she does not know what kind of Brazilian she is. When prompted to categorize herself, she says she is very white but cannot really categorize herself in the US.

> Sometimes I feel uncomfortable. But other times I don't even think about it because, as I said, I don't want to stay in their country for ever... Wow, I'm an immigrant. I have never thought of myself as one, but now whether I like it or not, I am one. My first feelings were not very pleasing. It was horrible. It was very strange. Almost as though I were a criminal.

Sônia, who acknowledges the ambiguity of her racial identity, is racialized as someone 'not from here' and to some extent no longer 'there' (in Brazil). The racialization discourse holds powerfully to the tension of belonging and not, of feeling neither here nor there. That theme surfaced regularly among our respondents.

One form of Brazilian resistance to racialization is the powerful tendency to attribute real or perceived social frictions to class or economic position rather than to race or racialization. It is perhaps less complicated and therefore more salutary to think of one's mistreatment as a result of the ephemeral condition of being 'poor' than as a result of the permanent condition of being 'of colour' or Latina or immigrant. After all, most Brazilians come to the United States with several goals, a main one being to increase their economic quality of life. The American dream includes the possibility that those who were poor will become less poor and those that are middle class will experience additional upward social mobility. Racialization is an obstacle to the American dream and one that takes many Brazilians by surprise. Yet, perceiving injustices as due to class alone belies the insidious force of racism that exists in the

United States. Moreover, invisibility, another consequence of the myth of racial democracy, is often reflected in both the inability of many of the women to articulate their racial identity and their outright denial of having encountered racism. Many women did respond to identity questions with comments about their social class. Many other women, as mentioned, knew they had been mistreated but were reluctant to say it was due to race.

For example, Ana (42, here twenty-two years) responds that she does not know if she has been mistreated here because of her race. She, who is 'Afro-descendente', also says that she has 'never had the ability to recognize discrimination ....No I don't believe I have been mistreated because ... I am of colour or I am Brazilian.' However, previously in the interview, Ana noted that, when she first arrived, she had encountered some tension presumably because of race.

### The Hispanic, Latin American and Latina element of racialization

Brazilian women also vary in their acceptance of Hispanic, Latin American and Latina identities, which are also racialized. Many of the excerpts suggest, at the very least, significant ambivalence, and sometimes outright resistance, about the merging of their actual identities with the various identification categories that exist in the imagination and in the bureaucracies of the US. Furthermore, many of the narratives show that resistance also occasionally leads to an insertion of 'Brazilian race' as a response. The respondents' response of Brazilian identity to a variety of questions seemed to suggest that asserting 'Brazilian' is a hedge, albeit a somewhat weak hedge, against the automatic racialization that occurs with an 'immigrant' identity.

Similar to Beserra's findings (2005), we cull from our interviews some ambivalence about Latina category, some confusion and certainly some irritation. We also note that some women prefer locating themselves in that ambiguous space of 'other' as preferable to all the other identity options. Brazilians' experience also includes, at least according to some of the women, the tendency for others to impose the Hispanic construction on them, a label that is not only inaccurate but is experienced as a pejorative. The interchangeable use of 'Hispanic' and 'Latino' in the United States reflects the one-size-fits-all categorization of everyone from Latin America who may or may not speak Spanish or a language sounding vaguely similar. The interchangeability of the labels also reflects a lack of knowledge on the part of the labellers. Brazilians' rejection of Hispanic, in addition to being historically and conceptually appropriate, is a form of resistance to racialization because, to many Brazilians, Hispanics are positioned close to blacks. Therefore, the rejection allows Brazilians to think of themselves as closer to white. Many of the women noted, consistently with common stereotypes, that Hispanics were somehow inferior and that is why some respondents disassociated themselves from that category. Several of the women when asked about whether the Hispanic label ever gets applied to them, responded with at least an attempt to show just how different/better Brazilians are and some contempt about being associated with inferior groups.

For example, Leticia (here five years, age 20) talked about the category Hispanic as it related to how she saw herself in the United States. Leticia thinks of herself as white but in Brazil thought of herself as Brazilian. Leticia engages in what we might think of as confused positioning of nationality, even ethnicity, for race, but this is precisely the device that allows some Brazilians to pre-empt negative judgement and slotting that they know is associated with being non-white, immigrant and even Latin American or Latino. Leticia has learned in a sociology class that the US has two racial categories, white and non-white. If one is not born in the US, she notes, one is automatically non-white and unequal. In asserting her Brazilian identity she is perhaps eschewing altogether the racial dichotomy. She first said that she did not think of herself as Hispanic because she doesn't 'like to speak Spanish' and doesn't 'really like the Spanish language'. When asked what she thought were the differences between Brazilians and Hispanics other than the language, Leticia says: 'I don't know. I think that Hispanics, it's not like they like to fight, but it's like, you know, we say that you shouldn't take dirty laundry home. . . . They don't care about it if they get along.' Leticia goes on to say that 'Hispanic' is a term describing the way people are and is a poor fit for Brazilians. Finally, Hispanics are somehow inferior to Brazilians. Vilma also talks about Hispanic traits, which she describes in the language of their cultural inferiority. Vilma, who sees herself as white, would even check 'other' before she would associate with Hispanic. Vilma, like many people, sees 'Hispanic' as representing something she is not; however, that category is inappropriate less because she does not fit its definition than because she does not identify with 'Hispanic', as defined by a set of stereotypes.

Helena (35, here sixteen years), in answer to the question about her racial identity in Brazil, said:

I am white. . . . It's only now that I've found out that I'm Hispanic [laughing]. I'm Latina. [Helena continues saying] No [she doesn't really accept Hispanic]. . . . .I think when you say Hispanic, you relate this to Puerto Rican. . . .. And there are also those stories, that Puerto Ricans don't work hard, that they just live off the government, that they have all kinds of rights and privileges, but today, you know, my husband says, "No, they're just stories".

Roberta (38, here nine months) said: 'Hispanic? I don't know. I think Hispanics are very bossy. They think they are better than Brazilians. So we stay apart from them.'

Alessandra (48, here seven years), in contrast, positions her identity closer to Hispanic than do most of the other women. Alessandra notes that most of the mistreatment or racialization she experiences is a result of her not yet speaking English perfectly. Alessandra notes that, although she is blonde and white skinned, her accent results in racist attitudes often directed at her. She said that Hispanics are latin[5] and, therefore, in the United States, but not in Brazil, she could identify with them.

The majority of responses defined Hispanics as having some kind of character or trait that made them inferior to Brazilians or allowed them to think they are better than Brazilians. Yet some women seemed casual and indifferent about their ideas of Hispanic by focusing on the reality of the language difference or focusing on perceived cultural differences. Renata's comment is a fairly good representation of the subset of women who saw Hispanics as being from different countries and speaking a different language than Brazilians do. Renata (44, here six years), who considers herself white in Brazil and white in the US but darker than US whites, says that she never used Hispanic when she was in Brazil and that Hispanics are people in the United States that speak Spanish. Adrianna (here eight years, 44) considered herself white in both Brazil and the United States, identified quite quickly, and without a prompt, as latin and then Latin American and Latin Brazilian. She does not consider herself Hispanic because 'our ethnicity as Brazilians is a little different'. And, although she considers Hispanics as 'latins', she does not consider herself to be 'the same as them' because the history of colonization of Brazilians is different from the history of colonization of other countries of South America.

In a variety of ways the women claim and disclaim Hispanic, Latin American, latin and Latina especially in relation to their claims to Brazilian identity. The process of racialization seems to be automatic for people whose first language is not English. The social distancing from Latina by some Brazilian women is consistent with Beserra's findings that Latina is perceived to be lower in the ethno-racial hierarchy. Many of the women position themselves against *Latinas* in a similar way as they did against Hispanics, implying, as they did with Hispanics, that Latinas are all one culture. On the other hand, many women seem to have no qualms about claiming Latina or Latin American, either with or without Brazilian added on to their self-identifications.

Cristina (22, here five years), who considers herself 'brown', was identified as white by a high school official on school documents because she is not black and they did not have Latino as a choice. She says that she often chooses 'other' because 'they must invent a race for Brazilians'. She says that Americans see her as latin and 'they don't know the difference between Spanish and Portuguese'.

Teresa (29, here five years), who considered herself white in both Brazil and the United States, says in response to questions about being Latina or Latin American: 'I define myself as a Brazilian.' She responds 'No' to whether she is a Latina. When asked what Latin American meant to her, Teresa says: 'Latin Americans? They are a people similar to the people of Brazil, but I consider myself to be more Brazilian and not a Latin American. I don't know how else to put it. I think it's a middle term [she says *meio-termo*] somewhere between the two.'

Guzmán and Diaz McConnell (2002) speculate that those with less established ties with the United States, as in people that have been here for relatively few years, may feel more rooted to their country of origin. Given the relative youth of the Brazilian movement to the United States, this may be one of the reasons why some women identify as Brazilian alone or in combination with a pan-ethnic term. That does not preclude the possibility that asserting 'Brazilian' positions women away from a more marginalized identity.

**Brazilians and race**

Questions about racial identity yielded a range of responses from almost complete silence, to long critiques of race as an identity, to comparisons with race in Brazil. As we reflect on our question about racial identity, we understand that the question itself becomes part of the racialization discourse that exists in the United States.

Sônia (40, here just one month this time, having been here before), the inspiration for the paper title, suggests that there is an essential Brazilian identity, one that rarely exists, but is connected to racial identity: 'someone totally Brazilian as you know, who is descendant of black, it is hard to find. So I would ask myself, "What kind of Brazilian race are we?" But here [US], no, I've never asked myself that question.'

Marta said that she was white in Brazil but when she first came to the US and even now, she thinks of herself as Brazilian, but 'I am not seen as white.' As mentioned above, Marta and several other women, perhaps as a form of resistance to racialization, overlay a national or country of origin identity on a racial identity.

Leticia (20, here for five years) notes that it was both the beginning of her college education and life in the US that brought her attention to her racialized identity. She also comments on 'the form':

It doesn't matter what colour your skin is, where you come from, you are non-white. That is what he said [referring to her sociology professor who was talking about racialization]. And for all of these places where you have to fill out the forms, you always have to say that you are non-white. Because that is the way they [Americans] were raised, that's how they think. Filling out those forms, you know. They [bureaucrats, etc.] look closely at this, what we fill out.

Leticia also made it clear that this was not how she thought about herself in general or, more specifically, when she was still living in Brazil. She noted that this identification was in part compliance with 'them', which we assume to be whoever was asking her to fill out the forms, the culture brokers of America. Leticia says that she always thought she was white and later white Brazilian, with the Brazilian coming only after she arrived in the US. She articulated the obvious but it is worth reporting as it speaks to a fundamental difference between the US and Brazil in the ways in which the official categories of identification come to be negotiated. She said that in Brazil she did not think about this division because in Brazil 'everyone was Brazilian'. This reinforces a previous point: if everyone is Brazilian, than everyone is treated the same at least in Brazil, reinforcing the idea of racial democracy. Thus, one unexpected result of the racialization of Brazilians in the United States is the way the racial democracy discourse is both a protection against racialization and reinforced by it.

Isabel (38, here for eight years) gave what seemed like a playful response to these questions, which began with what race she thought herself to be in Brazil:

For me I was Brazilian. At the time I didn't think about race. I don't know, was I ... yellow? [laughing]. When people talk about the three races, white, black and yellow, I thought I was yellow. No, I thought I was *morena* (brown), *morena clara* (a light brown), which is the best skin to have ....I didn't think much about this. I thought more about how I was in a country I did not belong to [no laughter here].

Flávia (22, here two years), in response to question about her racial identity in Brazil, said:

[chuckling] I don't remember. I think I was white. Isn't that what you would say? Yes, I think I was white. But after coming here I'm not white any more. I'm Hispanic or Latina.*I*: Right after you arrived in the United States, what race did you consider yourself? Latina.*I*: How do you think Americans see you racially speaking? As Hispanic. Hispanic.*I*: Have you noticed that to them [Americans] you are not white? Right, I'm not white to them. *I*: What are you then, immigrant, Hispanic, someone inferior or superior or equal? I think inferior. I think it can be very different depending on the person you are dealing with. Not everyone treats me as inferior. But they know that I'm not from here.

Flávia says that she feels that in America she has more options for her identity than she had in Brazil. She says, 'Here I don't think of myself as white because I have the option of being latin. In Brazil you don't have that option.' When asked if she felt white, she said 'No, latin. I don't feel white'. Flávia said that she was not a Latina 'ethnically speaking'.

Lucinda (43, here sixteen years) references her racial identity in terms of the 'form': 'People say, you know, when you go to fill in the little form where it asks you what your race is, I write in Brazilian. Because I am not any of the others. I'm not white, but I'm also not black. So I write in Brazilian or maybe Latina.'

The above excerpts reinforce previous comments showing that when the women seem uncomfortable with the identity categories they often assert Brazilian. They also transpose pan-ethnicity with national identity with racial identity. Furthermore, their remarks highlight an importance nuance about the racialization process. Some of the women are realistic, understanding well that US Americans will, as a matter of cultural and political practice, place them on the black-white continuum, more often that not, closer to black and sometimes regardless of where they might place themselves. However, their encounters with the same cultural and political practice do not preclude a different self-positioning that *distances* them to some degree from other marginalized sub-populations. One way this distancing manifests itself is through acknowledging 'non-white' rather than dark skinned, brown or black, which is an attempt to assert whiteness as a reference category for their identities. So, although they realize they will be slotted, they do find ways to insist on some self-determination of their location in the hierarchy.

Lucinda responded that when she lived in Brazil she was:

[W]hite, white. But here I'm black. Because of my hair and everything. And also because of my colour. Now my daughter is in reality white. ... But here you start to really see things. Here is when you begin to see ... .So it is here in the United States that I began to see I wasn't white.

Yet several women dismissed the idea of one's race as important to one's socioeconomic and cultural position; however, several of these same people saw their immigrant identity, which then connected to their racial identity, as being important to their general treatment and socioeconomic position. Marta perhaps is the most incisive and intellectual about her racialized identity as she talks about global racial classification systems and about how she change during her time in the United States. Marta's, perception and, no doubt, her reality, show that, even with fifteen years experience in the United States, racialization is automatic:

> when I first got here I found out in no time that I was not considered white [because of the colour of her skin she thought of herself as white in Brazil] because I come from Latin America ....And you begin to understand that you do not belong to that group and that you belong to the other group. What group do I belong to? Brazilian ....As something that does not belong here. Yes, something that comes from a country that they are not interested in.

## Conclusion

Racialization is the process of attaching racial meaning to people and social phenomena and often provokes a response from the people being racialized. We noted that many respondents were conscious of the racialization process and most of them were conscious of the ways they were excluded. Almost without exception, in responses to questions about their identities, the women obfuscated, denied and claimed categories that allow them to be comfortable to a degree with the United States system. In addition, almost all the women recognized the inevitability of racialization, even if they were not explicit about the process happening to them.

Racialization and exclusion are components of the same process. Some experienced racialization, the border of inclusion/exclusion, as Anzaldúa describes it, 'set up to distinguish *us* from *them*' (1987, p. 549, emphasis in original). Whether it was a deliberate form of resistance, many women pushed back through rejection or qualification of the label immigrant, through their rejection of 'Hispanic', through rejection or qualification of 'Latina' and 'Latin American', through their assertion of 'Brazilian' and through their framing of mistreatment due to their temporary class position rather than to race or immigrant status. To some, identifying as Brazilian may reflect their relative newcomer status. More importantly, asserting Brazilian may also be a psychological device used to enervate the racialization process. This may also be an ironic use of the 'myth' of racial democracy. Brazilian identity carries a powerful belief with a moral component that Brazilians do not have a place for racism and are therefore above judgement and racial categorization. As a counterforce to racialization, and the exclusion that comes from it, Brazilians devise ways to rise above the fray, including identifying as Brazilian. For Brazilians, however, the device may not be a match for the power of the racialization process that occurs in the United States.

Sônia asked herself the question: 'What kind of Brazilian are you?' Although we cannot presume to answer her question for her, we have attempted to contextualize it. In the United States, Brazilian seems to be an identity that is created in there to protect them against the forces of exclusion.

## Notes

1.   All demographic information is accurate as of the date of the interview.
2.   Each woman, unless she had significant difficulty answering the question, came up with her own terms and racial identifiers.
3.   These tensions have increased significantly since the events of September 11, a tragedy that occurred before our interviews, and now during the battle in the United States over the 'immigration' problem.
4.   In this specific case, the respondent used what would be the equivalent of *negro*, which is used interchangeably with 'Afro-descendente' and with Afro-Brazilian, the more acceptable terms for Brazilians of African descent. It is not pejorative like 'Negro' is in the US. In Brazil, it refers to the person's origin or ethnicity and it has been embraced by the black movement and people of African descent.
5.   Our interviews did not ask about Latin identity, yet several respondents used the term in their responses. When respondents used this label, we did not capitalize it so as to connote something that is less formal and less precise. We believe respondents' use of 'latin' reflects both the ambiguity in the way some women identify and a reflection of the popularized yet problematic use of the label as a casual reference to anyone of Latin American descent.

## References

ANZALDÚA, GLORIA 1987 'The new mestiza', excerpted in Charles Lemert (ed.), *Social Theory: The Multicultural and Classic Readings*, 3rd edn, Boulder, CO: Westview Press
BARLOW, ANDREW 2003 *Between Fear and Hope: Globalization and Race in the United States*, Lanham, MD: Rowman & Littlefield
BESERRA, BERNADETTE 2003 *Brazilian Immigrants in the United States: Cultural Imperialism and Social Class*, New York: LFB Scholarly Publishing LLC
—— 2005 'From Brazilians to Latinos? Racialization and Latinidad in the making of Brazilian carnival in Los Angeles', *Latino Studies*, vol. 3, pp. 53–75
BRAGA MARTES, ANA CRISTINA (ed.) 2000 *Brasileiros nos Estados Unidos: Um Estudo Sobre Imigrantes em Massachusetts*, São Paulo: Editora Paz e Terra
BRAGA MARTES ANA CRISTINA and RESENDE FLEISCHER, SORAYA 2004 *Fronteiras Cruzadas Ethnicidade, Gênero e Redes*, São Paulo: Editora Paz e Terra
CROUCHER, SHEILA 2004 *Globalization and Belonging: The Politics of Identity in a Changing World*, Lanham, MD: Rowman & Littlefield
GOLASH-BOZA, TANYA 2006 Dropping the hyphen? Becoming Latino(a)-American through racialized assimilation', *Social Forces*, vol. 85, no. 1, pp. 27–55
GUIMARÃES, ANTONIO SÉRGIO 2001 'Race, class and color behind Brazil's "racial democracy"', *NACLA Report on the Americas*, vol. 34, no. 6, May/June
GUINIER, LANI and TORRES, GERALD 2002 *The Miner's Canary: Enlisting Race, Resisting Power, Transforming Democracy*, Cambridge, MA: Harvard University Press

GUZMÁN, BETSY and DIAZ MCCONNELL, EILEEN 2002 'The Hispanic population: 1990–2000 growth and change', *Population Research and Policy Review*, vol. 21, nos 1–2, pp. 109–28

LEVITT, PEGGY 2001 *The Transnational Villagers, Berkeley and Los Angeles*, CA: University of California Press

—— 2003 '"You know, Abraham was really the first immigrant"': religion and transnational migration', *International Migration Review*, vol. 37, no. 3, pp. 847–73

LEWIS, AMANDA E. 2003 Everyday race-making', *The American Behavioral Scientist*, vol. 47, pp. 283

MARGOLIS, MAXINE 1994 *Little Brazil: An Ethnography of Brazilian Immigrants in New York City, Princeton*, NJ: Princeton University Press

—— 1998a *An Invisible Minority: Brazilians in New York City*, Boston, MA: Allyn & Bacon

—— 1998b 'We are *not* immigrants! A contested category among Brazilians in New York City and Rio de Janeiro', *Diasporic Identity, Selected Papers on Refugees and Immigrants*, American Anthropological Association, vol. 6, pp. 30–50

—— 2001 'Notes on transnational migration: the case of Brazilian immigrants', *Negotiating Transnationalism, Selected Papers on Refugees and Immigrants*, American Anthropological Association, vol. 9, pp. 202–22

MESSIAS, DEANNE K. HILFINGER 2002 'Transnational health resources, practices, and perspectives: Brazilian immigrant women's narratives', *Journal of Immigrant Health*, vol. 4, no. 5, pp. 183–200

OBOLER, SUZANNE 2006 'Racial ideologies, identities, and the question of rights', excerpts in Elizabeth Higginbotham and Margaret L. Andersen (eds), *Race and Ethnicity in Society*, Belmont, CA: Thomson Wadsworth, pp. 192–9

SALES, TERESA 1999 *Brasileiros longe de casa*, São Paulo: Cortez Editora

—— 2003 *Brazilians Away from Home*, New York: Center for Migration Studies

SANSONE, LIVIO 2003 *Blackness without Ethnicity: Constructing Race in Brazil*, New York: Palgrave Macmillan

DOS SANTOS, SALES AUGUSTAS and SILVA, NELSON FERNANDO INNOCÊNCIO 2006 'Brazilian indifference to racial inequality in the labor market', *Latin American Perspectives*, vol. 33, pp. 13–24

SILVERSTEIN, PAUL A. 2005 'Immigrant racialization and the new savage slot: race, migration, and immigration in the new Europe', *Annual Review of Anthropology*, vol. 34, pp. 363–84

WINANT, HOWARD 2004 *The New Politics of Race: Globalism, Difference, Justice*, Minneapolis, MN: University of Minnesota Press

# Cigar production: how race, gender and political ideology were inscribed onto tobacco

Gabriela Sandoval

**Abstract**

This paper examines the significance of race, gender and political ideology to tobacco production in the Dominican Republic. Using the economic crisis that gripped the Dominican tobacco sector in the late 1990s as a lens, this study argues that the tobacco crisis both elucidates Dominican society's dependence upon racialized and gendered structures and the significance of racial, political and gendered symbolism that is inscribed onto tobacco.

This paper uses the 1990s boom and economic crisis in tobacco production in the Dominican Republic to understand the significance of race, gender and political ideology in the Dominican context. I argue that the tobacco crisis sheds light upon the economy's dependence on racialized and gendered structures as well as upon the importance of racial, political and gendered symbolism historically inscribed on to tobacco.

## The crisis

The crisis in the Dominican tobacco sector that began in 1998 was the worst in memory, if not history. Never before has a price for tobacco gone un-negotiated, and therefore unpaid, for two years. Tobacco is prone to crisis, but even in the worst crises a price was always set. The causes of the 1998 crisis in the tobacco sector of the Dominican Republic – concentrated in the country's fertile Cibao region – are complex and intertwined, but their effects are undeniable. The societal implications of the crisis are embedded in the social organization of tobacco production.

The crisis in tobacco production at the end of the 1990s may have lasted only a few years, but it was distinguished, not by low levels of trade and investment but, rather, by a complete halt in trade and investment. Furthermore, the tobacco crisis presaged the larger national economic crisis faced by the Dominican economy just a few years later. Set off by the collapse of one of the country's largest banks, the repercussions included dramatic decreases in the Dominican government's annual budget and GDP, reversing the steady growth witnessed in the 1990s which had given the Dominican Republic its position as the most stable and fastest growing economy in the region.

In this paper I explore the reasons for and development of the tobacco crisis. I study the role of tobacco, not only as an export crop, but as a fundamental element in Dominican culture. I argue that a sectoral study of an agricultural product with deep, rich cultural and historical roots can provide important lessons about the social, political and economic structures that have governed its production. I hope to provide a picture of the way the history of tobacco production and recent trends in the world economy converged to create a crisis of unprecedented proportions and to understand why cultivators continue to produce tobacco despite overwhelmingly negative price signals – both during times of crisis and in periods of relative prosperity. This understanding is not attained through an economic analysis, however. Rather, my hypothesis is rooted in a cultural understanding of tobacco production in the Dominican Republic.

Although this study examines tobacco as a crop with a unique and peculiar history and symbolism, my argument about the reliance of the Dominican economy upon racialized and gendered structures can be seen in other sectors as well. The Dominican Republic's economy has experienced considerable growth in its tourist and export-processing sectors over the last several decades. Raynolds (1998, 2001), for example, has documented the gendered and raced nature of worker identity and labour segmentation in Dominican agriculture and export processing. Although agricultural production has decreased, it nevertheless continues to contribute significantly to the country's GDP. Tobacco presents an interesting case through which to understand Dominican race and gender dynamics.

## The study

This paper is about tobacco in the Cibao – a fertile valley located in the north-west portion of the Dominican Republic between the Cordillera Septentrional and the Cordillera Central mountain ranges.

It is a region that has been favourable to agricultural production since prior to colonization.

Data for this project were collected during the summer of 1999 as part of a research project examining land tenure, land use, urban agriculture and food security[1] in the Cibao region. I conducted twenty-three key informant interviews and eight group interviews ranging in size from two to eight people. I chose a purposeful sample of interviewees from the four research sites – Villa González, Licey, Tamboril and Salamanca – who spanned all aspects of tobacco production: exporters, factory managers, cultivators, land renters, landowners, Dominican and Haitian day labourers, warehouse owners, cigar-factory owners, cigar-factory workers specializing in every aspect of the process, *comines* (middlemen), health workers, the Director of the INTABACO and academics at the Center for Urban and Regional Studies (CEUR) at the Pontificia Universidad Católica Madre y Maestra.

Interviews were supplemented with observation, participant observation at factories and tobacco-centred events such as protests staged by tobacco workers and document review. Primary sources included technical reports published by the INTABACO and CEUR as well as newspaper articles documenting the tobacco crisis from the Dominican dailies: *Listín Diario, Hoy* and *El Siglo.*

The city nearest the four study areas is Santiago de los Caballeros (Santiago). Santiago is the largest urban centre in the Cibao, and the second largest city in the country, with 75 square kilometres of urban area. Santiago developed with tobacco as its economic focus (San Miguel 1995). The city has seen very rapid population growth over the last several decades. It has grown from 155,000 people in 1970 to 400,000 in 1990. During the crisis Santiago's population was estimated at 690,000.

In the following section, I examine the societal structures that allow tobacco production to continue. These are the constants of production: labour segmentation in tobacco production and raced and gendered divisions of labour in the tobacco industry. The second section shows how tobacco production and societal structures interact to manufacture national and political identities.

Tobacco has a long history in the Dominican Republic; from Taíno production to colonial production and prohibition and from independence to its present place in the country's economy. Furthermore, the history of the crop in different regions varies substantially, although traditionally production has taken place primarily in the Cibao. Of the four study areas, Villa González has had the strongest dependence on tobacco cultivation. Licey has poorer conditions for production, but many farmers planted there during the boom. Tamboril has a strong tobacco tradition in artisan cigar production, not cultivating. Lastly,

Salamanca does not have a long history of producing tobacco, but its soil is well suited for the crop and tobacco has gained significance in the community as part of a larger development strategy.

## Labour segmentation in tobacco production

### Production: processes

Once seen as a 'creole' crop, tobacco production has evolved into a complex series of production processes. The concentration of land into larger land holdings translates into larger areas of production. This often implies divisions within the system of labour that did not exist in the same way when smaller plots of land were cared for solely by a farmer and his family and neighbours. Unlike sugar-cane production, in which some aspects of the work (i.e. sugar-cane cutting) are seen as strictly the labour of Haitians and Haitian Dominicans, there is no part of tobacco or cigar production processes that is done exclusively by Haitians or Dominicans of Haitian descent. This section explores the processes of production in the tobacco industry with an examination of the way labour is stratified along racial and gender lines.

The processing that tobacco undergoes entails many different types of activities between the time it is planted and the moment it is exported as a cigar. An estimated 250,000 people are employed in the Dominican tobacco sector.

### Gender and race

The impacts of gender and race on the life chances of individuals in a racialized and gendered society cannot be separated, nor are the influences of race and gender additive. In this section I examine the way race and gender interact in the Dominican Republic's tobacco sector. This analysis is important for two reasons. First, it provides insight as to why and how the tobacco sector reproduces itself. Second, it is important for what it says about Dominican society as a whole.

For the purposes of this analysis race is an historical unit of analysis the understanding of which has undergone numerous iterations within the context of the Caribbean. Wagley and Harris's (1958) concept of 'social race' is helpful in analysing the way race in the 'New World' was historically understood. They see race as a concept constructed from an intricate system of legal codes and statutes that led to a more generalized understanding of race as a social construction. It follows then that race relations are about social structure (see, e.g., Mintz 1996, p. 10).

Wagley and Harris describe the principal differences between Latin American slavery and US slavery and how these variations have impacted on the differential treatment of black citizens of various countries. These differences include legal codes, legal status and timing in terms of the waxing and waning importance to the economy of plantation crops and how these coincide with the abolition of slavery in different colonies. The authors argue that, whereas in the US 'the status of the slave crystallized into that of a sub-human creature and, eventually, in some of the Southern states, into that of an inanimate piece of property' (1958, p. 123), the

> postulate of the Iberian codes was that all men are spiritually equal in the sight of God, that the condition of slave or master was an accident of material existence, and hence that the slave might be a better man than his master. ... Under the Latin codes, the slave was simply an unfortunate human being who had rights of his own which required protection by the law. (Wagley and Harris 1958, p. 125)

But possibly the most telling difference is in the human status given to freed slaves within these contexts. In Latin America, freed slaves received full – or fuller – citizenship and legal status, in contrast to freed slaves in the US.

Significant differences between the construction of race in mainland Latin America and in the Caribbean merit some discussion here. With respect to race relations in the Caribbean, Knight stresses that 'the historical experience of the Caribbean has been different *in degree as well as in kind*' (1995, p. 31, emphasis in original). He argues that the principal difference stems from the significant presence of indigenous populations in Latin American countries. This is in sharp contrast to the significantly reduced presence of indigenous peoples in the Caribbean (ibid., p. 29). He characterizes race relations in the following way:

> The peoples of the Caribbean were intrepid pioneers of necessity, and innate revolutionaries before it was fashionable to be revolutionaries. They have forever been pragmatic and eclectic. That is why considerations of race and class are so baffling when viewed throughout the Caribbean. Yet they are fundamental to what defines the region and its cultures. (Knight 1995, p. 31)

Hoetink (1967), Lozano (1992) and Oostindie (1996) examined the ways race is understood in the Dominican context. Through his work in the Dominican Republic and other parts of the Caribbean, Hoetink developed his psychosocial theory of the 'somatic norm image'. This theory departed from earlier understandings of race relations having some sort of linear trajectory dependent upon the type of slave system in place in a given country. His argument was based upon the fact that people are perceived differently in different places:

> one and the same person may be considered white in the Dominican Republic or Puerto Rico, and 'coloured' in Jamaica, Martinique, or Curaçao; this difference must be explained in terms of socially determined somatic norms. The same person may be called a 'Negro' in Georgia; this must be explained by the historical evolution of social structure in the Southern United States. (Hoetink 1967, p. xii)

He defines the somatic norm image as the somatic, or physical, characteristics that a group accepts as its norm or ideal (1967, p. 120). In the Dominican Republic, race is based on Hispanophilic conceptions of race as well as contrasts against Haiti.

Dominican society is profoundly invested in its contrast against Haiti and Dominican racial identities in particular are constructed in contrast to Haiti. Indeed, as Glenn (1992) argues, identities, racial and otherwise, are relational in nature. The categories 'Haitian' and 'Dominican' gain meaning in relation to one another and they are linked to one another in the complex intertwining of alignment with power and privilege.

There continues to be disagreement about how to define race relations in the Dominican Republic. Derby (1994) argues that 'many observers simplistically conflate anti-Haitianism with racism'. I argue that this is not a 'simplistic' conflation. Rather, it is the way that racism and racial prejudice in the Dominican Republic have evolved over time. Racism is a dynamic process that will be made manifest differently within different social, economic and historical contexts.

Derby argues that anti-Haitianism is instead a form of 'racialized nationalism'. As with the concept of 'social race', the idea of 'racial democracy' has received much attention especially as contrasted with the 'race problem' in the US. These ideas, in conjunction with understandings of the racial continuum and the 'whitening' effects of class upon race, have often been offered to explain why the Caribbean (and Latin America) is not 'racist' (in the way the US and South Africa, for example, are understood to be racist). However, simply because this racism is rooted in a different colonial past than, for example, US racism does not make 'anti-Haitianism' any less a racist ideology contributing to racial inequalities.

*Labour segmentation*

It is important to understand anti-Haitianism and its interplay with gender and the sexual division of labour and the way it has been used to establish an historical ethnic division of labour in which the present ethnic and gender divisions of labour within tobacco production are rooted. First, in terms of gender, issues of race and nationality played into the politics of the border between Haiti and the Dominican Republic, but even these were tied to the labour of Dominican and Haitian women. For example, Article 10 of Immigration Law No. 95 in the Dominican Republic particularly affected Dominican women working as prostitutes in Haiti and Haitian market women who brought most of the produce and manufactured goods to rural Dominican markets (Derby 1994, p. 504). With respect to an ethnic division of labour, Derby finds that it

> developed in the ranching areas, in which large ranchers employed Dominicans as foremen to raise cattle, sheep, or hogs. ... These [foremen] then employed Haitians to help as sharecroppers with the bean, corn, and coffee harvests. The ethnic division of labor was so entrenched that after the massacre,[2] some of these middle ranchers abandoned the border and sought urban wage labor, unable to imagine cultivating crops without Haitian help. (Derby 1994, p. 511)

Other occupations, such as domestic work and selling at market, across the country also became 'ethnically encoded' as work done by Haitians (ibid., p. 514). Thus, the ethnic division of labour has historical precedents.

This is further evidenced in the labour stratification and segmentation present within the different labour activities involved in the cultivation of tobacco and the manufacture of cigars. Race and racism, gendered and ethnic divisions of labour combine with a culture of tobacco production to foster and perpetuate raced and gendered labour segmentation. When seen in the context of the most recent crisis, the way these factors interact to perpetuate the reproduction of the tobacco sector becomes increasingly clear.

The wide range of labour required – from unskilled to highly skilled – impacts on the way tobacco production is perceived and these aspects of labour influence who does what work. This division provides a glimpse of Dominican society and social relationships on the island using tobacco as a lens. Furthermore, as the global economy continues to impact on markets and communities, tobacco allows us to see a slice of these transformations as it is impacted upon and as it impacts on the people involved at every step of production.

The high level of differentiation between labour activities associated with tobacco production and cigar making has allowed the process to become very segmented. Dominican men, Haitian men, Dominican women and Haitian women are all concentrated in certain tasks and locked completely out of others. People are socialized into the different productive and reproductive roles of tobacco production and cigar making, usually based on their nationality, race and gender. This aspect of tobacco production interacts with the traditional gender- and ethnic-based divisions of labour, which are themselves rooted in histories of discrimination, to maintain the rigid structure of labour segmentation present in tobacco production in the Dominican Republic today.

For example, when asked why Haitians are often pigeonholed into the more labour intensive, lower-skilled jobs, producers often respond by explaining that, because Haiti does not produce tobacco, most Haitians in the Dominican Republic do not come from this tradition. They do not have the expertise certain tasks require. Similarly, factory owners and managers say that there are few Haitian workers in cigar factories because they lack expertise or do not have proper documentation.

The treatment of Haitians and Dominico-Haitians in the Dominican Republic has been well documented by human rights organizations. Indeed, this population has been described as 'illegal people' and their plight as one of 'permanent illegality' (Inter-American Commission on Human Rights 1999; Human Rights Watch 2002). Children born to Haitian immigrants in the Dominican Republic are routinely denied birth certificates. Article 11 of the Dominican Constitution grants Dominican citizenship by birth to persons born in the Dominican Republic. However, Dominican officials have found loopholes in the interpretation of this constitutional right in order to refuse Dominican-born children of Haitian migrant workers this right. Dominico-Haitians often find themselves in a kind of political limbo; neither are they granted Dominican citizenship at birth nor are they recognized as Haitian citizens.

This lack of documentation is a source of conflict for many Dominicans of Haitian descent (Lozano 1992; Inter-American Commission on Human Rights 1999; Human Rights Watch 2002). They face deportation and mass expulsion, racial profiling and prejudice. Another troubling consequence of the citizenship 'limbo' faced by Dominico-Haitians has to do with access to education. Although undocumented children are not prohibited by law from attending school, they are routinely denied access to classrooms by Dominican officials (Human Rights Watch 2002).

Haitians also have a history as contract labourers in the Dominican Republic. They are seen as cheap, abundant and exploitable labour. Their ambiguous citizenship allows them to be further exploited since they have no homeland to turn to for help in enforcing their rights. Their lack of access to education all but ensures their entry into low-skilled jobs, thus restricting access to the social mobility that might be enabled by citizenship and effectively inhibiting any of the 'whitening' effects that are often thought to accompany upward mobility in the Caribbean racial continuum. This, and the idea that their treatment is somehow justified due to their racial, ethnic and/or national status, has profound implications for the jobs they are able to obtain, their working and living conditions and ultimately their life chances.

In the tobacco sector, Dominican men tend to do work seen as requiring more skill such as tending to the seedbeds and fertilizing. Haitian men are concentrated in weeding and hilling, although increasingly they are being hired to help with harvesting. Application of fungicides and insecticides is performed by both Dominican and Haitian men. This aspect of the work is essential, but it entails exposure to dangerous toxins. Workers are not always made aware of the ramifications of inhaling and otherwise coming into contact with these chemicals. Dominican women do most of the tying, although younger workers, both male and female, help with the tying and occasionally Haitian women are also hired to tie the *sartas* (braids of palm frond leaves by which tobacco leaves are hung to dry). Women perform two other activities before the tobacco leaves the field. These are particularly invisible: production of *serones* (the sacks in which tobacco leaves are packaged) and cooking meals for tobacco workers.

A small family-owned field can employ the whole family and six or seven additional workers. The women and children in the family usually tie *sartas* without pay, while a woman who is hired to do this work will be paid about RD$2.50 (about US$0.15) per *sarta*. A worker can tie anywhere between 50 and 150 *sartas* in a day. Workers hired to pick leaves are paid RD$150 per day plus breakfast and lunch. Women in the tobacco producer's home cook breakfast and lunch for anywhere between ten and twenty people during the harvest, but the producers interviewed never mentioned this work as part of the production process.

Once the tobacco leaves the field it is handled by male *comines*, or middle men, and male warehouse workers. When the leaf arrives at a cigar factory, Dominican women – with few exceptions – will remove its stems. Dominican men and some women wrap the leaves into a cigar. The number of women has increased in this part of the work due to the mythology surrounding their hands and the delicate touch they are believed to bring to the work table. Women do much of the final packaging as well. Although Haitian workers are beginning to take on some of the more skilled jobs in the field, they are rarely found in the factories.

Rollers are an important example of the type of skilled worker required in cigar production. They were also instrumental during the boom and the crisis. A trained roller is an asset to the cigar manufacturer. Training a roller requires a minimum of one year, but, on average, this process takes between one and two years. Since this is not simply a skill, however, the actual art of cigar rolling takes a minimum of several years to master (Vaughan 1998), and not everyone is said to have the 'natural talent' to attain this level of mastery. During the crisis, experienced rollers were often lured away from jobs they had had for years, sometimes decades, by higher salaries, vehicles and even homes (Mott 1998). Some rollers left their old jobs as new companies were established closer to their homes, making their daily commutes shorter. This also had repercussions for the quality of cigars produced (Suckling 1997).

Labour segmentation in the tobacco industry ensured that the opportunities created by the boom would have differential impacts on the lives of women, men, Haitians and Dominicans of Haitian descent. There is some evidence that the boom created opportunities for women to earn increased wages in a sector outside the export-processing zones. On the other hand, the newest hires are often the most vulnerable. Therefore, workers who might have gained jobs from a boom in the industry were the most susceptible to losing them.

Although historically perceived as a creole crop, tobacco production evolved and survived through the use of exploitative societal structures that justify hiring, training and paying labourers differentially according to their gender, race, nationality, age or some combination thereof. These structures have been present for centuries, but tobacco production has come to rely more and more heavily upon them over time. This is particularly so for raced labour segmentation in the industry.

For example, the labour of Haitians is almost always considered low skilled. Although this is mostly due to the racist perception of Haitians as unable to do skilled work, the perception is reinforced by ethnic Haitians' lack of documentation. Tobacco is seen as a knowledge-intensive practice requiring labour ranging from the very low skilled to highly skilled. Allowing Haitians to participate in some aspects of the tobacco-growing and cigar-manufacturing processes would cause this work to be perceived as low skilled. Ultimately, this raises questions about who benefits from these perceptions. It behoves Dominican tobacco growers to exclude Haitian labourers to maintain the perception of their work as knowledge intensive. This does not mean that if Haitians did the work it would be any less skilled, but that the perception of the work, as artisan and skilled, would shift. The societal structures that allow tobacco production to survive are maintained by the benefit they provide to certain groups of participants in the processes.

## Identity and politics

*Tobacco as symbol*

This section examines the development of the symbols ascribed to tobacco and tobacco growers in order to understand the ways in which tobacco became implicated in the exploitative societal structures that contribute to labour segmentation. It does this by looking at the way tobacco came to be seen as a liberal, democratic crop grown by small landowning, autonomous farmers whose race was socially constructed as 'white'.

In the Dominican Republic tobacco carries a very heavy symbolic and ideological weight. Because it was grown mainly by small, autonomous landowners in the north who pushed for open international trade, it came to be associated with small holding, liberal ideology and democracy.

Tobacco played an important role in the ideological rivalry that developed between the northern and the southern regions of the Dominican Republic. This rivalry contributed to the definition of Dominican regional and national identity, as well as to the social and political segregation of the country (Moya Pons 1995). During the 1860s, the elites of the south of the country typically had large land holdings. In the north, there were many small landowners. Regional differences resulted in antagonisms that manifested in the ideological struggles between the northern liberals and southern conservatives (Baud 1996, p. 128). In 1861 when President General Pedro Santana placed the Dominican Republic under Spanish rule once again, this action was supported by the cattlemen of the south while the northern elites opposed it.

By attributing the liberal political thought of the north to tobacco production, several authors helped to establish its reputation as a 'democratic' crop (Demorizi 1964; Yunén 1985; Moya Pons 1995; Baud 1996; Cassá 1996; Hoetink 1997). 'In the fabrication, the fire and spiraling of smoke of a cigar, there was always something revolutionary, a kind of protest against oppression, the consuming flame and a liberating flight into the blue of dreams' (Ortiz 1947, p. 14). While *Cuban Counterpoint*, Ortíz's whimsical essay on the contrasting meanings of sugar and tobacco, was written from a Cuban perspective, it provides insight into the Dominican Republic as well. Ortíz sees Cuban history as a juxtaposition of the tobacco and sugar industries on the island.

Pedro F. Bonó wrote a comparable reflection on tobacco and cacao in 1880.[3] At that time these two crops were competing for primacy in the Cibao's economy. Bonó argues that tobacco is democratic because any worker, no matter how poor, with access to just a small piece of land can easily obtain credit and that, because tobacco requires only half of the year to cultivate, the other half can be used to grow subsistence crops. He takes the characterization further and states that tobacco 'es la base de nuestra infantil democracia por el equilibrio en que mantiene a las fortunas de los individuos, y de ahí viene siendo el obstáculo más serio de las oligarquías posibles; fue y es el más firme apoyo de nuestra autonomía' ('is the base of our young democracy due to the equilibrium with which it maintains the fortunes of individuals and from that point, is the most serious obstacle to potential oligarchies. It was and is the strongest support to our autonomy') (Demorizi 1964).

Yunén (1985) identifies several decisive political events inspired by the 'democratic' and 'liberal' plant, among them: the fall of President Santana in 1856, caused in part by the drop in tobacco exports, the Revolution of 1857 provoked by speculative acts of President Báez against the Cibao's tobacco cultivators and, in 1863, the defence of national sovereignty initiated, promoted and maintained mostly by tobacco cultivators during the Restoration War. This war resulted from the annexation of the Dominican Republic to Spain. After the annexation, the government attempted to impose trade policies and set up a monopoly on tobacco in the interest of the Spanish. Resentment built up among tobacco cultivators, and in February 1863 war erupted (Moya Pons 1995).

The democratic and liberal ideals of free trade and small, autonomous land holdings worked by farmers who were imagined as hard working, thrifty and self-sufficient, as well as the events they inspired, came to be associated, not only with the tobacco trade, but also with the whole of the Cibao, and ultimately with the 'best' characteristics of the Dominican people (Baud 1991). As in Ortíz's account of Cuba, tobacco and sugar represented competing interests:

Nicotine stimulates the mind, giving it diabolical inspiration; the excess of glucose in the blood benumbs the brain and even causes stupidity. For this reason alone tobacco would be of the liberal reform group and sugar of the reactionary conservatives. (Ortiz 1947, p. 10)

Tobacco continues to carry romantic connotations of democracy and autonomy, as Gaspar Polanco, director of INTABACO, made clear, but tobacco production is no longer an autonomous activity. It is no longer a small traditional business, but a project that requires a business mentality (Polanco 1999). This transformation is also reflected in the cigar industry. For example, the León Jimenes tobacco enterprise is now administered by Guillermo León, a 36-year-old with a degree in business administration and a fourth-generation tobacco man (Tamayo 1996–7, p. 132).

The system of land tenure also changed since these ideological ascriptions to regions were formed. During the 1920s and 1930s land was abundant. A producer in need of land had only to ask a nearby landowner for permission to cultivate. Rent was not paid since land acquired value only through use. The producer simply demarcated a *conuco* (small plot of land used to grow food and herbs) and planted it. In the 1930s land prices began to increase. A system similar to sharecropping known as '*arriendo en media*' developed. At the beginning of the next decade, tobacco prices dropped drastically. Many small landowners sold their plots. Ultimately, this led to the concentration of land into the hands of a few rich families (Baud 1984).

At present, most producers no longer own the land they work. However, the long-standing perception of the plant as the domain of small-scale, autonomous landowners is so deeply rooted that it continues to colour the way people, including policy-makers, see and understand tobacco cultivation.

Ortíz (1947) also contrasts sugar and tobacco by investing them with race and gender: tobacco is dark and masculine, sugar 'high yellow' (or white, depending on how far up the 'social ladder' [processing] it has managed to climb) and feminine. The two crops symbolize contrasting values: artisan production/mass production, city/country, democracy/slavery and native/foreign.

## The island at racial odds with itself

Tobacco contributes to a national, as well as regional construction of identity in the Dominican Republic in other ways. For numerous and complex reasons, Dominican national identity is often constructed in opposition to its eastern neighbour, Haiti. Maingot (1996) argues that the Dominican Republic, and particularly 'white'[4] Dominicans, generated a kind of racial fear of Haiti and Haitians, or what he calls a 'terrified consciousness'. He states:

> Driven by this fear, the whites unleash a 'regimen of terror' which, as might be sociologically predicted, generates not only a self-fulfilling prophecy but a grotesque inversion of logic: you justify the terror against the black on the grounds that what you perceive to be his intrinsic and natural barbarity terrorizes you. (Maingot 1996, p. 53)

This fear, coupled with contempt and a racialized nationalism, has its roots in several historic events, particularly the impact of Haiti's independence and Haiti's invasion and occupation of the Dominican Republic. Haiti's successful revolt for independence set off a general wave of fear in the slaveholding American colonies. 'The fear of "Haitianization" had survived the events in Haiti to become the dominant metaphor behind the terrified consciousness of the [European] whites' (ibid., p. 57).

Baud (1991) argues that Santo Domingo had developed a 'profound inferiority complex' due to French Saint Domingue's success as a plantation colony. In fact, the French colony grew so much in the eighteenth century that it became the richest colony in the world. This 'inferiority complex' was further exacerbated by the invasion and twenty-two-year occupation of Santo Domingo by Haiti. Baud (1996) states that Dominican resentment of Haiti was heightened by the fact that the Dominican Republic's independence was ultimately won with the help of Haiti's own independence fighters and Toussaint Louverture. Thus, with the roots of the Dominican Republic's 'inferiority complex' firmly established, it comes as no surprise that the country's national identity was often contrasted with international perceptions of Haiti: black/white and civilization/barbarism.

The stage for a 'terrified consciousness' in the Dominican Republic was set with the Haitian revolution, but racism and anti-Haitian sentiment rooted in racism was prevalent in Europe and the US (Maingot 1996, p. 55). However, the panic and repugnance was much more tangible in Santo Domingo. Not only did the Spanish colony feel a very real imperialist threat from Haiti, Haitian occupation served to exacerbate the sentiment.

The relationship between the two countries eventually stabilized. They signed the Treaty of Peace and Friendship, Commerce and Navigation in 1867, just two years after the Restoration Wars. Economic, cultural and political ties between the two countries were strong. Girault states that 'era de uso común entre las dos naciones ser refugio de exiliados políticos. Cuando un partido tomaba el poder en una parte de la isla, los oponentes se podían refugiar en la otra parte' ('it was common practice between the two nations to provide refuge for political exiles. When one political party took power on one side of the island, the opponents could take refuge on the other side') (1992, p. 71). This all changed with the US military occupation of Haiti in 1915 and the Dominican Republic in 1916 as did the whole nature of the Haitian-Dominican border and the relationship between the two countries.

The US military invaders used the 'terrified consciousness', but it was fully invoked for and applied in the construction of Trujillo's racist nationalist programme. This continued under Balaguer (1966–78, 1986–96) and is best exemplified in his book *La Isla al Revés* (1983). He conjures the fear of Haiti by re-imagining the primary goal of the Haitian Revolution as full conquest of the island, associating disease with Haitians and Haitian immigration and stating that Haitians cause the decay of Dominican morals and ethnic composition: all to inspire a nationalist and patriotic sentiment in the Dominican population.

Since the US occupation, fear has been mostly replaced with contempt and this contempt has been increasingly expressed in racial and ethnic terms.

> The racial differences between the (predominantly) black Haitian population and the (predominantly) mulatto population of the Dominican Republic had always been a factor in relations between the two countries, but the transformation in social and economic structure which occurred after 1870 made the racial factor more important. (Baud 1996, p. 31)

Even though the majority of the Dominican Republic's population is of mixed heritage – indigenous, African and European – Dominican elites nevertheless went to great lengths to establish their whiteness. Again, in contrast to Haiti:

> But I have to warn you, madam, that the Dominicans are Constitutionally white, and that is the reason we have established this Republic, which you must not confuse with that of Haiti, where the people eat human flesh, speak creole French (*patois*) and where voodoo gods abound. (Moscoso Puello quoted in Baud 1996, p. 126)

Thus, Dominican identity is constructed as the antithesis of what is perceived as Haitian (Yunén 1985; Baud 1996).

### Identity and crisis in a Dominican context

Race and place were also linked within the Dominican Republic. The northern area of the nation came to be seen as a 'whiter', so much so, that Trujillo adopted *merengue*, the popular music developed in the north, to push his racist nationalist agenda (Pacini 1995; Lipsitz 1998). Lipsitz states:

> Trujillo put the power of the state behind *merengue* because he viewed it as an emblematic icon of the nation's white, Spanish, and Catholic traditions, a source of national unity that provided a sharp contrast with the Dominican Republic's black, French, and Vodoun neighbors in Haiti. (Lipsitz 1998, pp. 299–300)

Yet even this piece of history regarding the country's popular culture cannot be divorced from tobacco. One of the principal instruments used in *merengue* was the Hohner button accordion. This instrument's arrival in the Dominican Republic can be traced to the nineteenth century when tobacco producers in the Cibao traded tobacco for accordions with German merchants. Significantly, tobacco is present in most aspects of Dominican life, from its politics and history to its music (Lipsitz 1998).

The place of tobacco in the contemporary Dominican imagination is linked to its history: the racial implications of slavery, the liberal ideals implicit in tobacco producers' dependence upon the free trade of their crop, their ability to acquire land and the history of conflict with Haiti. These factors and others contributed to the formation of particular Dominican identities: racial, regional and political. But, as time has passed and globalization developed, little remains of the obvious benefits of tobacco production. Land tenure has changed drastically. Economies of scale continue to emerge. Export-processing zones encroach upon traditional production. To survive, tobacco production has had to acquire the traits of other types of agricultural production. For example, tobacco now requires large landholdings, higher levels of technology and capital, and an infusion of more easily exploitable labour. Over the years, tobacco has become increasingly dependent upon structures of inequality.

Identity acquires increasing significance, not only in the history of tobacco production, but in the present stubbornness with which it continues to be planted. During the crisis, it was not uncommon for identity to come to the forefront of discussions. For example, many tobacco growers from Villa González based their response to the tobacco sector's crisis on their identity as tobacco growers. On several occasions I asked cultivators why they did not go to Santiago in search of work as cultivators from other areas had. The most common answer was, 'Soy agricultor' ('I am a farmer'). Some elaborated that this meant they did not identify with any other type of work. Their identity as 'tobacco producer' is salient enough to compel traditional farmers to weather the crisis without looking too far for other alternatives. This in turn pressures the government to step in with a bail-out solution.

Finally, I examine the ways tobacco production is reproduced. Tobacco is not usually an economically profitable crop. So why do producers continue to plant tobacco year after year? I argue that non-economic values associated with tobacco production contribute to the maintenance and reproduction of tobacco cultivation. Given the romantic ideals and cultural values associated with tobacco production, it comes as no surprise that life-long tobacco producers see their whole identities as tied inextricably to their crop and continue to plant tobacco in even the worst of crises. Conversely, those Dominicans who cultivated tobacco solely in response to the high prices of the 1996–7 boom had no qualms about returning to previous crops or other employment when the boom gave way to crisis.

Other benefits of tobacco production include a network that provides several different safety nets available only to tobacco producers. It would be foolish to believe that tobacco producers and their families have no other sources of income than tobacco. Some producers have jobs that do not interfere with their fieldwork, such as *concho*[5] driving. Tobacco producers often have family members with jobs outside the tobacco sector. Many Dominicans also have relatives in the US who send them remittances.

Del Rosario (1999) identifies three principal reasons for the continuing push to plant tobacco, when, even after two years without sale, producers, particularly those in traditional tobacco producing areas, have *still* planted tobacco. These are also what he calls 'the secret of tobacco'. First, although quality tobacco grows best under certain climactic and soil conditions, it is basically a weed that can grow anywhere (see also Rogozinski 1992, p. 66). So, if planted, it does not matter what the conditions, it *will* be harvested. Second, the producer might not know when, but tobacco *will* sell (see also Ramos 1999).

Last, and most important, tobacco is a source of credit. The same way that tobacco cultivators have faith that they will get paid for their harvest, so the *colmado* (small store that carries staple foods often sold in very small quantities) owner believes the producer will pay him/her. No other crop affords its producer this benefit. Credit, broadly speaking, extends even further: one producer spoke of a large tobacco warehouse owner in Villa González who advanced him money when a family member was ill and had to be hospitalized during the production cycle. Exporters and warehouse owners in other crops do not extend this courtesy to producers. Similarly, Henke Kelner, the maker of Davidoff Cigars and a renowned tobacconist, is said to treat his long-term contract farmers more like family than business associates 'since he knows that he has to get the best possible tobacco from them' (Suckling 1996, p. 110). There are similar relationships within cigar factories. In the León Jimenes factory, workers receive a free uniform and pay only half the cost of two meals on work days in the company cafeterias. They also get two free car washes each week and thirty packs of cigarettes every month and they are allowed to smoke as many cigars in the factory as they like (Tamayo 1996–7).

Unlike other agricultural products and the manufacture of other goods, tobacco and cigar production require an enormous amount of work and expertise. Tobacco production is a culture into which many people and workers have been born and socialized. Most of the tobacco producers I interviewed have participated in the cultivation and warehousing of tobacco or the production of cigars since the time they were very small children. Cultivation and cigar manufacturing are trades that have been passed down from generation to generation. One factory manager called work in tobacco an 'inheritance'.

The conception of tobacco as an inheritance is rooted in its long agricultural and political history. This also affects the way that institutions such as the INTABACO interact with producers. For example, Kelner states: 'I am convinced that the only way to make quality cigars is to have control through the entire process. The problem with the cigar business has been a question of tradition' (Suckling 1996, p. 110). His statement shows that, although tradition has been instrumental in the continuing production of tobacco and cigars, it also hampers the establishment of institutional norms and structures for maintaining the quality of tobacco products.

Kelner also cites tradition, or the lack of, as a reason for the crisis: 'The problem is that a lot of people in the business now are just in it for the money. ... They don't care about tobacco. They are not really interested in cigars' (Suckling 1997, p. 121). This tradition is also tied to family production. Many cigar companies have been passed from fathers to sons for generations. Some of these families emigrated from Cuba and maintain, along with a sense of tradition, a strong sense of nostalgia. In an interview for *Cigar Aficionado*, Carlos Fuente Jr., the president of Tabacalera A Fuente y Cia, said: 'The cigar business is about families, about people who have their hearts in the business, people that sleep, breathe, live and dream tobacco' (Shanken 1998, p. 116). Guillermo León, the president of León Jimenes Cigars, also attributed the failure of the new cigar factories to their lack of tradition: 'the business of making tobacco is not something that you can just start up from here to tomorrow if you don't have traditions, and so on' (Mott 1998, p. 91).

For this type of production to continue, the legacy must be passed down to progressive generations of tobacco cultivators. But what happens when outside values infiltrate another culture and the process of bequeathing work from one generation to the next is disrupted? Most producers to whom I spoke have found their children reject their fathers' work. Sons no longer want to 'get dirty' in the field. They prefer to study and stay indoors. The next few decades will be telling for the future of tobacco production if this work is taken out of the hands of traditional producers. It is difficult to tell, however, if children's choices are due to a temporary distaste for their parents' trade or more permanent career choices.

## Conclusion

Not long ago, Baud asked 'how and why do peasant households continue to produce for the market when it is clear for outsiders that they receive too little for their product?' He problematized perceptions of peasants as 'hapless victim[s]' of capitalism and 'rational' entrepreneur[s] (1991, p. 9). Similarly, in this paper, I ask: how has tobacco production survived? Except that, instead of looking to the *campesinato* (population of farmworkers) for answers, I question raced and gendered social structures in the Dominican Republic. Specifically, I examine labour segmentation by race, gender and nationality in tobacco production as well as raced and gendered divisions of labour in the tobacco industry. Furthermore, I show the reciprocally reinforcing relationships among tobacco production, raced and gendered social structures and the construction of national, political and racial identities.

The 1990s boom/bust cycle in the tobacco sector of the Dominican Republic provides a unique lens through which race, gender and Haitian-Dominican relations in the Dominican Republic can be understood, I argue that structures of inequality have been appropriated by the tobacco production process in order to allow it to continue to adapt. As part of an intricate web of survival strategies in the Cibao, tobacco provides unique insights into the Dominican development process, societal relationships and the place of a traditional crop in an ever-globalizing world.

## Acknowledgements

The author wishes to gratefully acknowledge the financial support provided by Cornell University's Institute for International Food, Agriculture and Development, the Mario Einaudi Center for International Studies, the Department of City and Regional Planning and the Latin American Studies Program; institutional support provided by the Centro de Estudios Urbanos y Regionales (CEUR), Pedro Juan del Rosario, Luis Polanco, Neeta Misra, Barbara Lynch and all of the project's key informants without whom this project would not have been complete; and editorial assistance provided by colleagues and friends, especially Cheryl Beredo for insightful commentary. Any errors are the sole responsibility of the author.

## Notes

1.    Tobacco has an unusual role in agricultural production in the Dominican Republic. It is a non-edible product that significantly enhances food security, counted by scholars among such edible crops as cassava, plantains and beans (del Rosario 2000). Yet it is always at the mercy of whims and taste, addiction and campaigns opposing its production and marketing.
2.    Reference to the 1937 massacre of Haitians commissioned by President Trujillo on the Haitian-Dominican border.
3.    In addition to Ortíz's sugar/tobacco and Bonó's tobacco/cacao counterpoints, a piece on cattle-raising and sugar in the Dominican Republic in Las Patrias de Santo Domingo (1975) offers another counterpoint.

4. Specifically, Dominican elites who define themselves as white (see Baud 1996, pp. 124, 128).
5. The *concho* is a form of public transportation very particular to the Dominican Republic. Small passenger cars follow set routes around the city picking people up and dropping them off from any location along their route for a small set fee.

# References

BALAGUER, JOAQUIN 1983 *La Isla al Revés: Haiti y el Destino Dominicano*, 3rd edn, Santo Domingo: Libreria Dominicana

BAUD, MICHIEL 1984 'La gente del tabaco: Villa González en el siglo veinte', *Ciencia y sociedad*, vol. 9, no. 1, pp. 101–37

—— 1991 'Peasant Society under Siege: Tobacco Cultivators in the Cibao (Dominican Republic), 1870–1930', PhD dissertation, Rijksuniversiteit Utrecht, Utrecht, Holland

—— 1996 '"Constitutionally white": the forging of a national identity in the Dominican Republic', in Gert Oostindie (ed.) *Ethnicity in the Caribbean: Essays in Honor of Harry Hoetink*, London: Macmillan Caribbean, pp. 121–51

CASSÁ, ROBERTO 1996 *Historia Social y Económica de la República Dominicana*, Vol. 2, Dominican Republic: Alfa & Omega

DEL ROSARIO, PEDRO JUAN 1999 Interview by author. Ithaca, NY

—— 2000 'Urban food systems', International Studies and Planning Seminar, Cornell University, Ithaca, NY

DEMORIZI, EMILIO R. (ed.) 1964 *Papeles de Pedro F. Bonó: Para la Historia de las Ideas Políticas en Santo Domingo*, Santo Domingo: Editora Caribe

DERBY, LAUREN 1994 'Haitians, magic, and money: raza and society in the Haitian-Dominican borderlands, 1900 to 1937', *Comparative Studies in Society and History*, vol. 36, no. 3, pp. 488–526

GIRAULT, CRISTIAN 1992 'Las relaciones entre la República de Haití y la República Dominicana: un enfoque geographico', in Wilfredo Lozano (ed.) *La Cuestión Haitiana en Santo Domingo: Migración Internacional, Desarrollo y Relaciones Inter-Estatales Entre Haiti y República Dominicana*, Santo Domingo: FLACSO, Centro Norte-Sur de la Universidad de Miami, pp. 69–77

GLENN, EVELYN N. 1992 'From servitude to service work: historical continuities in the racial division of paid reproductive labor', *Signs*, vol. 18, no. 1 pp. 1–43

HOETINK, HARRY 1967 *Caribbean Race Relations: A Study of Two Variants*, New York: Oxford University Press

—— 1997 *El Pueblo Dominicano: Apuntes para su Sociología Historica*, 4th edn, Santo Domingo: Ediciones Librería La Trinitaria

HUMAN RIGHTS WATCH 2002 *Dominican Republic: 'Illegal People' Haitians and Dominico-Haitians in the Dominican Republic*, vol. 14, no. 1 (B)

INTER-AMERICAN COMMISSION ON HUMAN RIGHTS 1999 *Country Report: Dominican Republic*, http://www.cidh.oas.org/countryrep/DominicanRep99/Table.htm

KNIGHT, FRANKLIN W. 1995 *Race, Ethnicity, and Class: Forging the Plural Society in Latin America and the Caribbean*, The Seventeenth Charles Edmonson Historical Lectures, Baylor University Waco, TX, 27–8 March, Waco TX: Markham Press Fund

LIPSITZ, GEORGE 1998 'Their America and ours: intercultural communication in the context of "Our America"', in Jeffrey Belnap and Raúl Fernández (eds) *José Martí's 'Our America': From National to Hemispheric Cultural Studies*, Durham, NC: Duke University Press, pp. 293–316

LOZANO, WILFREDO (ed.) 1992 *La Cuestión Haitiana en Santo Domingo: Migración Internacional, Desarrollo y Relaciones Inter-Estatales Entre Haiti y República Dominicana*, Santo Domingo: FLACSO, Centro Norte-Sur de la Universidad de Miami

MAINGOT, ANTHONY P. 1996 'Haiti and the terrified consciousness of the Caribbean', in Gert Oostindie (ed.) *Ethnicity in the Caribbean: Essays in Honor of Harry Hoetink*, London: Macmillan Caribbean, pp. 53–80

MINTZ, SYDNEY 1996 'Ethnic difference, plantation sameness', in Gert Oostindie (ed.) *Ethnicity in the Caribbean: Essays in Honor of Harry Hoetink*, London: Macmillan Caribbean, pp. 39–52

MOTT, GORDON 1998 'An interview with Guillermo León, President León Jimenes Cigars', *Cigar Aficionado*, August, pp. 80–97

MOYA PONS, FRANK 1995 *The Dominican Republic: A National History*, New York: Hispaniola Books

OOSTINDIE, GERT 1996 'Introduction: ethnicity, as ever?', in Gert Oostindie (ed.) *Ethnicity in the Caribbean: Essays in Honor of Harry Hoetink*, London: Macmillan

ORTIZ, FERNANDO 1947 *Cuban Counterpoint: Tobacco and Sugar*, Durham, NC: Duke University Press

PACINI HERNANDEZ, DEBORAH 1995 *Bachata: A Social History of a Dominican Popular Music*, Philadelphia, PA: Temple University Press

POLANCO, GASPAR 1999 Interview by author. Santiago, DR. 14 June

RAMOS, PEDRO ARROYO 1999 'La producción nacional del tabaco', *Listín Diario* 28 April, El Cibao, p. 6

RAYNOLDS, LAURA T. 1998 'Harnessing women's work: restructuring agricultural and industrial labor forces in the Dominican Republic', *Economic Geography*, vol. 74, no. 2, pp. 149–69

—— 2001 'New plantations, new workers: gender and production politics in the Dominican Republic', *Gender and Society*, vol. 15, no. 1, pp. 7–28

ROGOZINSKI, JAN 1992 *A Brief History of the Caribbean from the Arawak and the Carib to the Present*, New York: Meridian

SAN MIGUEL, PEDRO 1995 *Los Campesinos del Cibao: Economia de Mercado y Transformación Agraria en la República Dominicana, 1880–1960*, San Juan, PR: Editorial de la Universidad de Puerto Rico

SHANKEN, MARVIN R. 1998 'An interview with Carlos Fuente Jr., President, Tabacalera A Fuente y Cia', *Cigar Aficionado*, December, pp. 108–29

SUCKLING, JAMES 1996 'Tobacco man: Henke Kelner, maker of Davidoff Cigars, is a true lover of the leaf and a demanding connoisseur of a good smoke', *Cigar Aficionado*, Summer, pp. 106–17

—— 1997 'The Dominican cigar explosion', *Cigar Aficionado*, August, pp. 112–21

TAMAYO, JUAN O. 1996–7 'Reviving a tradition', *Cigar Aficionado*, Winter, pp. 130–9

VAUGHAN, BRENDAN 1998 'Swisher sweet dreams', *Cigar Aficionado*, October, pp. 108–17

WAGLEY, CHARLES and HARRIS, MARVIN 1958 *Minorities in the New World*, New York: Columbia University Press

YUNÉN, RAFAEL E. 1985 *La Isla Como Es: Hipotesis para su Comprobación*, Santiago: Universidad Católica Madre y Maestra

# Religiosity and gender equality: comparing natives and Muslim migrants in Germany

Claudia Diehl, Matthias Koenig and Kerstin Ruckdeschel

**Abstract**

In European public debates, Islam is often described as an impediment to gender equality. By using data from surveys conducted in Germany, we analyse the role of high levels of individual religiosity in explaining Turks' and Germans' approval of gender equality and the way Turkish and German couples share household tasks. Results suggest that, for both groups, individuals with strong religious commitments are less likely than secular individuals to hold egalitarian gender role attitudes. At the behavioural level, this correlation between religiosity and gender egalitarianism only holds true for Turkish respondents. Furthermore, strong religious commitments contribute to generational stability in attitudinal and behavioural gender-traditionalism among Turks. However, when explaining Germans' more egalitarian gender-related attitudes and behaviours, religiosity turns out to be just one factor among others – and not a particularly important one. Further research is needed to disentangle the different cultural and religious aspects of Muslim migrants' attitudes and behaviours.

## Introduction

The religious dimension of migrants' integration receives growing public and academic attention in Western immigration countries. European debates notoriously focus on the integration of Muslims. Not unlike Spanish in the US (Zolberg and Long 1999), Islam is publicly conceived as a major symbolic boundary distinguishing both Christian and secular Europeans from their country's immigrants (Césari 2004; Alba 2005; Casanova 2006; Koenig 2007). Of crucial importance for this symbolic boundary is the perceived incompatibility of Islam with the modern principle of gender equality. Alleged violations of this principle belong to the standard repertoire of those who ask for less tolerance *vis-à-vis* Muslim claims for recognition, as evinced by recurrent controversies over the Muslim headscarf which is often seen as a symbol of female oppression. Given its prominence in public discourse, this presumably negative relationship between Islam and gender equality merits close attention. In this article, we investigate how high levels of individual religiosity affect gender attitudes and gender role behaviour among first and second generation migrants from countries with a predominantly Muslim population. In order to grasp the specifics of Muslim religiosity, we compare these migrants with a native, predominantly Christian control group.

We focus on the situation in Germany where increasing public visibility of approximately 3 million Muslims is subject to growing controversy. Most of the Muslims are of Turkish origin, either having immigrated as low-skilled labour migrants during the period of 'guest-worker' recruitment in the 1960s and 1970s, or belonging to the second generation, i.e. those who immigrated as children or were born in Germany. Previous research has shown that both Turks in Turkey and Turkish immigrants in Germany do in fact hold substantially more conservative gender role attitudes than Germans (see Nauck 1990; Inglehart and Norris 2003; Gerhards 2007). However, it has not yet been systematically assessed to what extent these traditional orientations are related to the strength of Turkish immigrants' religiosity and to their religious background as Muslims.

This research lacuna is at least partly due to data limitations. However, the German 'Generation and Gender Surveys' [GGS], which were conducted as part of an internationally comparative panel study on family relationships and are based on large samples of Germans and Turks, offer new and unique opportunities for the systematic study of the relationship between Muslim religiosity and gender equality. They provide information on both groups' individual levels of religiosity as well as on gender attitudes and behaviours, i.e. individuals' approval of gender equality as well as more practical features of gender relations such as the way couples share household tasks.

Using these new data sets, we ask to what extent between- and within-group differences in gender-related attitudes and behaviours of Turks and Germans are attributable to differences in religiosity. The two groups vary with respect to many other characteristics known to affect gender equality such as education, female labour force participation, and broader socialization contexts. We thus need to assess the relative extent to which group differences are attributable to degree and content of religiosity as compared to other factors. Since it may be expected that exposure to more egalitarian gender values during formative years attenuates the influence of Muslim religiosity, we also need to scrutinize how the nexus between religiosity and gender-related attitudes and behaviours changes in the generational succession among Turkish immigrants.

We start with an overview of theoretical arguments and previous empirical findings on the relationship between religion and gender relations in general and among Muslim migrants in particular. We then present our data and measurements and give a descriptive overview of the distribution of our relevant variables for Germans and first and second generation Turks. Based on this, we present our analysis of how religiosity impacts on gender-related attitudes and behaviours among the groups under consideration. A critical discussion of our findings concludes the article.

## Religion and gender in the context of migration: theoretical arguments and empirical findings

The intersection between religion and gender relations has long attracted attention among social scientists. Within the specific context of migration, researchers have focused on the role of gender in religious identity construction among migrants (Alumkal 1999; Amir-Moazami and Jouili 2006), on female activism in religious diasporas (Werbner 2002), and on the influence of religious socialization goals on the transmission of gender role values in migrant families (Idema and Phalet 2007). However, as Cadge and Ecklund (2007, p. 365) argue in their review of US scholarship about religion and migration, 'there are few studies that examine the way religion and gender intersect more broadly outside of particular religious organizations'. In European scholarship there is a rich literature on public discourses about religion and gender (Gaspard and Koshrokhavar 1995; Bowen 2006), but few studies systematically scrutinize their relationship on the individual level.

In the following, we discuss potential hypotheses about the influence of religious traditions and of individual religiosity – broadly understood as the commitment to religious values and norms – as potential factors for subscribing to more traditional gender role orientations and gender-related behaviours such as the division of household labour. Doing this, we draw on standard paradigms of secularization and assimilation as well as on alternative theories of religious culture and reactive ethnicity, assess their prima facie plausibility against the background of existing empirical findings on Turkish migrants in Germany, and discuss arguments about religiosity's changing pertinence in the generational succession.

## Religion's impact on gender attitudes and behaviour

There are many factors that affect gender attitudes and behaviour, including most notably the degree of societal modernization (Inglehart and Norris 2003, p. 47). Gender attitudes are strongly related to *individual social background*, with the better educated, female, and younger parts of the population holding more egalitarian attitudes. Gender behaviour – e.g. the division of household tasks between men and women, decision making in the household, or couples' money arrangements – is similarly related to *partners' resourcefulness*, such as income differences and life circumstances (Blood and Wolfe 1960; Becker 1981; Treas 1993; Bianchi *et al* 2000; Blossfeld and Drobnic 2001; Breen and Cooke 2005; Grunow, Schulz and Blossfeld 2007). Nevertheless, since many of these studies show that an increase in women's resources does not necessarily lead to more equality, people's gender behaviour seems also to be influenced by *cultural values* and *social norms*.

Within the broad range of values and norms, religious traditions have long been a prime suspect for explaining the unequal distribution of power between men and women. Many religions regulate the sphere of reproduction, and female sexuality in particular, by linking gender to symbolic distinctions between sacred and profane and to ritual norms of purity and impurity. In doing so, they tend to legitimize inequalities and hierarchical relationships between the sexes both within religious institutions and within broader society (Brinkerhoff and MacKie 1985). Individuals with strong religious commitments may therefore be assumed to share more traditional gender attitudes and behaviour. And, indeed, strong religiosity tends to be correlated with overall less egalitarian gender role attitudes even after controlling for other individual level factors such as education (Inglehart and Norris 2003, p. 670; for ethnic group variation in this association see Kane 2000, p. 434).

Now, standard theories of secularization predict that increasing societal modernization contributes to both a decline in religiosity and a decrease in the practical relevance of religion and, in both ways, facilitates more egalitarian gender relations. Within the context of presumably secularized European societies, it can therefore be hypothesized that migrants from less modernized countries with higher levels of general religiosity exhibit less egalitarian attitudes than those shared by the majority, other things being equal.

The stereotypical argument that Muslim immigrants are ill-equipped to adapt to Western norms of gender equality, however, does not just refer to their strong religiosity. Rather, it assumes that there are also differences in the *content* of religiosity. There is indeed a long-standing literature which highlights denominational variations in attitudes toward women's roles and women's socioeconomic status and family-related behaviour (Lenski 1963; Porter and Albert 1977; Heaton and Cornwall 1989). Islamic discourses and practices such as Qur'anic scripture and the legal rules of shari'a are in particular perceived to entail inherently non-egalitarian gender relations (for a discussion see Mir-Hosseini 2000). And, in fact, Inglehart and Norris (2003, p. 47) have found that contemporary Jews, Protestants and Catholics – along with non-affiliated individuals – show higher mean scores on the gender equality scale than Buddhists and Muslims even after controlling for individual and societal background variables. Whereas religious cultures are here considered to affect the values and norms of most religious adherents, in general one would have to hypothesize *a fortiori* that Muslim migrants with particularly high degrees of religiosity hold more conservative gender role orientations than strongly religious Christians or Jews, other things being equal.

Available empirical evidence on Turkish Muslims in Germany is inconclusive with respect to these hypotheses. Previous findings confirm that immigrants from Turkey are substantially more religious than native Germans and other groups of former guest-workers (Fuchs-Heinritz 2000; Frick 2004; for more ambivalent results based on girls and young females, see Boos-Nünning and Karakaşoğlu 2005). Besides, existing data support the assumption that Turkish migrants, most of whom come from rather traditional rural contexts and who only rarely hold higher educational degrees, are overall less egalitarian than natives. There is also some preliminary evidence that religiously committed Muslim migrants (but not Christians) are substantially less approving of gender equality than secular migrants (for high school students see Brettfeld and Wetzels 2003, p. 331). At the behavioural level, previous research has shown that higher levels of religiosity are related to less female autonomy in Turkish immigrant households (Nauck 1985). In sum, however, the existing literature does not reveal to what degree traditional gender attitudes and behaviours among Muslim immigrants are best explained by their socioeconomic background, by their degree of religiosity, or by some particular characteristics of Islam.

*Religion and gender among second generation immigrants*

We now turn to the implications of straight-line theories of secularization and assimilation for the role of religion and gender among second generation migrants. Higher levels of education and labour force participation are usually connected to lower levels of religiosity (van Tubergen 2006). Many migrants born in the host society have left the educational and occupational ethnic niches occupied by the first generation and can therefore be expected to be *less religious* than those who immigrated as adults. Changes in the cultural and economic context of female migrants in particular (Jones Correa 1998) and exposure to more egalitarian gender norms may also alter the practical relevance of religious norms in the generational succession. As life in a secular society raises the social and economic (opportunity-)costs of strict adherence to religious gender norms, migrants' religiosity may not only weaken over time, but also become more private and 'symbolic' (Gans 1994). One would therefore hypothesize that the relationship between migrants' religiosity and their gender attitudes and behaviours differs markedly between the first and the second generation.

However, theories of secularization and assimilation have met considerable criticism. Thus, it is claimed that, depending on the circumstances in the host society, ethnic ties and identities may be maintained or even revitalized among the second generation (Portes and Rumbaut 2001, p. 148). These 'reactive' forms of identity formation may compensate for a lack of social approval and are most likely to emerge in hostile reception contexts marked by discrimination and a lack of upward mobility, which create the need for alternative sources of social status and identity. Since religion is an important foundation of ethnicity for many immigrant groups, this should also apply to religious acculturation processes (Greeley 1971). As generational persistence may affect both the strength of religious commitments and their grip on migrants' attitudes and behaviours in other, non-religious spheres, one would hypothesize that the relationship between religiosity and gender-related attitudes and behaviour remains strong or becomes even stronger for second generation migrants.

Again, empirical evidence is inconclusive for deciding between these two alternative arguments. At first sight, it seems that religiosity is declining in the generational succession, as evinced by data from the German Socio-Economic Panel (SOEP) which show that second generation immigrants from Turkey and the former Yugoslavia are less religious than first generation migrants in terms of indicators such as religion's subjective importance or attendance at religious services (Frick 2004; Diehl and Schnell 2006). However, it is not clear to what extent these changes are merely due to differences in group composition (e.g. age and education). In fact, one might well expect that Turkish migrants in Germany would follow patterns of 'reactive ethnicity' or at least 'ethnic maintenance' rather than straight-line assimilation, since they face larger social and cultural distances than other groups of labour migrants such as Italians or Greeks. Although second generation Turks in Germany have higher levels of education and labour force participation and more contacts with natives than the first generation, their structural, cognitive, and social assimilation progresses more slowly than that of other labour migrants (Kalter and Granato 2002; Diehl and Schnell 2006), and they remain subject to negative stereotypes (Wasmer and Koch 2003). This may slow down acculturation processes and further the maintenance or even reactivation of ethnic and religious identifications and norms.

Moreover, there is evidence that migrant parents feel a greater need to put more effort into the maintenance of cultural heritage than non-migrants. Intergenerational continuity in the transmission of religious norms within Turkish families is indeed high, particularly in the relationship between fathers and sons (Nauck 1995, 2000). Existing findings also reveal that children of immigrant parents with religious socialization goals hold more conservative gender role orientations than children who were raised in a more secular socialization climate. Again, this applies particularly to father–son dyads (Idema and Phalet 2007).

Empirical research on generational change at the behavioural level is so far limited to qualitative studies which suggest that religion has indeed changed its meaning for second generation Muslim migrants. Supposedly, Turkish women who grew up in Germany, not unlike young urban female Muslims in Turkey (Göle 1996), draw a sharp line between religious and traditional norms and rules and consider the former as a source of identity and emancipation rather than of oppression. 'Neo-Muslimas' tend to choose partners who follow the 'true Islam', and even though gender roles are still far from interchangeable the asymmetry in the privileges of the sexes is limited (Nökel 2002, p. 251). There is no evidence, however, about the quantitative relevance of this group.

This brief outline shows that existing empirical evidence cannot settle the contradictory theoretical assumptions about the role of religiosity in explaining gender role orientations and gender-related behaviour of natives and first and second generation immigrants. Therefore, we now turn to our own empirical analyses.

## Data and measurements

The German 'Generation and Gender Surveys' were conducted in 2005 and 2006 at the German Federal Institute for Population Research. In two separate surveys, 10,000 Germans and 4,000 Turks aged between 18 and 79 were interviewed on topics such as relationships with partners, parents and children, gender role orientations and family life, religious attitudes, and socio-demographic characteristics. The survey instrument was the same for both groups, except for some additional questions on migrants' immigration history and their individual integration (for data and methods see Ruckdeschel et al. 2006; Ette et al. 2007). In the German sample respondents were identified by random route; the survey of Turks was based on a probability sample from the local registration offices. Accordingly, only Turkish citizens were interviewed. About 20 per cent of all persons of Turkish origin living in Germany, especially those whose assimilation is more progressed, have acquired German citizenship during the last decade (see Salentin and Wilkening 2003; Diehl and Blohm 2007). Thus, findings cannot be generalized to the whole Turkish origin population in Germany.[1]

The survey contains several suitable indicators for migrants' gender role attitudes and behaviours and for their religious affiliations and orientations.[2] In order to measure gender role attitudes, we adapted Inglehart and Norris's Gender-Equality Scale [GES] (see Inglehart and Norris 2003) and constructed an index based on five items measuring approval of gender equality.[3] On the behavioural level, gender equality is measured by the division of household tasks between the partners. Gender division of labour is labelled 'traditional' if the female partner is responsible for typical women's tasks (doing the dishes and cooking) and the male partner does typical men's tasks (maintenance repairs and paying the bills). All other forms of household division of labour (man does typical women's tasks and vice versa, third party does the work, man or woman does all the work) are categorized as 'non-traditional'.

With regard to religious affiliation, the survey distinguishes between self-identified Christians, Muslims, others, and those belonging to no religion. Individual religiosity is measured by three standard indicators: attendance at religious services; approval of the statement that religious ceremonies related to the life-cycle events such as weddings and funerals are important; and the mentioning of religion as one of the three most important socialization goals for children. In terms of Glock's (1962) seminal statement, these indicators measure the ritual and ethical dimensions of religiosity, respectively. Cognitive, belief, and experiential dimensions of religiosity were, unfortunately, not included in the survey. However, even a moderate multi-dimensional concept of religiosity is desirable, when comparing Christians and Muslims who vary substantially with regard to the doctrinal and practical importance of various dimensions. For instance, religious service attendance, the standard indicator for the public ritual dimension of religiosity, has very different meanings within Christian and Islamic traditions and, as our data show, it is also less important for Muslim women than for Muslim men. To measure strong religious commitment, we therefore used a composite index that takes group-specific manifestations of religiosity into account. Thus, we code all those respondents as 'religious' who display strong religious commitments according to at least two of the three indicators mentioned above (attendance at religious services at least once a week; agreement that religious ceremonies are important; religion mentioned as one of the three most important socialization goals out of a list of eleven).

As outlined above, relevant social background variables need to be taken into account when assessing the relative impact of religion on gender-related attitudes and behaviour. Age, sex, and family status (married or cohabiting with partner versus living alone) are thus included in the analyses. As indicators for respondents' resourcefulness, individual level variables such as education (CASMIN classification, recoded into low for those who completed no school or basic education versus high for all others),[4] employment status (full-/part-time employment or unemployment versus not employed or retired), and the presence of children are added. Additional indicators for partners' resourcefulness at the household level are the age difference between the partners (female more than three years younger than male versus female about the same age as male or older) and the employment status of the couple (only one partner is employed versus both partners are employed).

In order to measure respondents' exposure to the overall more egalitarian gender values of majority members, additional analyses for Turks include measurements of their social assimilation (Idema and Phalet 2007, p. 85). Since the latter is not measured directly we use the language spoken most of the time (German versus Turkish) and – at the household level – the origin of the partners as proxies (partner is first generation Turk or Turkish origin versus partner is second generation Turk or Turkish origin versus partner has German or other non-Turkish origin).

## Empirical findings

We start out with a descriptive overview of the different variables for first and second generation Turks and Germans. We then take a closer look at the relationship between religiosity, nationality, and generation. Against this background, we scrutinize the role of religiosity in explaining between- and within-group difference in gender-related attitudes and behaviour of Germans and first and second generation Turks.

*Gender, religion, and socio-structural background characteristics: a descriptive overview*

The three groups differ substantially in terms of the characteristics under consideration. In accordance with much of the existing literature, we find that first generation Turks approve of gender equality less often and are less likely to practise an egalitarian division of household tasks than Germans. Second generation Turks are somewhere in between Germans and Turkish immigrants with respect to the attitudinal aspects of gender equality, while on the behavioural level the dividing line is still between first and second generation Turks and Germans (see Table 1).

The three groups also differ in terms of our most important independent variable, religion. Analyses not displayed here reveal that 70 per cent of the Germans claim to be Christians, while more than 90 per cent of the Turks identify as Muslims. Of greater interest to our analysis, however, are the respective shares of religiously committed or 'orthodox' persons among the three groups. Against the background of existing research on religious affiliation, it should not come as a surprise that only 6 per cent of Germans are religiously committed in terms of at least two of our three indicators (regular attendance, importance of religious ceremonies, religious socialization goals), as compared to 21 per cent of second generation Turks and 27 per cent of those Turks who immigrated after childhood. It should be noted here that the religiously committed constitute a minority not only within the German population (see for example Norris and Inglehart 2004, p. 74), but also, in accordance with the 'polarization thesis' (Merkens 1997, p. 63), within the Turkish population.

Second generation Turks are younger than the other two groups and accordingly less likely to be married or cohabiting and to have children. The share of individuals with higher educational degrees and the share of those who are employed are larger among second generation than among first generation Turks. Germans, however, are the group with the largest share of employed individuals. Those Turks who were born in Germany or immigrated as children speak mostly German more often than first generation migrants, probably because they have German friends.

In terms of the indicators for the resource asymmetry within the household, the figures show that first and second generation Turks live substantially less often in a relationship in which both partners are employed than Germans. Females are about the same age or older than their partners in two-thirds of second generation Turkish and German couples, while this proportion is smaller among Turkish immigrants. In addition, less than 10 per cent of first generation Turks have a partner of non-Turkish origin, whereas the proportion is twice as high for second generation Turks. The proportion of those with a partner from another immigrant generation (i.e. first generation migrants with a partner who was born in Germany or immigrated at an early age or vice versa) is also larger among second generation migrants.

*Generational change in migrants' religiosity*

Before turning to the impact of religiosity on gender role attitudes and gender equality, it is worth taking a closer look at generational change

**Table 1.** *Distribution of dependent and independent variables by nationality and generational status (means or per cent)*

| | Turks 1st generation (n = 2,721) | Turks 2nd generation (n = 1,161) | Germans (n = 8,594) |
|---|---|---|---|
| *Dependent variable (individual level)* | | | |
| Gender index (means)* | 2.5 | 2.9 | 3.4 |
| | | | |
| *Dependent variable (household level)** | | | |
| Egalitarian division of labour | 42 | 45 | 59 |
| | | | |
| *Independent variables (individual level)* | | | |
| Highly Religious | 27 | 21 | 6 |
|   Attendance at least once a week | 28 | 19 | 8 |
|   Religious ceremonies very important | 38 | 35 | 21 |
|   Religious socialization goals | 30 | 26 | 5 |
| | | | |
| Female | 48 | 45 | 54 |
| Age (means) | 42 | 28 | 49 |
| Married or cohabiting | 82 | 50 | 62 |
| Parent | 82 | 46 | 67 |
| Education: more than basic school | 28 | 49 | 63 |
| Employment status: employed | 41 | 47 | 51 |
| Assimilation: speaks mostly German | 20 | 49 | |
| | | | |
| *Independent variables (household level)** | | | |
| Partners about the same age/women older | 56 | 67 | 65 |
| Both partners employed | 17 | 25 | 42 |
| | | | |
| Partner's origin | | | |
|   German | 9 | 22 | |
|   Other generation than respondent | 17 | 39 | |

\* Gender index: 1 = rejection of gender equality, 5 = approval of gender equality
\*\* Cohabiting couples only

in migrants' religious orientations. While bivariate results suggested that there is generational change in religiosity Figure 1 reveals that this is exclusively due to the different age composition of first and second

**Figure 1.** *Gross and net differences in religiosity between first and second generation Turks and Germans (odds ratios)*

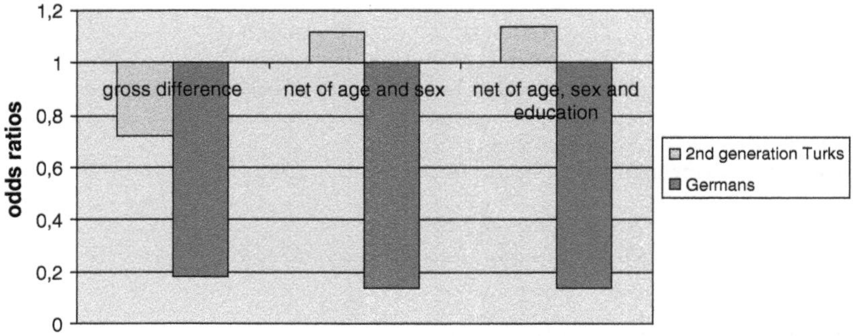

Note: Differences statistically significant except for second generation net differences (p < .10), reference category: first generation Turks.

generation migrants. If this is taken into account, second generation migrants are about as religious as first generation migrants.

Separate analyses for males and females not presented here show that second generation Turkish men are even slightly more religious than first generation males whereas second generation women are slightly (though not significantly) less religious than female immigrants. Moreover, while the difference between first and second generation Turks disappears after controlling for the demographic composition of the groups, the difference between Turks and Germans becomes larger. If Germans were as young and predominantly male as first generation Turks, they would be even less religious than they already are. Additional controls for education do not change the picture substantially.

In sum, our findings show that, contrary to assumptions of straight-line theories of assimilation and secularization, religiosity does not decline in the generational succession, at least not when the share of those with strong religious commitments is considered. On the other hand, popular statements about a religious revival among second generation migrants are also without empirical evidence.

*Religion and the approval of gender equality*

As already discussed, second generation Turks are more approving of gender equality than first generation Turks but still less approving than Germans. But to what extent do these differences merely reflect group variation in relevant individual background variables? And how far are they attributable to migrants' strength or content of religiosity? In order to answer these questions, we start out by presenting regression models on the approval of gender equality, first excluding and then including religion (models I and II). A model with interactions between group belonging and religiosity allows us to study the *differences* in the attitudinal repercussions of strong religious commitments for Muslims and Christians and for first and second generation migrants (model III). Separate models for the three groups complete the picture by providing more detailed insight into the relative importance of religious commitments, background variables on the individual and household level, and – for the Turkish group – degree of social assimilation (models IV to VIII, see Table 2).

The models confirm, first, that Turkish immigrants and, to a lesser degree, second generation Turks hold substantially more conservative gender role attitudes than Germans even after controlling for individual background variables known to affect these orientations. Furthermore, we can see in model II that high religiosity has a rather strong negative impact on the approval of gender equality. However, results also show that group differences in the approval of gender equality remain fairly stable when religiosity is included. Obviously, it is only to a very small extent that the nationality gap shown in model I can be attributed to migrants' religious commitment.

In order to assess if and to what extent the relationship between religiosity and traditional gender role orientations is stronger for Muslim as compared to Christian believers and for first as compared to second generation Turks we insert interactions between religiosity and generation/nationality (dummy variables for religious and non-religious first and second generation Turks and Germans) into model III. Results show very clearly that high religiosity has a negative impact on the approval of gender equality for *all three* groups – albeit the overall lower level of approval is lower among Turks in general: religious Germans are still more approving of gender equality than secular Turks. Furthermore, generational change towards more egalitarian gender role orientations is limited to secular Turks.

Separate models for first and second generation Turks and for Germans provide more detailed insight into the relative importance of the factors under consideration here. For the Turkish group, these models also allow us to look into the role of social contacts with majority members who on average hold more egalitarian gender role attitudes. Results show some substantial similarities between the groups (see Table 2). As we have already seen, the role of strong religious beliefs reduces the likelihood of approving of gender equality for each group. Furthermore, being female and better educated is accompanied by more egalitarian gender role orientations for all three groups. This is especially the case for second generation Turks and for Germans. However, only Turks hold more conservative gender role attitudes when they are married or cohabiting and have children. As

**Table 2.** *Approval of gender equality (unstandardized linear regression coefficients)*

| | All | | | Turks 1st generation | | Turks 2nd generation | | German |
|---|---|---|---|---|---|---|---|---|
| | M I | M II | M III | M IV | M V | M VI | M VII | MVIII |
| **Group:** | | | | | | | | |
| *Turks 1st generation* | — | — | — | — | — | — | — | — |
| Turks 2nd generation | .185 (.023) | .181 (.023) | — | — | — | — | — | — |
| Germans | .731 (.015) | .676 (.016) | — | — | — | — | — | — |
| Religious | — | -.258 (.018) | — | -.234 (.028) | -.230 (.028) | -.225 (.048) | -.209 (.048) | -.299 (.027) |
| Female | .247 (.011) | .242 (.011) | .247 (.011) | .115 (.027) | .133 (.027) | .260 (.041) | .271 (.041) | .272 (.013) |
| Age | -.006 (.000) | -.005 (.000) | -.005 (.000) | -.002 n.s. (.001) | -.001 n.s. (.001) | .006 n.s. (.003) | .007 (.003) | -.007 (.000) |
| Married or cohabiting | -.077 (.013) | -.071 (.013) | -.078 (.013) | -.174 (.035) | -.157 (.034) | -.204 (.055) | -.197 (.055) | -.039 (.014) |
| Parent | -.030 (.014) | -.028 (.014) | -.035 (.014) | -.097 (.035) | -.090 (.034) | -.105 n.s. (.057) | -.099 n.s. (.057) | .003 (.016) |
| Education: > basic school | .261 (.012) | .258 (.012) | .270 (.012) | .182 (.028) | .157 (.028) | .286 (.040) | .268 (.040) | .259 (.014) |
| Employment status: Employed | .136 (.012) | .130 (.012) | .133 (.012) | .090 (.027) | .071 (.027) | .076 n.s. (.042) | .067 n.s. (.041) | .125 (.014) |
| Assimilation: speaks mostly German | — | — | — | — | .234 (.031) | — | .148 (.040) | — |
| Interactions: 1st gen. relig. Turks | — | — | — | — | — | — | — | — |
| 1st gen. secular Turks | — | — | .089 (.026) | — | — | — | — | — |

Table 2 (Continued)

| | All | | | Turks 1st generation | | Turks 2nd generation | | German |
|---|---|---|---|---|---|---|---|---|
| | M I | M II | M III | M IV | M V | M VI | M VII | MVIII |
| 2nd gen. relig. Turks | – | – | −.011 n.s. (.043) | – | – | – | – | – |
| 2nd gen. secular Turks | – | – | .276 (.030) | – | – | – | – | – |
| religious Germans | – | – | .326 (.030) | – | – | – | – | – |
| secular Germans | – | – | .771 (.023) | – | – | – | – | – |
| Constant | 2.610 | 2.656 | 2.540 | 2.734 | 2.647 | 2.617 | 2.524 | 3.345 |
| $R^2$ | .32 | .33 | .32 | .08 | .10 | .15 | .16 | .18 |
| N | 12,053 | 12,053 | 12,053 | 2,607 | 2,607 | 1,080 | 1,080 | 8,366 |

Note: $p < .05$ (coefficients significant unless noted otherwise), *reference categories in italics*, SE in parentheses.

expected, those Turks who speak German most of the time are more likely to approve of gender equality.[5]

In general, the attitudes of first generation Turks seem to be more 'diffuse', i.e. less explicable by the variables under consideration here (see low model fit). This suggests that unobserved heterogeneity with regard to factors related to the country of origin, e.g. urban versus rural background, might play an important role for this group.

*Religion and gender-related behaviour*

We now turn to the impact of religion on gender-related behaviour. Here, we limit our analyses to cohabiting and/or married couples and look into the factors that influence how they divide the tasks in the household. Apart from that, we run similar models to the ones presented in the last section.

The models displayed in Table 3 show that Germans are much more likely to share household tasks in an egalitarian manner than Turks, whereas there is no significant difference between first and second generation Turks when background variables on the individual and household level are taken into account. The sizeable difference between Germans and Turks is partly due to the fact that both first and second generation Turks included in the analyses on the household level are a somewhat selective subsample. As we saw in the previous section, Turks who are married or cohabiting hold considerably more conservative gender attitudes than single Turks, whereas the difference between married and single Germans is very small. Accordingly, if this selectivity in the subsample considered here was taken into account, the differences between Germans and Turks would most likely diminish whereas the differences between first and second generation would remain rather stable.

The model including religiosity shows once more that the differences between Turks and Germans are only marginally attributable to differences in the two groups' levels of religiosity (see rather stable group coefficients in model II as compared to model I). The group interactions that we added in model III reveal an important difference between gender-related attitudes and behaviour: religious commitments seem to be accompanied by a traditional division of household tasks only for Turks but less so for Germans (the dummy-coefficients for religious and secular Germans are rather similar in model III). Furthermore, we can see that the absence of generational change in gender-related behaviour is mostly due to the fact that second generation religious Turks are just as conservative with regard to their gender-related behaviour as first generation religious Turks, while there is at least some generational change for secular second generation Turks.

**Table 3.** Non-traditional division of household tasks (logistic regression coefficients)

| | All | | | Turks 1st generation | | Turks 2nd generation | | Germans |
|---|---|---|---|---|---|---|---|---|
| | M I | M II | M III | M IV | M V | M VI | M VII | M VIII |
| **Group:** | | | | | | | | |
| *Turks 1st generation* | — | — | — | — | — | — | — | — |
| Turks 2nd generation | .053 n.s. (.099) | .052 n.s. (.099) | — | — | — | — | — | — |
| Germans | .331 (.068) | .285 (.070) | — | — | — | — | — | — |
| Religious | — | -.251 (.071) | — | -.369 (.104) | -.329 (.108) | -.378 n.s. (.212) | -.219 n.s. (.224) | -.105 n.s. (.116) |
| Female | .186 (.048) | .183 (.048) | .180 (.048) | -.225 (.093) | -.103 n.s. (.098) | .520 (.180) | .548 (.192) | .328 (.060) |
| Age | .005 (.002) | .005 (.002) | .005 (.002) | .007 (.004) | .014 (.004) | .040 (.014) | .040 (.015) | .002 n.s. (.002) |
| Parent | -.314 (.063) | -.309 (.063) | -.310 (.063) | -.400 (.140) | -.315 (.149) | -.231 n.s. (.243) | -.164 n.s. (.253) | -.292 (.075) |
| Education: > basic school | -.047 n.s. (.052) | -.044 n.s. (.052) | -.037 n.s. (.052) | -.056 n.s. (.103) | -.088 n.s. (.109) | .160 n.s. (.185) | .084 n.s. (.195) | -.074 n.s. (.065) |
| Approval of gender equality | .305 (.039) | .290 (.039) | .303 (.039) | .335 (.075) | .302 (.078) | .399 (.141) | .419 (.146) | .236 (.049) |
| Assimilation: speaks mostly German | — | — | — | — | .229 n.s. (.127) | — | .210 n.s. (.194) | — |
| Female same age or older | .102 (.048) | .106 (.048) | .107 (.048) | .187 (.092) | .167 n.s. (.095) | .241 n.s. (.188) | .279 n.s. (.198) | .048 n.s. (.060) |
| Both employed | .139 (.054) | .133 (.054) | .140 (.054) | .458 (.123) | .434 (.129) | .290 n.s. (.211) | .329 n.s. (.226) | .008 n.s. (.063) |

**Table 3** (*Continued*)

|  |  | All | | | Turks 1st generation | | Turks 2nd generation | | Germans |
|---|---|---|---|---|---|---|---|---|---|
|  |  | M I | M II | M III | M IV | M V | M VI | M VII | M VIII |
| Partner's origin: | *same generation* |  |  |  |  |  |  |  |  |
|  | German | – | – | – | – | .959 (.203) | – | .364 n.s. (.319) | – |
|  | different generation | – | – | – | – | .032 n.s. (.137) | – | .384 n.s. (.209) | – |
| Interactions: | *1st gen. relig. Turks* | – | – | – | – | – | – | – | – |
|  | 1st gen. secular Turks | – | – | .257 (.099) | – | – | – | – | – |
|  | 2nd gen. relig. Turks | – | – | -.160 n.s. (.188) | – | – | – | – | – |
|  | 2nd gen. secular Turks | – | – | .319 (.128) | – | – | – | – | – |
|  | religious Germans | – | – | .350 (.125) | – | – | – | – | – |
|  | secular Germans | – | – | .493 (.096) | – | – | – | – | – |
| Constant |  | -.162 | -.093 | -.406 | -.086 | -.517 | -.850 | -.316 | -.443 |
| Nagelkerkes $R^2$ |  | .05 | .06 | .06 | .05 | .08 | .09 | .10 | .02 |
| N |  | 7,719 | 7,719 | 7,719 | 2,092 | 1,980 | 557 | 516 | 5,070 |

Note: $p < .05$ (coefficients significant unless noted otherwise), *reference categories in italics*, SE in parentheses.

Again, we present separate models (IV to VIII) in order to assess the relative importance of the factors under consideration here for all three groups and look into the impact of migrants' exposure to natives' overall more egalitarian gender norms. These models confirm that religion is negatively related to an egalitarian division of household tasks only for Turks, not for Germans. Religious Turks of both generations are less likely to pursue an egalitarian division of labour in their household than secular Turks. And again, the influence of religiosity seems to be just as strong for second as for first generation Turks.[6] The impact of religion for second generation migrants is moderated if respondents' social context is taken into account: having a partner from a different generation is marginally positively related to more liberal gender division of labour for second generation migrants. This effect seems somewhat surprising but is easy to explain: analyses run separately for both sexes show that it is exclusively caused by second generation females whose partner migrated from Turkey (first generation). These couples are very likely to share household tasks in a non-traditional way which probably reflects the better bargaining position of those females who have been living in Germany for longer and who often sponsored their husband's immigration (for a similar finding, see Nauck 1985).

The positive effects of age for first and second generation Turks show once again that conservative young Turks are more likely to live in a relationship than more egalitarian ones who may have adapted to the 'Western' pattern of late marriages. In all three groups, those who approve of gender equality are more likely to show a non-traditional division of labour. The positive impact of egalitarian gender attitudes is particularly strong for second generation Turks. Obviously, 'cultural' factors such as religious commitments or gender role orientations matter more for Turks than for natives whose gender division of labour seems to hinge primarily on factors not considered here (see low model fit for this group).[7]

## Conclusion

In this article, we have asked to what extent between- and within-group differences of Germans and first and second generation Turks in gender attitudes and behaviour can be attributed to religious commitment. In sum, our analyses establish four key findings. First of all, whereas previous research has described the assimilation process of Turkish migrants in Germany as comparatively slow but steady, their religiosity seems to be rather stable across the generations. This applies at least to immigrants with strong religious commitments – who are a minority even within the Turkish population – and particularly to young Turkish males.

Secondly, our findings suggest that religious individuals hold more conservative gender role attitudes than more secular individuals among both Turks *and* Germans – even if relevant social background characteristics are taken into account. However, strong religious commitments do not affect the division of household tasks among German couples, while this continues to be the case among Turkish couples. Furthermore, the repercussions of religious commitments in everyday life are just as strong for those who grew up in Germany as for those who immigrated later in life. Turkish migrants' religiosity thus seems to be less 'symbolic' than in the case of Germans in so far as its grip on everyday life is tighter.

Thirdly, we could demonstrate very clearly that in explaining why Turkish immigrants hold more conservative gender role orientations and exhibit more traditional ways of organizing the household, strong religious commitment is just one among several factors – and not even a particularly important one. Even secular Turks are more conservative than Germans with similar background characteristics. One might argue that this is just another piece of evidence for the strong indirect impact of the Islamic heritage on cultural norms of gender relations even of secular Turks. However, existing research suggests caution in drawing such far-reaching conclusions: populations of many other non-Islamic countries in southern and eastern Europe have similar traditional gender orientations to Turkey (Gerhards 2007), and parents' gender-specific expectations of their children's involvement in household tasks are rather conservative for all labour migrants (Greeks, in particular, see Nauck 2000, p. 369). Clearly, further research is needed to assess the relative impact of the Islamic culture and to disentangle it from other aspects of migrants' cultural background.

Fourthly, despite religiosity's moderate role in explaining gender-related differences between Turks and Germans our analyses show that strong religious commitments contribute to generational stability in attitudinal and behavioural gender-traditionalism. Only secular second generation migrants hold more egalitarian gender role attitudes than first generation migrants, and generational change in gender-related behaviour – albeit small – is also limited to secular Turks. Strong religiosity seems to be an effective barrier to generational change towards gender equality in attitudes and in everyday life among Turkish migrants, or so our analyses suggest.

It has to be emphasized that our findings cannot be generalized to the whole Turkish origin population living in Germany. Since naturalized Turks who are often less religious are not included in our analyses, the overall level of religiosity for the Turkish origin population might be overestimated (note, however, that naturalization is equally prevalent among first and second generation Turks; see Diehl and Blohm 2008). Besides, nationality differences on the behavioural level might be somewhat overstated because Turks who live in relationships tend to be more conservative than single Turks.

Notwithstanding these reservations, the baseline of our argument is rather clear-cut: religious commitment has considerable influence on gender attitudes of *all* groups considered here, whereas it has repercussions on everyday behaviour only for the Turkish population. These findings are in accordance with decades of research showing that the religious factor matters in the sphere of gender relationships. With regard to the role of Islam in explaining the more conservative gender attitudes and behaviours of Turks as compared to natives, however, our findings call for a revision of popular and easy-at-hand attributions: the large attitudinal and behavioural differences even between secular Turks and Germans suggest that the factual explanatory power of migrants' religiosity lags far behind its prominence in public debates.

## Acknowledgements

We would like to thank Teresa Jurado, Pia Schober and Peter Preisendörfer for carefully reading and commenting on the manuscript.

## Notes

1.    Although naturalized Turks were included in the German sample, they were strongly underrepresented. We therefore had to exclude them from the analyses.

2.    The questionnaires are available under: www.bib-demographie.de/publikat/frame_material.html

3.    The four GES items are: (1) On the whole, men make better political leaders than women (agree coded low); (2) When jobs are scarce, men should have more right to a job than women (agree coded low); (3) Do you think that a woman has to have children in order to be fulfilled or is this not necessary? (agree coded low); (4) If a woman wants a child as a single parent but she doesn't want to have a stable relationship with a man, do you approve or disapprove? (disapprove coded low). The fifth item was not in the original GES: (5) Taking care of household and children is just as satisfying as to work for money (agree coded low).

4.    This was necessary due to the large differences between the groups. Most first generation Turks have no educational degree or have only completed elementary education while only a small share of Germans fall into this category.

5.    Note, however, that it is impossible to assess the causal relationship between migrants' social assimilation and their adoption of liberal gender attitudes with cross-sectional data.

6.    The statistically non-significant coefficients ($p = .9$) for the second generation are primarily due to the small number of cases for this group.

7.    In analyses not presented here we inserted into the models several indicators that have proven to be an important determinant in explaining changes in the gender division of labour over time (duration of partnership, marriage-migration, large educational gap between the partners) (see Grunow, Schulz and Blossfeld 2007), but this did not increase their explanatory power. Including income differences between the spouses was impossible due to missing cases.

# References

ALBA, R.D. 2005 'Bright vs. blurred boundaries: second generation assimilation and exclusion in France, Germany and the United States', *Ethnic and Racial Studies*, vol. 28, pp. 20–49

ALUMKAL, A.W. 1999 'Preserving patriarchy: assimilation, gender norms, and second-generation Korean American evangelicals', *Qualitative Sociology*, vol. 22, pp. 127–40

AMIR-MOAZAMI, S and JOUILI, J. 2006 'Knowledge, empowerment and religious authority among pious Muslim women in France and Germany', *The Muslim World*, vol. 96, pp. 617–42

BECKER, G.S. 1981 *A Treatise on the Family*, Cambridge, MA: Harvard University Press

BIANCHI, S.M., *et al.* 2000 'Is anyone doing the housework? Trends in the gender division of household labor', *Social Forces*, vol. 79, pp. 191–234

BLOOD, R.O. Jr. and WOLFE, D.M. 1960 *Husbands and Wives: The Dynamics of Married Living*, New York: Free Press

BLOSSFELD, H.-P. and DROBNIC, S. 2001 'Theoretical perspectives on couples' careers', in H.-P. Blossfeld and S. Drobnic (eds), *Careers of Couples in Contemporary Societies: From Male Breadwinner Households to Dual Earner Families*, Oxford: Oxford University Press, pp. 16–50

BOOS-NÜNNING, U. and KARAKAŞOĞLU, Y. 2005 *Viele Welten leben. Zur Lebenssituation von Mädchen und jungen Frauen mit Migrationshintergrund*, Münster: Waxmann

BOWEN, J.R. 2006 *Why the French Don't Like Headscarves*, Princeton: Princeton University Press

BREEN, R. and COOKE, L.P. 2005 'The persistence of the gendered division of domestic labour', *European Sociological Review*, vol. 21, pp. 43–57

BRETTFELD, K. and WETZELS, P. 2003 'Junge Muslime in Deutschland: Eine kriminologische Analyse zur Alltagsrelevanz von Religion und Zusammenhängen von individueller Religiosität mit Gewalterfahrungen, -einstellungen und -handeln', in *Islamismus. Texte zur Inneren Sicherheit*, Berlin: Bundesministerium des Inneren, pp. 221–316

BRINKERHOFF, M.B. and MACKIE, M. 1985 'Religion and gender: a comparison of Canadian and American student attitudes', *Journal of Marriage and the Family*, vol. 27, pp. 415–29

CADGE, W. and ECKLUND, E.H. 2007 'Immigration and religion', *Annual Review of Sociology*, vol. 33, pp. 359–79

CASANOVA, J. 2006 'Religion, European secular identities, and European integration', in T. Byrnes and P. Katzenstein (eds), *Religion in an Expanding Europe*, Cambridge: Cambridge University Press, pp. 65–92

CÉSARI, J. 2004 *When Islam and Democracy Meet*, New York: Palgrave

DIEHL, C. and BLOHM, M. 2008 'Die Entscheidung zur Einbürgerung: Optionen, Anreize und identifikative Aspekte', in F. Kalter (ed.), Migration, Integration und ethnische Grenzziehungen. *Kölner Zeitschrift für Soziologie und Sozialpsychologie*, Special Issue 48, in print

DIEHL, C. and SCHNELL, R. 2006 '"Reactive ethnicity" or "assimilation"? Statements, arguments, and first empirical evidence for labor migrants in Germany', *International Migration Review*, vol. 40, pp. 786–816

ETTE, A., *et al.* 2007 *Generations and Gender Survey. Dokumentation der Befragung von türkischen Migranten in Deutschland*, Wiesbaden: Bundesinstitut für Bevölkerungsforschung

FRICK, J.R. 2004 *Integration von Migranten in Deutschland auf Basis national und international vergleichbarer Mikrodaten*, im Auftrag des Sachverständigenrats für Zuwanderung und Integration

FUCHS-HEINRITZ, W. 2000 'Religion', in A. Fischer, Y. Fritzsche and W. Fuchs-Heinritz (eds), *Jugend 2000. 13. Shell Jugendstudie*, vol. 1, Opladen: Leske & Budrich, pp. 157–80

GANS, H.J. 1994 'Symbolic ethnicity and symbolic religiosity: towards a comparison of ethnic and religious acculturation', *Ethnic and Racial Studies*, vol. 17, pp. 577–92

GASPARD, F. and KOSHROKHAVAR, F. 1995 *Le foulard et la République*, Paris: Éditions la Découverte

GERHARDS, J. 2007 *Cultural Overstretch: Differences Between Old and New Member States of the EU and Turkey*, London: Routledge

GLOCK, C.Y. 1962 'On the study of religious commitment', *Religious Education*, vol. 57, pp. 98–110

GÖLE, N. 1996 *The Forbidden Modern: Civilization and Veiling*, Ann Arbor: University of Michigan Press

GREELEY, A.M. 1971 *Why Can't They Be Like Us? America's White Ethnic Groups*, New York: E.P. Dutton

GRUNOW, D., SCHULZ, F. and BLOSSFELD, H.-P. 2007 'Was erklärt die Traditionalisierungsprozesse häuslicher Arbeitsteilung im Eheverlauf: soziale Normen oder ökonomische Prozesse?', *Zeitschrift für Soziologie*, vol. 36, pp. 162–81

HEATON, T.B. and CORNWALL, M. 1989 'Religious group variation in the socioeconomic status and family behavior of women', *Journal of the Scientific Study of Religion*, vol. 23, pp. 283–99

IDEMA, H. and PHALET, K. 2007 'Transmission of gender-role values in Turkish-German migrant families: the role of gender, intergenerational and intercultural relations', *Zeitschrift für Familienforschung*, vol. 19, pp. 71–105

INGLEHART, R. and NORRIS, P. 2003 *Rising Tide: Gender Equality and Cultural Change Around the World*, Cambridge: Cambridge University Press

JONES CORREA, M. 1998 'Different path: gender, immigration and political participation', *International Migration Review*, vol. 32, pp. 326–49

KALTER, F. and GRANATO, N. 2002 'Demographic change, educational expansion, and structural assimilation of immigrants. The case of Germany', *European Sociological Review*, vol. 18, pp. 199–216

KANE, E.W. 2000 'Racial and ethnic variations in gender-related attitudes', *Annual Review of Sociology*, vol. 26, pp. 419–39

KOENIG, M. 2007 'Europeanizing the governance of religious diversity – Islam and the transnationalization of law, politics and identity'', *Journal of Ethnic and Migration Studies*, vol. 33, pp. 911–32

LENSKI, G. 1963 *The Religious Factor. A Sociological Study of Religion's Impact on Politics, Economics, and Family Life*, Garden City, NJ: Doubleday

MERKENS, H. 1997 'Familiale Erziehung und Sozialisation türkischer Kinder in Deutschland', in H. Merkens and F. Schmidt (eds), *Sozialisation und Erziehung in ausländischen Familien in Deutschland*, Hohengehren: Schneider, pp. 9–100

MIR-HOSSEINI, Z. 2000 *Islam and Gender*, London: I.B. Tauris

NAUCK, B. 1985 '"Heimliches Matriarchat" in Familien türkischer Arbeitsmigranten? Empirische Ergebnisse zu Veränderungen der Entscheidungsmacht und Aufgabenallokation', *Zeitschrift für Soziologie*, vol. 14, pp. 450–65

—— 1990 'Eltern-Kind-Beziehungen bei Deutschen, Türken und Migranten', *Zeitschrift für Bevölkerungswissenschaft*, vol. 16, pp. 87–120

—— 1995 'Educational climate and intergenerative transmission in Turkish families: a comparison of migrants in Germany and non-migrants', in P. Noak, M. Hofer and J. Youniss (eds), *Psychological Responses to Social Change. Human Development in Changing Environironment*, Berlin: De Gruyter, pp. 67–85

—— 2000 'Eltern-Kind-Beziehungen in Migrantenfamilien – ein Vergleich zwischen griechischen, italienischen, türkischen und vietnamesischen Familien in Deutschland', in Sachverständigenkommission 6. Familienbericht (ed.), *Empirische Beiträge zur Familienentwicklung und Akkulturation. Materialien zum 6. Familienbericht*, Vol. 1., Opladen: Leske & Budrich, pp. 347–92

NÖKEL, S. 2002 *Die Töchter der Gastarbeiter und der Islam. Zur Soziologie alltagsweltlicher Anerkennungspolitiken. Eine Fallstudie*, Berlin: Transcript

NORRIS, P. and INGLEHART, R. 2004 *Sacred and Secular. Religions and Politics Worldwide*, Cambridge: Cambridge University Press

PORTER, J.R. and ALBERT, A. 1977 'Subculture or assimilation? A cross-cultural analysis of religion and women's role', *Journal of the Scientific Study of Religion*, vol. 16, pp. 345–59

PORTES, A. and RUMBAUT, R.G. 2001 *Legacies: The Story of the Immigrant Second Generation*, Berkeley: University of California Press

RUCKDESCHEL, K., *et al.* 2006 *Generations and Gender Survey. Dokumentation der ersten Welle der Hauptbefragung in Deutschland*, Wiesbaden: Bundesinstitut für Bevölkerungsforschung

SALENTIN, K. and WILKENING, F. 2003 'Ausländer, Eingebürgerte und das Problem einer realistischen Zuwanderer-Integrationsbilanz', *Kölner Zeitschrift für Soziologie und Sozialpsychologie*, vol. 55, pp. 278–98

THRÄNHARDT, D. 1999 'Germany's immigration policies and politics', in G. Brochmann and T. Hammar (eds), *Mechanisms of Immigration Control: A Comparative Analysis of European Regulation Policies*, Oxford: Berg, pp. 29–57

TREAS, J. 1993 'Money in the bank: transaction costs and the economic organization of marriage', *American Sociological Review*, vol. 58, pp. 723–34

VAN TUBERGEN, F. 2006 'Religious affiliation and attendance among immigrants in eight Western countries: individual and contextual effects', *Journal for the Scientific Study of Religion*, vol. 45, pp. 1–22

WASMER, M. and KOCH, A. 2003 'Foreigners as second-class citizens? Attitudes toward equal civil rights for non-Germans', in R. Alba, P. Schmidt and M. Wasmer (eds), *Germans or Foreigners? Attitudes toward Ethnic Minorities in Post-Unification Germany*, New York: Palgrave Macmillan, pp. 119–41

WERBNER, P. 2002 'The place which is diaspora: citizenship, religion and gender in the making of chaordic transnationalism', *Journal for Ethnic and Migration Studies*, vol. 28, pp. 119–33

ZOLBERG, A.R. and LONG, L.W. 1999 'Why Islam is like Spanish: cultural incorporation in Europe and the United States', *Politics and Society*, vol. 27, pp. 5–38

# Suicidal behaviour of young immigrant women in the Netherlands. Can we use Durkheim's concept of 'fatalistic suicide' to explain their high incidence of attempted suicide?

Diana van Bergen, Johannes H. Smit, Anton J.L.M. van Balkom and
Sawitri Saharso

## Abstract

Young immigrant women of South Asian, Turkish and Moroccan origin
in the Netherlands demonstrate disproportionate rates of non-fatal
suicidal behaviour. Suicidal behaviour is usually explained from a
psychological or medical tradition. However, we would like to emphasize
sociological correlates, by examining the relevance of Durkheim's *fatalistic suicide*, characterized by overregulation. We conducted a retro-
spective analysis of 115 case files of young women who demonstrated
suicidal behaviour, to illuminate their living conditions. The analysis
included a comparison of class factors as well as psychiatric and
psychological risk factors. In at least half of the cases, South Asian,
Turkish and Moroccan women experienced specific stressful life events
related to their family honour. Women's lives were often characterized by
a lack of self-autonomy. It is concluded that the archetype of *fatalistic
suicide* should be re-evaluated when interpreting the suicidal behaviour of
young immigrant women in the Netherlands, and incorporated into
strategies of prevention.

## Introduction

Two epidemiological studies carried out in the city of The Hague
showed that young women from certain ethnic minority groups more

often demonstrate non-fatal suicidal behaviour than Dutch young women (Schudel et al. 1998; Burger et al. 2005). This suggests that a substantial group of young immigrant women in the Netherlands suffer from severe difficulties and distress in life. In the late 1990s, the rates of suicidal behaviour of South Asian, Turkish and Moroccan women in the age range 15–24 years appeared to be two to four times higher than those of majority Dutch young women.[1] By 2005, the rates for South Asian and Turkish young females continued to be disproportionate, while those for Moroccan young women were still high compared to Dutch young women, but not statistically signifi-cant. The reports on the alarming rates of suicidal behaviour of young immigrant women occasioned research into the background of this phenomenon.[2]

Suicidal behaviour is defined by the World Health Organization (WHO) as: 'a non habitual act with a non-fatal outcome that the individual, expecting to, or taking the risk to, die or inflict bodily harm, initiated and carried out with the purpose of bringing about wanted changes' (De Leo et al. 2006). It concerns behaviour including self-poisoning by taking an overdose of pills, or cutting the wrist(s). The desired change includes, but is often not limited to, the intent to die. In addition, desired changes may include a wish to escape from an unbearable situation or thoughts, the search for peace of mind, or the wish to communicate to others how much they are in mental pain (Hjelmelandt, Knizek and Nordvik 2002).

Research in suicidology usually explains suicidal behaviour almost exclusively by psychiatric and psychological risk factors, e.g. mental illness and dysfunction in personality. However, studies have pointed at the possible relevance of Durkheim's sociological theory of *fatalistic suicide*, by arguing that suicides of many young women world-wide originate in overregulated lives and their discontent with their social roles (see, for instance, Iga (1981) on suicidal behaviour of Japanese women, or Davies and Neal (2000) on the suicide of women in rural China). Two Dutch studies based on interviews with female South Asian students aged between 16 and 24 indicated that such women are often faced with high levels of control exercised by their parents (Krikke, Nijhuis and Weesenbeek 2000; Salverda 2004). This led us to analyse the relevance of Emile Durkheim's concept of *fatalistic suicide* for understanding the suicidal behaviour in young South Asian as well as Turkish and Moroccan women in the Netherlands (van Bergen et al. 2006).

Durkheim's work was based on an investigation of records of suicide in the late nineteenth century, when registration of non-fatal cases of suicidal behaviour did not yet occur. Across all ethnic groups in the Netherlands, men commit suicide twice as often as women, while more women than men attempt suicide.[3] This disparity is known as the *gender paradox* in suicidology. This pattern of male to female ratio (ranging from 2:1 up to 3:1) can be observed world-wide (with the exception of rural China, where more women than men die by suicide) (Canetto and Lester 1995; Beautrais 2003).

Durkheim's focus on lethal cases, as well as the male to female ratio in suicide statistics, precipitates the question whether it is justified to use Durkheim's concepts for examining the non-fatal suicidal behaviour of young women. However, recent research indicates that those young individuals who die by suicide and those who attempt suicide are not two distinct populations but rather a similar group. Beautrais (2003) established by a case control study that those youngsters (aged 15–24 years) who die by suicide and those who attempt suicide share common sociological characteristics and psychiatric diagnostic and psychiatric history features. These features concern exposure to recent stressful life events, lack of formal educational qualifications, mood disorder and history of psychiatric care. Beautrais argues that the fact that men more often die by suicide than women could hence be attributed to their choice of more lethal methods. This proposition is supported by the fact that female youth suicides in New Zealand more than doubled from 1977 to 1996, notably due to the increased use of hanging and vehicle exhaust gas by women. These findings argue against a rigid separation of lethal versus non-lethal suicidal behaviour. Therefore, we believe it is justified to use Durkheim's theory for our focus on the non-fatal suicidal behaviour of immigrant women.

In this paper, our research procedures and research subjects will be described first. Subsequently we investigate the contribution of psychiatric and psychological risk factors and incidences of abuse, and compare the results. Durkheim's archetype of *fatalistic suicide* will be described next. Since the registration of suicidal behaviour indicates a relation between suicidal behaviour, gender and ethnicity we also verify how regulation can be understood in the light of these markers. Subsequently, we demonstrate the cultural context of South Asian, Turkish and Moroccan young women who demonstrated suicidal behaviour by providing a number of case file summaries. We conclude by discussing the relevance of Durkheim's theory for explaining and preventing the suicidal behaviour of young minority women.

## Methodology and description of the sample

Durkheim was criticized for the fact that he solely categorized on the basis of external and observable characteristics by using aggregated level data (for instance on divorce rate, income level or urbanization rate). By neglecting to study the individual dispositions, suicides are treated as occurring in a social void, without reference to the values and beliefs that constitute the cultural milieux of individuals (Hamlin and Bryn 2006). By contrast, in our study we focused on collecting data that could illuminate the specific social environment and living conditions of young women. We thus chose to investigate medical case files consisting of accounts of mental health care workers of the lives of young women.

We selected case files (N = 115, mean age 23.5, SD = 6.6) of females between 12 and 41 years old of South Asian (N = 24, mean age 25.3, SD = 5.9),[4] Turkish (N = 32, mean age 23.7, SD = 6.7), Moroccan (N = 30, mean age 23.7, SD = 6.4) and Dutch (N = 29, mean age 21.7, SD = 6.7) origin on the basis of the WHO definition of suicidal behaviour, non-native-Dutch last name, and age. Two researchers assessed which files belonged in the selection. The files were available from the archives of a public mental healthcare centre (95 per cent of the cases for the years 1995–2005) and an academic hospital in the city of Amsterdam (5 per cent of the cases for the years 2003–2005). Permission was granted from the Medical Ethical Committee. The case files were a collection of notes of the treatment provided by psychiatric nurses, psychologists or social workers and psychiatrists (in training). Although the files were not filled out systematically, since several professionals were involved with one patient and wrote the notes, this functioned as a cross-check and increased triangulation. Research indicated that immigrant females were most at risk in the 15 to 24 years age group, yet our research subjects were aged between 12 and 41 years. The rationale behind this is that suicidal behaviour is known for its repetitive character (Arensman and Kerkhof 2003).

To clarify the extent to which social and economic class could possibly be related to overregulation, we selected Dutch control cases where the parents had a low professional status, since it is known that non-western immigrant groups in the Netherlands often belong to the lower social-economic strata. We initially chose to investigate topics that are known in suicidology to be clear risk factors for suicidal behaviour (Beautrais 1998), e.g. demographics, childhood, relationship with parents, social support, relationship with partner, life events,

**Table 1.** *The marital status of female outpatients of four ethnic groups in Amsterdam*

|                | Turkish N = 32 N (%) | Moroccan N = 30 N (%) | South Asian N = 24 N (%) | Dutch N = 29 N (%) |
|----------------|----------------------|------------------------|---------------------------|---------------------|
| Single         | 6 (19)               | 7 (23)                 | 9 (38)                    | 12 (41)             |
| With a partner | 9 (28)               | 9 (30)                 | 6 (25)                    | 10 (34)             |
| Married        | 11 (34)              | 6 (20)                 | 3 (13)                    | 2 (7)               |
| Divorced       | 4 (13)               | 6 (20)                 | 6 (25)                    | 5 (17)              |
| Separating     | 2 (6)                | 2 (7)                  | 0 (0)                     | 0 (0)               |

**Table 2.** *Method used in suicidal behaviour of female outpatients of four ethnic groups in Amsterdam*

|  | Turkish<br>N = 32<br>N (%) | Moroccan<br>N = 30<br>N (%) | South Asian<br>N = 24<br>N (%) | Dutch<br>N = 29<br>N (%) |
|---|---|---|---|---|
| Auto-intoxication with medication and/or alcohol | 24 (75) | 22 (73) | 15 (63) | 20 (69) |
| Self-cutting | 7 (22) | 4 (13) | 6 (25) | 9 (31) |
| Self-poisoning with acid | 0 (0) | 0 (0) | 4 (17) | 1 (3) |
| Other method | 3 (9) | 7 (23) | 7 (29) | 5 (17) |
| *Multiple methods* | 3 (9) | 5 (17) | 8 (33) | 6 (21) |

sexual and physical abuse, as well as psychiatric and psychological disorders. In addition, we also recorded the occasion and method used for suicidal behaviour. At a later stage, by shifting back and forth through the data on the life events of ethnic minority women, the principal researcher recognized elements of *fatalistic suicide* and subsequently included factors of overregulation in the analysis.

### The relevance of risk factors of psychiatric or psychological disorders and physical or sexual abuse

A plausible contribution to the suicidal behaviour of young immigrant women is the manifestation of psychiatric and psychological disorders. In addition, the rates of suicidal behaviour are elevated amongst those having multiple diagnoses of psychiatric disorders (co-morbidity). Some studies into psychiatric diagnoses among immigrants in the Netherlands hint at increased rates of certain psychiatric diagnoses, e.g. an elevated prevalence of anxiety disorder and depression for Turkish immigrants aged 12 to 65, while schizophrenia appears to be more often diagnosed in Surinamese and Moroccans, whether born in the country of origin or in the Netherlands (de Wit 2005; Van Oort et al. 2007). However, research from the United Kingdom indicated

**Table 3.** *Extent of repetitive suicidal behaviour and lethal intent of suicidal behaviour of female outpatients of four ethnic groups in Amsterdam*

|  | Turkish<br>N = 32<br>N (%) | Moroccan<br>N = 30<br>N (%) | South Asian<br>N = 24<br>N (%) | Dutch<br>N = 29<br>N (%) |
|---|---|---|---|---|
| Repetitive suicidal behaviour | 18 (56) | 14 (47) | 16 (67) | 16 (55) |
| Lethal intent | 8 (25) | 5 (17) | 6 (25) | 4 (14) |

that psychiatric disorders were significantly more common among majority British women than among South Asian immigrant women who had demonstrated suicidal behaviour (Bhugra et al. 1999). These contradictory findings prompted us to examine the psychiatric and psychological risk factors of majority Dutch young women versus the ethnic minority women who displayed suicidal behaviour (see Table 4).

Overall, having a psychiatric or personality disorder appears more relevant as a risk factor for Dutch (79 per cent) in comparison to Turkish (59 per cent) and Moroccan women (60 per cent), while South Asian women differ less substantially from Dutch women (71 per cent). This difference in the Dutch majority as opposed to minority women originates in seemingly higher incidences of mood and anxiety disorder in Dutch majority women. Co-morbidity is notably more often found in Dutch women (59 per cent) compared to South Asian (33 per cent), Turkish (28 per cent) and Moroccan women (27 per cent).

Research into the role of sexual and physical abuse unanimously shows that these experiences are a serious risk factor for suicidal behaviour (McHolm, Macmillan and Jamieson 2003; Salander-Renberg, Lindren and Osterberg 2004). These findings motivated us to examine their contribution in the case of our research subjects and compare the results (see Table 5).

**Table 4.** *Risk factors of psychiatric and personality disorders of female outpatients who displayed suicidal behaviour, in four ethnic groups*

|  | Turkish<br>N = 32<br>N (%) | Moroccan<br>N = 30<br>N (%) | South Asian<br>N = 24<br>N (%) | Dutch<br>N = 29<br>N (%) |
|---|---|---|---|---|
| Mood disorders* | 12 (38) | 11 (37) | 11 (46) | 17 (59) |
| Anxiety disorders** | 7 (22) | 5 (17) | 3 (13) | 10 (34) |
| Psychotic disorders | 2 (6) | 2 (7) | 3 (13) | 4 (14) |
| Borderline personality disorder/traits | 7 (22) | 6 (20) | 8 (33) | 13 (45) |
| Substance abuse*** | 3 (9) | 1 (3) | 5 (21) | 6 (21) |
| Other psychiatric disorders | 4 (13) | 7 (23) | 5 (21) | 5 (17) |
| *No disorder* | 13 (41) | 12 (40) | 7 (29) | 6 (21) |
| *One or more disorders* | 19 (59) | 18 (60) | 17 (71) | 23 (79) |
| *Co-morbidity**** | 9 (28) | 8 (27) | 8 (33) | 17 (59) |

*Mood disorders reported on include depression, depressive mood, dysthymia and bipolar disorder
**Anxiety disorders reported on include generalized anxiety, panic disorder, phobias, social anxiety disorder, obsessive-compulsive disorder and posttraumatic stress disorder
***Substance abuse include the abuse of alcohol, hard drugs or soft drugs
****Co-morbidity refers to having two or more disorders

**Table 5.** *Risk factors of sexual and physical abuse in female outpatients who displayed suicidal behaviour, in four ethnic groups in Amsterdam*

|  | Turkish N = 32 N (%) | Moroccan N = 30 N (%) | South Asian N = 24 N (%) | Dutch N = 29 N (%) |
|---|---|---|---|---|
| Sexual abuse or sexual harassment | 6 (19) | 5 (17) | 5 (21) | 11 (38) |
| Physical abuse | 10 (31) | 11 (37) | 10 (42) | 6 (21) |
| *No abuse* | 19 (59) | 18 (60) | 13 (54) | 17 (59) |
| *Either physical or sexual abuse* | 13 (41) | 12 (40) | 11 (46) | 12 (41) |
| *Both physical and sexual abuse* | 3 (9) | 4 (13) | 4 (17) | 5 (17) |

In correspondence with previous research findings, the frequency of sexual abuse and physical abuse in our sample is quite high. Sexual abuse is more often mentioned in the files of Dutch young women compared to ethnic minority women, whereas physical abuse is equally reported across ethnicities. This may reflect actual disparities, but it seems plausible that a taboo around sexual abuse in cultures that value chastity and virginity, such as the Turkish, Moroccan and South Asian cultures (Brouwer et al. 1992), has resulted in some underreporting.

In sum, previous research findings of immigrants being more vulnerable to psychiatric disorders were not confirmed in our study, and incidences of abuse were equally distributed as risk factors across ethnicities. These findings led us to suggest that psychiatric or psychological illnesses and abuse are not the key to explaining why minority women demonstrate suicidal behaviour more often than majority Dutch women. Hence, we turn to explore the relevance of *fatalistic suicide.*

### Durkheim's fatalistic suicide

A theoretical prism that continues to be beneficial in suicidology today is Durkheim's standard work *Suicide* (Kushner and Sterk 2005; Hamlin and Bryn 2006). Durkheim's goal was to account for the suicide rate by studying characteristics of individuals in their societal structure and social context. By emphasizing that suicide is a social manifestation and positing that individual motives could not explain the suicide rate, Durkheim went against previous beliefs that suicide resulted from entirely personal phenomena, such as the existence of mental illness (Durkheim 1952). Durkheim's work, which resulted in a typology of suicide, must be understood in terms of Weberian ideal types (Acevedo 2005). *Suicide* focuses on two core elements: the amount of social integration and the amount of social regulation.

Social integration refers to the degree to which people in society are connected to each other, through the possession of shared beliefs, sentiments and interest in one another, and a sense of devotion to common goals. Social regulation points to the extent to which society or a social group has control over the emotions, motivations and behaviours of its individual members through government by norms, rules and customs. According to Durkheim, the emergence of a severe lack *or* a very strong manifestation of either aspect could put individuals at risk for suicidal behaviour (Acevedo 2005).

*Fatalistic suicide* is characterized by a situation of extremely high levels of social regulation, while simultaneously social integration is low. Mutual ideas and shared feelings that should safeguard social bonding and connectedness no longer exist, yet strong regulation is present. It concerns suicide as a result of overregulated and thus unrewarding lives: 'futures are pitilessly blocked and passions violently choked by oppressive discipline' (Durkheim 1952, p. 276). Unfortunately, Durkheim himself wrote very little about *fatalistic suicides*; he mentioned only briefly that suicides of slaves were expected to fall into this category, as well as those of childless wives in the west (Durkheim 1952). Durkheim found *fatalistic suicide* hardly relevant for the west. His moral position led him to emphasize the social effects of underregulation or *anomic suicide* following from the decline of the importance of social norms due to processes of modernization.

Despite the underreporting in Durkheim's work on *fatalistic suicide*, we have indicators that its features of overregulation are highly relevant to the suicidal behaviour of young immigrant women in the Netherlands. For reflections on the mechanisms involved in *fatalistic suicide*, we turn to the arguments of scholars who have discussed the subject.

Pearce (1989) described the subservient situation of slaves, who were considered the property of their masters, as inferior and dehumanizing, and he described them as lacking control over the course of their life. *Fatalistic suicide* refers to environments where there is total coercion by an overwhelming force that has control over individual action (Acevedo 2005). For the accomplishment of human desires and to arrive at satisfaction, however, it is evident that individuals need to possess agency in determining their life course. When individuals experience serious oppressive forms of regulation, a consistent belief in human agency to realize social change becomes unimaginable (Acevedo 2005). Hopelessness arises: 'the individual's existence has been completely demystified and drained of possibility. [...] Excessively controlled by social-cultural prescriptions, individual freedom and improvement of life would become non-existing' (Douglas in Pearce 1989, p. 122). There is too little space for individuality because collective life is too intense to allow for individual development. The individual counts for little or nothing and does not have control over his/her fate, which results in a sense of powerlessness and meaninglessness.

One of the few other examples of *fatalistic suicide* mentioned by Durkheim is the suicide of housewives who remain childless. Even though at first the example seems rather outdated in the twenty-first century, for the sake of the argument we investigate it. Durkheim (1952) argues that motherhood protects wives from suicide through its effect of social integration into family life. Durkheim thought that a childless wife could have no personal bonding with a role as merely a housewife and that she could not derive meaning from it: 'Fatalists do not derive protection from their role, for them it comes from the outside. Others that surround her reproduce the role, but not the individual who occupies it' (Bearman 1991, pp. 520–1). This touches upon a crucial aspect. The experience of constraint begins when the regulation is not (any more) based on accepted norms, and when these norms are not (any longer) internalized, but judged as external, and hence they can only be upheld through force. *Fatalistic suicide* is a reaction to a force coming from outside, which is perceived as unjust and which is not integrated in one's inner self. This results in feelings of individual isolation and alienation. Furthermore, an individual needs to have awareness of his/her own alienation in order to perceive it as problematic (Halbwachs in Travis 1990).

More recently, Davies and Neal (2000) investigated the suicides of young women in rural China and described these as a clear case of *fatalistic suicide*, mostly because of the restricted sex roles for women. Central to these restrictions is the practice of marrying off daughters by all-powerful families. These daughters subsequently live in unhappy marriages under the tyranny of their mother-in-law, who expects total compliance. Suicide rates for Chinese young women are much lower in the cities, which underscores that the risk for suicidal behaviour is associated with the rural family system, as well as demonstrating the pivotal role of the method commonly employed in rural China, i.e. pesticide poisoning.

In sum, the work of scholars who discussed Durkheim's *fatalistic suicide* defined it as involving overregulation originating from harsh moral demands, upheld through force. As a result, individuals are faced with a lack of agency and develop a sense of powerlessness and dehumanization. When norms are considered external, demanding and obtrusive and fail to be internalized by the individual, a sense of alienation is created. The individual does not experience having meaningful relations and lacks a sense of connectedness.

## Overregulation in young immigrant women's lives: intersections of gender and culture

Since we are concerned with females from specific ethnic minority immigrant groups in the Netherlands who display disproportionate rates of suicidal behaviour in comparison to majority Dutch women, gender and ethnicity seem important factors. Having established the make-up of a *fatalistic suicide*, the subsequent question that emerges is whether there is a relation between gender and ethnicity on the one hand, and overregulation on the other. Hierarchical and oppressive structures of gender and ethnicity intersect in different ways for different groups. Identities cannot be reduced to a single marker because they are interlocked. Because of this entanglement, it should be investigated how the gender system and its relation with other systems of inequality and oppression may function. Multilayered and routinized forms of domination that often converge in women's lives prompt analysis of multiple grounds of identity when considering how the social world is constructed (McCall 2005).

Ethnic minority groups deploy cultural practices that originate in distinct sets of behaviour and beliefs that often distinguish groups from a larger culture of which they are a part. As Geertz (1973) argued, cultural practices are symbolized and enacted by social actors and the context that gives such practices meaning and significance. Some cultural practices seem to have a much greater influence on the lives of (young) women than on the lives of men. In particular, in the domain of sexual and reproductive life that is central in many cultures, women's role is often pivotal (Yuval Davis 1997). The sphere of sexuality and reproduction is a crucial theme in cultural practices since it enables the continuity of the ethnic group. As a result, it is women in particular who are 'considered to be the guardians of the collectivity's identity and honor and who demarcate with their behaviour the moral boundaries of their group' (Yuval Davis 1997, p. 25). In addition, cultural traditions and sometimes the re-invention of traditions are often used as ways of legitimizing the control and oppression of women in situations in which individual men as well as the collectivity feel threatened by others.

## Empirical findings on fatalistic suicide in the lives of young immigrant women

After analysing the accounts of young immigrant women, eight factors of overregulation emerged that related to *fatalistic suicide*. These factors were not established a priori but emerged cross-culturally as a result of the analysis of the case files when we studied the circumstances that led these young women into suicidal behaviour.

Table 6 shows that factors of overregulation emerged in about 50 per cent of cases for Moroccan, Turkish and South Asian young women, as opposed to 28 per cent in the Dutch cases. Issues around demands of upholding chastity were found almost equally in all ethnic minority groups. (The fear of) being outcast appeared to be relevant to Turkish and Moroccan young women in particular. Incidences of forced marriages were observed mostly in Turkish young women, whereas the impossibility of opting for a divorce because of family pressure to stay in an unwanted marriage was observed in Turkish as well as Moroccan young women. Rejection of the partner by their families was found in particular in South Asian women. The threat of death could be found across ethnicities, but most notably among Moroccan women. Being stalked by an (ex-) partner emerged as a cross-cultural problem for women. Being forced into prostitution happened to two Dutch women and one Turkish woman. In sum, three factors were found that affected both minority and majority women, while five factors to do with family honour were observed in ethnic minority

**Table 6.** *Factors of overregulation in female outpatients who displayed suicidal behaviour, in four ethnic groups in Amsterdam*

|  | Turkish N=32 N(%) | Moroccan N=30 N(%) | South Asian N=24 N(%) | Dutch N=29 N(%) |
|---|---|---|---|---|
| Chastity jeopardized | 8 (25) | 9 (30) | 4 (17) | 0 (0) |
| (Fear of being) outcast by family | 3 (9) | 4 (13) | 0 (0) | 0 (0) |
| Pressure to maintain unwanted marriage | 2 (6) | 3 (10) | 0 (0) | 0 (0) |
| Threatened with death | 2 (6) | 4 (13) | 2 (8) | 1 (3) |
| (Threatened with a) forced marriage* | 7 (22) | 2 (7) | 1 (4) | 0 (0) |
| Rejection of partner/Being rejected as partner | 3 (9) | 3 (10) | 6 (25) | 1 (3) |
| Stalking by (ex-) partner | 3 (9) | 1 (3) | 3 (13) | 3 (10) |
| Forced prostitution | 1 (3) | 0 (0) | 0 (0) | 2 (7) |
| Forced abortion | 0 (0) | 1 (3) | 0 (0) | 1 (3) |
| Locked up at home/Forced housekeeping | 0 (0) | 1 (3) | 0 (0) | 0 (0) |
| Restrictions on activities outside the home | 2 (6) | 0 (0) | 0 (0) | 1 (3) |
| Forced by family to give up education | 0 (0) | 1 (3) | 0 (0) | 0 (0) |
| *No factors of regulation* | 14 (44) | 14 (47) | 11 (46) | 21 (72) |
| *One or more factors of regulation* | 18 (56) | 16 (53) | 13 (54) | 8 (28) |
| *Multiple factors of regulation* | 7 (22) | 8 (27) | 3 (13) | 1 (3) |

*In a forced marriage one or both partners do not have agency in the marriage arrangement and disagree with the marriage arrangement. This includes those partners who have cooperated under physical or psychic threat.

women only. To illustrate how overregulation originating in honour-related issues emerges and to illuminate the extent to which a lack of agency exists, case summaries of minority women are discussed below.

### Chastity regulation: accusations, control and the threat of being outcast

Accounts indicate how safeguarding the family honour through maintaining a chaste (decent) reputation is felt deeply by young minority women, who face serious consequences if they fail to live up to this prescription. The case files demonstrate how the status of a chaste woman was jeopardized, and how the women were subsequently faced with repercussions that appear to be associated with their suicidal behaviour. As a result, some women felt they had little choice but to run away from home.

> Her mother migrated to the Netherlands just before giving birth to her. She used to be dad's favourite, although she knows that he would have preferred to have a son. Later there were severe conflicts between them. She used to be very angry with him, because he would not allow her all sorts of things, like going on school trips. Her father beat her up and she tried to hit him back. Her mother was isolated and sad, because her family was in Morocco and her husband did not give her any money. Her parents' marriage was bad. Her mother cried on her shoulder instead of the other way round. When her mother was pregnant with her sister, her mother had a fight with her father and left home, but returned later. In her mid-puberty one day her father hit her on the head. She then went to stay with friends in the city. She got introduced to drugs and criminals. At a party, she met a young man with whom she had sex for the first time. Her parents found out about this when they discovered a letter with the results of her pregnancy test. They were furious and never wanted to see her again. They pretended not to know her when they bumped into her, and thought of her as a whore. She then stayed with foster parents. At some point she contacted her family again, because she wanted to see how her younger sister was doing. Her father appeared to regret all the things that had happened between them, but her mother was jealous of this and therefore criticized her to her father. She concludes that her parents see her as a bad child.
>
> (Moroccan student, aged 20, who took an overdose)

The account above shows how violent repercussions in the family follow from the loss of a woman's virginity, a cultural value of chastity, which is a woman's responsibility to bear.

## Marital regulation: rejection of the partner and (threats of) being forced into marriage

Some parents and family members of young minority women who demonstrated suicidal behaviour rejected their partners. In South Asian families, this often concerns a rejection on the basis of caste, religion or ethnic background. When family members attempt to control a woman's spouse choice, they attempt to safeguard ethnic and cultural reproduction, and such efforts are often reinforced after migration. Rejection of the partner choice is also interlocked with agreements with family members, e.g. a match between cousins. This is often thought to guarantee a match between upbringing, religion or class and expected to result in the continuation of steady family relations (Sterkx and Bouw 2005). The following example illustrates the rejection of the daughter's partner by a South Asian family.

Her partner, of Surinamese Creole background, cheated on her and she then took many pills. They have now ended their relationship, which lasted three years. Her family have always been against her relationship, because of his ethnic background. They have forbidden her to ever meet him again. Asked about her family background, she describes how her father avoided the family and let her mother take care of everything. She had never got on well with her mother, since she felt her mother was more in favour of her brother than her. Also her mother always claimed that she resembled her father's family, which she understood as a criticism. She gets on really well with her brother. Except that when she had her first boyfriend he had remarked that this was something she could not do to her mother.
(22-year-old South Asian woman who took an overdose of pills on at least two occasions; employment status unknown)

An account of a Turkish young woman also demonstrates lack of individual choice in partner selection.

She arrived in the Netherlands when she was 12 years old and she lives with her mother. She introduced her boyfriend to her father two weeks ago. Her father is against her spouse choice because he already has a partner for her in mind, and he threatened to deport her mother from the Netherlands back to Turkey when she proceeded with her relationship and marriage. Her father has a Dutch partner now. Possibly, her father wants to save his honour by marrying his daughter off to his village friend. After consulting a counsellor she found out that she would need to wait two years before she could be married, otherwise her mother could indeed be expelled. During these two years, she feared she would be married off to her father's choice of spouse from his village in Turkey. She subsequently took an overdose.

> (17-year-old Turkish woman who took an overdose
> of pills; employment status unknown)

The effect of migration in the above account is that the young woman's mother is dependent on her husband for her residence permit. The father who wants to force a marriage upon the daughter exploits this dependency. In the next account of a Moroccan woman, it is shown that cultural value regarding what is considered to be respectable female behaviour does not end when a woman is divorced.

> Her family is against her relationship with a Moroccan man who has been married twice before. Previously, her aunt supported her, but now her entire family is against the marriage. She has demonstrated serious life-threatening behaviour. She does not want her family to find out about this because she feels that they could blame her suicidal behaviour on her relationship. She also has serious worries about her infertility and she feels bad about the fact that her parents are divorced and her mother does not want contact any more. She used to be married herself but went through a divorce after six years of marriage, even though her husband did not agree; her family supported this, since the two of them had very different personalities. She herself is very outgoing and active, while her ex-husband was more timid and preferred to stay at home. She was married at a very young age to a Moroccan, since she felt this was the appropriate thing to do for a Moroccan woman. She is described as someone with big circle of multi-ethnic friends.

> (28-year-old Moroccan woman, method unknown;
> employed and part-time student)

Interestingly, we observed that the woman featured above had internalized certain cultural demands around her spouse choice earlier in her life, i.e. that he should be a Moroccan and that she should marry young. Later in her life, her choice of partner clashes with the wishes of her family who want to control her partner selection in order for her to become respectable again.

## Forced to maintain an unwanted marriage by threats of violence or death

The following account illustrates how family members of a Turkish woman exercise control through threatening her with isolation, and how physical abuse intersects with gender and culture.

She reported the physical abuse she suffered from her husband at the police station. She lives with her husband at her mother's house. Three months ago, she underwent a forced marriage to her cousin, which was done in a sly way: her parents told her she needed to sign documents to report her missing passport, while in fact they were the papers for an Islamic marriage. Her family put her under great pressure to stay married and she withdrew her police report when she learnt about the consequences of her act for her family: social isolation and outcasting. Her parents threatened to kill her when she wanted to opt for a divorce. She then took an overdose. To the psychologist, her suicidal behaviour seems to be a way out of her powerless position.

(20-year-old Turkish woman who took an overdose of pills; employment status unknown)

In the following account of a Moroccan woman, it is highlighted how cultural negative attitudes towards divorced women precipitate a conflict between loyalty towards the family and a woman's personal wishes as an individual.

She grew up in Morocco with many siblings and was her father's favourite. Her father was sweet and kind, while her mother was very strict and punished her often. She hardly has a support system; all her family members live in Morocco. She married her first husband when she was 21 years old. She wanted to continue her education, but had to get married and then move to the Netherlands to be with her husband. Her husband had a job in education, yet he did not want her to continue her studies in the Netherlands. Her husband already had children from his previous marriage. He put pressure on her to take birth control pills and to have an abortion when she got pregnant. Her relationship with her husband has not turned out as she had hoped. Since she has given birth to a child, her husband has changed substantially. He has become a very religious man and this clashes with her own views. She struggles with what to do now. If she stays in her marriage, she will have to give up her own perspective on raising the children. If she follows her heart, she will lose her family and family honour.

(Moroccan woman, aged 34 who took an overdose on several occasions; employed in education)

## Conclusion and discussion

Our data show that well known risk factors in suicidology such as psychiatric and psychological illness as well as sexual and physical abuse do not appear to be sufficient to clarify the rationale of the suicidal behaviour of young women of Turkish, Moroccan and South Asian origin. We observed that many minority women reported living conditions characterized by overregulation, which is a central feature of fatalistic suicide. Our aim was subsequently to illuminate the role and mechanisms of overregulation with regard to their suicidal behaviour. By studying individual cases (ranging in number from 24 to 32 per ethnic group) that provided details of the values and beliefs in their cultural milieu and family context, we wanted to overcome the pitfalls of studying aggregated level data that often place subjects in a social and cultural vacuum.

Elements of fatalistic suicide were shown to be important in at least half of the cases of suicidal behaviour among Turkish, Moroccan and South Asian young women. Honour-related life events were inter-twined with excessive regulation and pressure by family members to ensure that a woman abided by cultural norms. This led to an absence of freedom to create one's own life course and an underdeveloped sense of autonomy, which is characteristic of fatalistic suicide. Highly demanding norms in crucial domains in life (e.g. marriage, divorce, partnership, sexuality) were experienced as oppressive. These cultural and moral practices had a huge influence on the lives of some minority young women. For instance this occurred when doubts around the reputation and virginity status of young women emerged. As a consequence of (being suspected of) violating cultural norms on appropriate female behaviour, violence and sometimes (threats of) a forced marriage took place. In addition, some minority women had to choose between continued abuse (e.g. by the husband) on the one hand and opting for divorce and involving the police. The latter, however, subsequently rendered some women an outcast in their own community, or led to them losing their residency permit.

Strict control by parents over their daughter's future spouse also emerged as central to the distress in a number of minority women. These regulatory measures originated in efforts to ensure continuation of the family and ethnic community. The honour-related rules prevented young women from achieving individuation and goal fulfilment. Their suicidal behaviour thus bears elements of fatalistic suicide. It seems plausible that suicidal behaviour of females in these ethnic groups can be understood as an expression of a deeper underlying need to influence their life course.

Since we matched a group of majority Dutch women with low social and economic status it seems safe to assume that the factors of overregulation are not a result of class background. Our data indicated that Dutch young women who displayed suicidal behaviour did not experience as much overregulation in their lives compared to minority women. On the occasions when they did face overregulation, it concerned forced prostitution and stalking by partners rather than honour-related events. It appears that overregulation that originates in honour protection is culture-bound.

Durkheim (1952) asserted that the suicide rates found in various cultures were indicative of the level of social pathology. This precipitates the question why some immigrant families maintain such strict enforcement of rules and moral guidelines. It appears that many immigrant communities in the west are undergoing a process of cultural transition towards more individualism and greater freedom for women. Durkheim also argued that the suicide rate is a proxy for social solidarity (Bearman 1991). Hence, the alarming rates of suicidal behaviour and the fatalistic components we discovered hint at prevailing contestation in certain immigrant communities around cultural prescriptions, and imply gendered traditional power relations. Tensions develop when parents employ a traditional culture rationale for exercising honour-related regulations in spheres where young women wish to follow their own life. This process may also be influenced by 'a general frigidity of cultures which takes place in diasporic communities' (Yuval Davis 1997, p. 67), as a response to their localization in the dominant society at large which is character-ized by modernization and individualization. The honour regulation exercised prevented young women from experiencing connectedness with their family and ethnic community and appeared to precipitate disintegration rather than the cultural stability desired by the family.

The information on the lives of the young women was not reported systematically and exhaustively. However, the fact that psychologists and psychiatrists wrote the notes in the files rather than sociologists renders underreporting plausible on social and cultural factors of overregulation. In addition, we focused on young women who were seen for treatment by mental health services. It may be expected that societal regulatory factors play an even larger role among ethnic minority women who are not in touch with mental health care.

Difficulties exist in translating the background and social meaning of suicidal behaviour across different cultures. Anthropological studies into attitudes on suicidal behaviour could help to illuminate if suicidal acts are recognized in an ethnic community as a response to certain kinds of distress. South Asian women are known to be vulnerable to suicidal behaviour world-wide, which may indicate a lower threshold and cultural rationale for suicidal behaviour since it is engrained in their cultural repertoire (Raleigh, Bulusu and Balarajan 1990; Patel and Gaw 1996). By contrast, since Islam fiercely forbids suicide, the threshold for suicidal behaviour seems higher in Moroccan and Turkish women.

On the basis of our data, we have shown that overregulation is central to the accounts of many young suicidal minority women in the Netherlands. In line with the work of Kushner and Sterk (2005,

p. 1141), who asserted that: 'Durkheim's definition of fatalism described the psychological and social condition of many women [...] who inhabit the globe today', we would like to emphasize how fatalistic suicide needs to be re-evaluated as a concept in suicidology. The reason why there has been a lack of attention to fatalistic suicide may be that, although women attempt suicide more often than men, since the suicidal behaviour of males is more often lethal, it is frequently taken as a yardstick for research on suicidal behaviour (Canetto and Lester 1995). In conclusion, factors of overregulation should be borne in mind for future directions in suicidology as well as for developing strategies for suicide prevention for Turkish, South Asian and Moroccan young immigrant women in the Netherlands.

## Notes

1.   Turkish and Moroccan immigrants arrived as guest labourers in the 1970s and the majority stayed in the Netherlands. The South Asian migration history goes back to the late nineteenth century when contract labourers were shipped from India to the previous Dutch colony of Surinam to work in agriculture. Shortly before Surinam gained its independence in the 1970s, many Surinamese moved to the Netherlands. The South Asian-Surinamese mostly settled in The Hague. It is therefore expected that the ethnic group among the Surinamese that is at risk for suicidal behaviour is mostly South Asian. Approximately 85 per cent of the South Asian-Surinamese population are Hindu and 15 per cent are Muslim.
2.   Incidences of suicidal behaviour as registered by hospitals and emergency agencies in the city of The Hague in 2002–2003: Turkish young women aged 15–19: 5.0 incidences per 1,000 per year, and aged 20–24: 7.0 per 1,000 per year. Surinamese young women aged 15–19: 4.5 per 1,000 per year, and aged 20–24: 4.0 per 1,000 per year. Moroccan young women aged 15–19: 2.3 per 1,000 per year, and aged 20–24: 2.0 per 1,000 per year. Majority Dutch women aged 15–19: 1.0 per 1,000 per year, and aged 20–24: 1.5 per 1,000 per year.
3.   Statistics show that men commit two to three times more suicide than women in the Netherlands. South Asian men have increased rates compared to Dutch men, while rates for Moroccan and Turkish men are about 80 per cent of that for Dutch men. South Asian and Turkish men commit suicide three times as often as women in these groups. Moroccan and Dutch men commit suicide about twice as often as women in their ethnic groups (Garssen, Hoogeboezem and Kerkhof 2006).
4.   Two women, from India and Bangladesh, were added to the sample of South Asians because of commonalities in their region of origin.

## References

ACEVEDO, GABRIEL A. 2005 'Turning anomie on its head. Fatalism as Durkheim's concealed and multidimensional alienation theory', *Sociological Theory*, vol. 23, no. 1, pp. 75–85
ARENSMAN, ELLA and KERKHOF, A.J.F.M. 2003 'Repetition of attempted suicide: frequent, but hard to predict', in Diego de Leo, Unni Bille Brahe, A.J.F.M. Kerkhof and Armin Schmidtke (eds), *Suicidal Behavior. Theories and Research Findings*, Gottingen: Hogrefe & Hubers Publishers

BEARMAN, PETER S. 1991 'The social structure of suicide', *Sociological Forum*, vol. 6, no. 3, pp. 501–24

BEAUTRAIS, ANNETTE L. 1998 'Risk factors for suicide and attempted suicide among young people', in *Commonwealth Department of Health and Aged Care, National Youth Suicide Prevention Strategy – Setting the evidence-based research agenda for Australia (A literature review)*, Canberra

—— 2003 'Suicide and serious suicide attempts in youth: a multi-group comparison study', *American Journal of Psychiatry*, vol. 160, pp. 1093–9

BHUGRA, DINESH, DESAI, MANISHA, BALDWIN, DAVID S. and JACOB, K.S. 1999 'Attempted suicide in west London 2. Intergroup comparisons, *Psychological Medicine*, vol. 29, p. 1131

BROUWER, LENIE, LALMAHOMED, BEA and JOSIAS, HENNA 1992 *Het Weglopen van Turkse, Marokkaanse, Hindostaanse en Creoolse meisjes*, Utrecht: Van Arkel

BURGER, IRENE, HEEMERT, BERT VAN, BINDRABAN, CLAUDIA A. and SCHUDEL, JOOST 2005 'Parasuicides in Den Haag: Meldingen in de Jaren 2000–2004', *Epidemiologisch Bulletin*, vol. 40, no. 4, pp. 2–8

CANETTO, SILVIA SARA and LESTER, DAVID 1995 'Epidemiology of women's suicidal behavior', in Silvia Sara Canetto and David Lester (eds), *Women and Suicidal Behavior*, New York: Springer, pp. 35–57

DAVIES, CHRISTIE and NEAL, MARK 2000 'Durkheimian altruistic and fatalistic suicide', in W.F.S. Pickering and Geoffrey Walford (eds), *Durkheim's Suicide, a Century of Research and Debate*, pp. 36–53, London: Routledge

DE LEO, DIEGO, BURGIS, SHELLY, BERTOLOTE, JOSE M., BILLE BRAHE, UNNI and KERKHOF A.J.F.M. 2006 'Definitions of suicidal behavior', *Crisis: The Journal of Crisis Intervention and Suicide Prevention*, vol. 27, no. 1, pp. 4–15

DE WIT, MATTY 2005 *Psychische Stoornissen bij Migranten*, Amsterdam: GGD

DURKHEIM, EMILE 1952 *Suicide*, New York: Free Press

GARSSEN, JOOP M., HOOGEBOEZEM, JAN and KERKHOF, A.J.F.M. 2006 'Zelfdoding onder Migrantengroepen en Autochtonen in Nederland', *Nederlands Tijdschrift voor Geneeskunde*, vol. 150, no. 39, pp. 2143–9

GEERTZ, CLIFFORD 1973 *The Interpretation of Culture. Selected Essays*, New York: Basic Books

HAMLIN, CYNTIA L. and BRYN, ROBERT J. 2006 'The return of the native: a cultural and social-psychological critique of Durkheim's Suicide based on the Guarani-Kaiowa of southwestern Brazil', *Sociological Theory*, vol. 24, no. 1, pp. 42–57

HJELMELANDT, HEIDI, KNIZEK, BIRTHE and NORDVIK, HILMAR 2002 'The communicative aspect of nonfatal suicidal behavior – are there gender differences?' *Crisis: The Journal of Crisis Intervention and Suicide Prevention*, vol. 23, no. 4, pp. 144–55

IGA, MIMORU 1981 'Suicide of Japanese youth', *Suicide and Life Threatening Behavior*, vol. 11, no. 1, pp. 17–30

KRIKKE, HANS, NIJHUIS, HANS and WEESENBEEK, RIANNE 2000 *Aan de Grenzen. Suïcidaal Gedrag onder Allochtone Meisjes en Jonge Vrouwen*, Den Haag: Public Health Service Bureau

KUSHNER, HOWARD and STERK, CATHERINE 2005 'The limits of social capital: Durkheim, suicide and social cohesion', *American Journal of Public Health*, vol. 95, no. 7, pp. 1139–43

MCCALL, LESLEY 2005 'The complexity of intersectionality', *Signs: Journal of Women in Culture and Society*, vol. 30, no. 3, pp. 1771–800

MCHOLM, ANGELA E., MACMILLAN, HARRIET L., JAMIESON, ELLEN 2003 'The relationship between childhood physical abuse and suicidality among depressed women: results from a community sample', *American Journal of Psychiatry*, vol. 160, no. 5, pp. 933–8

PATEL, S.P. and GAW, A. 1996 'Suicide among immigrants from the Indian subcontinent: a review', *Psychiatric Services*, vol. *47*, no. *5*, pp. 517–21

PEARCE, FRANK 1989 *The Radical Durkheim*, London: Unwin Hyman

RALEIGH, V.S., BULUSU, L. and BALARAJAN, R. 1990 'Suicides among immigrants from the Indian subcontinent', *British Journal of Psychiatry*, vol. 156, pp. 46–50

SALANDER-RENBERG, ELLINOR, LINDREN, SYBILLA and OSTERBERG, INGER 2004 'Sexual abuse and suicidal behaviour', in Diego de Leo, Unni Bille Brahe, A.J.F.M. Kerkhof and Armin Schmidtke (eds), *Suicidal Behavior. Theories and Research Findings*, Gottingen: Hogrefe & Hubers Publishers

SALVERDA, ELIZABETH 2004 *Laat me los hou me vast. Een kwalitatieve studie naar het welbevinden van Hindostaanse meisjes in Den Haag*, Den Haag: GGD rapport

SCHUDEL, J., STRUBEN, H.W.A. and VROOM-JONGERDEN, J.M. 1998 'Suïcidaal gedrag en etnisch-culturele ofkomst. Den Haag: 1987–1993', *Epidemiologisch Bulletin*, vol. 33, no. 4, pp. 7–13

STERKX, CAROLIEN and BOUW, LEEN 2005 *Liefde op Maat. De Partnerkeuze van Turkse en Marokkaanse jongeren*, Amsterdam: Het Spinhuis

TRAVIS, ROBERT 1990 'Suicide in cross cultural perspective', *International Journal of Comparative Sociology*, vol. 16, no. 3–4, pp. 237–48

YUVAL DAVIS, NIRA 1997 *Gender and Nation*, London: Sage Publications

VAN BERGEN, DIANA D., SMIT, JOHANNNES H., KERKHOF, A.J.F.M. and SAHARSO, SAWITRI 2006 'Gender and cultural patterns of suicidal behavior. Hindustani young women in the Netherlands', *Crisis: The Journal of Crisis Intervention and Suicide Prevention*, vol. 27, no. 4, pp.181–8

VAN OORT, FLOOR A., JOUNG, I.M.A, VAN DER ENDE, JAN, MACKENBACH JOHAN P., VERHULST, FRANK C. and CRIJNEN, ANTON A.M. 2007 'Development of ethnic disparities in internalizing and externalizing problems from adolescence into young adulthood, *Ethnicity and Health*, vol. 48, no. 2, pp. 176–84

# Marriage in colour: race, religion and spouse selection in four American mosques

Zareena A. Grewal

## Abstract

In this study, marriage serves as the point of entry into discussions about race, religion, and identity in American mosques. The experience of minority status in the US shapes the ways Muslim immigrants construct difference. The intersections of race, class, gender and religion emerge as Arab and South Asian Muslim Americans talk about interracial marriage and preferences for lighter-skinned mates. Muslim American children of immigrants test the boundaries of what constitutes an eligible spouse by drawing on religious sources that challenge their parents' ideologies of colour and racial prejudices. Islam serves as a common moral ground between generations that came of age in different cultures, creating a space for negotiating conflicting visions. Long after religion has faded as the cornerstone of social protest against racism in the US, Muslim youth in American mosques revive it in debates about race and colour.

## Culture vs. religion: a generational conflict

In some ways, Rashid's[1] relationship with his parents is not all that different from that of many 22-year-old Americans. His parents worry that he does not spend enough time on his schoolwork. They do not like the way he dresses. They do not like his friends. And they do not approve of the woman he loves.

Rashid is the son of Pakistani immigrants who came to Ann Arbor, Michigan, more than forty years ago. He rejects the word Pakistani wedged between hyphens in his identity. He identifies only as a Muslim. He would much rather pore over his books on Islam than those for his classes. He has grown a beard and wears a *kufi*, a Muslim skullcap. He carries a Quran with him at all times. Most of his friends are Muslim and black, as is the woman he wants to marry.

> I use the term "so-called Pakistani" because ... I don't like to identify myself on a race or nationality. ... As long as we carry the cultural baggage ... "We're Pakistani ... or Arab-American" ... we're identifying ourselves with the artificial names of geography. Once we get over that, we're Muslim first. Then we can relieve all the problems we have in our community. Not the "so-called problems" of who my kids can and cannot marry. These are things our parents distract themselves with. I mean real problems, like carrying [Islam] in this country. (Rashid)

The spirit of religious reform that underscores Rashid's critique is echoed by young Muslim Americans throughout mosque-based communities in the US, communities established by their immigrant parents. Most of these immigrants, typically Arabs from the Middle East and *Desi* immigrants from South Asia, arrived during the 1960s and 1970s and included large numbers of educated professionals who realized their dreams of financial success and quiet family life in American suburbs.[2] (I prefer the local term *Desi* to South Asian, which is not used by the subjects. Desi, literally 'of the country' in Hindi-Urdu, is used interchangeably with terms referencing nationality, like 'Indo-Pak').

The renewed interest in religion throughout American mosque communities is part of the global Islamic revival[3] that emerged in the latter half of the twentieth century, which coincided with the influx of large numbers of post-'65 Muslim immigrants to the US as well as the increasing influence of western cultural models and social norms in Muslim societies. Although it is often misrepresented as a simple backlash against westernization, the global Islamic revival is a product and agent of the complex forces of globalization, fuelled by the increase in religious literacy, the speed and ease of communication and the fluid movement of people, practices and ideas across national borders (Roy 2004). Key features of the reformist discourse are consistent across the wide spectrum of revivalist Muslims throughout the world; however, the specific preoccupations and particularities of a religious community always inform religious debates and give them local character.

The rediscovery of Islam in diaspora[4] takes a range of interesting forms. For many Muslim immigrants their religious identity takes on a prominence it did not have when they lived in Muslim societies. The 'Muslim first' identification is often even stronger for their children (Naber 2005). The ethnographic material presented here demonstrates the extent to which arguments about religion lace intergenerational debates about marriage and identity in four American mosques. My focus is not on *why* first- and second-generation Muslim immigrants find Islam increasingly appealing, but on *how* they draw on Islam as a discursive resource. Marriage serves as a point of entry into examining the ways the experience of diaspora shapes their constructions of difference. I argue that religion must be integrated into an intersectional analysis that brings race, gender and class together as systems that mutually construct and interpenetrate one another.

As American-born children of immigrants, such as Rashid, come of marriageable age, they often have different ideas from their parents about the measures of a good spouse. The first generation grew up in Muslim societies where particular cultural practices (constructions of beauty, marital endogamy, etc.) are naturalized and taken for granted. However, the second generation, raised in the US, often dismisses its parents' practices as both racist and 'un-Islamic'. Interestingly, the term 'culture' sometimes takes on a negative connotation as a pollutant of 'pure' Islam in reference to first-generation Muslims in a number of diasporic communities (Glynn 2002; Schmidt 2002; Naber 2005). Ironically, the second generation often does not recognize its own American sensibilities as cultural and constructed in the same way as those of their parents. Setting their parents' 'cultures' in opposition to Islam, Muslim American children assume a moral higher ground and assert their own religious authority in the face of their parents' 'cultural' authority. Examining perspectives on interracial marriage and intra-racial colour preferences sheds light not only on the nature of the generational tug-of-war between 'cultural' parents and 'religious' children, but also on the complex ways that constructions of identity are transformed in culturally fragmentary contexts such as the US. The second generation's moral claims are persuasive because they draw on the same religious sources that their parents consider authoritative (Quranic verses, Prophetic examples, sermons at their mosques, etc.) rather than secular anti-racist logics.

Although they may perceive race as natural and fixed in nature, many in the second generation defensively invoke Quranic verses and colonial history in order to challenge ideologies of colour and race, insisting that an individual's worth is determined by faith and righteousness. The following Quranic verse is frequently invoked as evidence of the egalitarian spirit of Islam: 'O men! Behold, We have created you all out of a male and a female, and have made you into nations and tribes, so that you might come to know one another. Verily, the noblest of you in the sight of God is the one who is most deeply conscious of Him. Behold, God is all-knowing, all-aware' (49, p. 13) (Asad 1980, p. 794). Interestingly, for many of these Muslims issues of race are arguably under overt religious scrutiny in ways that class and gender discrimination are not.[5] Although there are religious debates about gender and class discrimination in these mosques, these issues are peripheral when compared to the energy and attention devoted to talking about racial unity and egalitarianism in Islam.[6] Clearly, Islam is not a static import in immigrant communities; it is a dynamic discursive resource for young adults who challenge their parents' ideologies of colour and racial prejudices as well as the racism that envelops the contemporary US. At a time when the edgy urgency of hip hop has made religious articulation of social protest, so prevalent in the civil rights era, sound antiquated and hollow, Muslim youth reinvigorate it, challenging the assumption that religion has ceased to be a compelling vehicle in the fight against racism.

## Study methods

Muslims are now the fastest growing religious population in the US, primarily constituted by three ethnic/racial sub-groups: black American converts, Desi immigrants and Arab immigrants and the subsequent generations in each sub-group.[7] The four Sunni mosque-based communities examined here are scattered throughout the greater Detroit area and overlap in terms of membership. The mosques in Ann Arbor, Canton, Troy and Franklin, Michigan, serve as social and religious centres for immigrants from the Middle East and South Asia and smaller numbers of black and white American-born Muslims and immigrants from other parts of the Muslim world. All four communities are largely middle to upper-middle class, and the children of immigrants are usually college bound regardless of their parents' educational level or economic standing. Muslim immigrants in the US tend to be upwardly mobile and better educated than their co-religionists in other western countries.[8] 'Mosqued' communities such as these represent only a small segment of Muslim Americans.[9]

The research presented here is based on ninety in-depth interviews with college-educated, second-generation Arab and Desi Muslims between the ages of 18 and 30, supplemented with several interviews with their black and white Muslim peers, and with first-generation immigrants from these communities.[10] The sense of a 'shortage' of eligible mates in these mosques characterizes many minority communities. Most of the subjects in this study rely heavily, sometimes exclusively, on family and community networks in order to isolate potential Muslim mates, although university groups (like the Muslim Students Association), religious conferences and internet matchmaking or social networking services (like naseeb.com or facebook.com) expose young people to potential Muslim mates beyond their parents' social circles. In this context, questions about conflicting notions of desirability and where to draw the boundaries of the pool of eligible Muslim mates become particularly important.

## Immigration, Islam and whiteness

Arab and Desi immigrants have a long and tortured history in relation to American 'whiteness', as a legal and biological category and as a social or political construction. Whiteness was a prerequisite to naturalization in the US until 1952. Throughout the twentieth century, European immigrants suffered discrimination in the US and as an act of self-preservation became white by essentially choosing whiteness, deciding they were white and then struggling to be recognized as white (Roediger 1994). Joan Jensen (1988) and Ian Lopez (1996) provide detailed histories of the discourse of legal whiteness in US courts and analyse a number of early cases of Arab and Indian immigrants who contested the biological logic of race in order to be naturalized as US citizens, albeit unsuccessfully. In contrast to whites who trace their lineage to Europe, Middle Eastern immigrants continue to be perceived and defined as non-whites socially although they are also currently defined as whites and/or Caucasians legally (Naber 2000, p. 51). Desi immigrants straddle the vexed boundary between Asian and Caucasian in a similar fashion. First- and second-generation Muslim immigrants examined here consistently characterize the exclusion they feel as racial, although other Americans might identify their 'difference' from the white majority as merely ethnic.

The racially motivated hatred Muslim immigrants experienced throughout the twentieth century has intensified in the last half of the century due to the tenor of US foreign policy in the Middle East, particularly since September 11 (CAIR 2003; Volpp 2003). Nadine Naber (2000) perceptively directs our attention to the social and political 'racialization of religion', premised on the intrinsic inferiority of Islam, which *racially* marks Muslim immigrants in the US. I prefer Naber's argument and terminology to similar arguments made by Garbi Schmidt (2002) and others about the 'ethnification' or 'ethnogenesis' of Islam by second-generation Muslims in the west because of the softening effects of the language of ethnicity. In the 1970s, the category of ethnicity increasingly displaced race as the primary unit of academic analyses, shifting the focus from constructions of difference to internal group formation and the symbols of inclusion. This trend also, inadvertently, sparked a neo-conservative glorification of ethnicity and a self-celebratory nativism that boasted a 'new' American mosaic that extended beyond black and white, ultimately reducing ethnicity to a euphemism for race or a kind of racial subset. Making ethnicity the master concept over race often glosses over exclusions and hostilities with racial undercurrents, particularly in the ethnographic analyses of those groups ranked between the poles of black and white (Omi and Winant 1994; Sanjek 1994).

In many Arab and Desi communities, whiteness is simultaneously coveted and disparaged. Although most Arabs and some Desis regularly check the 'white' box on official forms and may even enjoy the privilege of whiteness in particular contexts, they often reject that identification in other situations. Nayef, a blond Syrian, explains that whiteness is more than appearance.

> The way being Arab manifests itself racially is [that] we see ourselves as different, as Arab Muslims. ... To be labeled a white boy, it's the worst. You're like, "I ain't white ... I'm Arab!" And everyone that's teasing you [might be] light-skinned [Arabs] but it's irrelevant. It's white, meaning American [whites].

Even those Arab Americans who have physical characteristics typically considered definitive attributes of whiteness (blond or red hair, fair skin, etc.) often reject whiteness as their racial identity within the spaces of their communities. Their rejection entails a political claim to the right to protection from discrimination as well as the reclamation of self-definition 'on their own terms, in the face of the state's and the media's distortions of their identities' (Naber 2000, p. 51). Furthermore, phenotype does not always guarantee the power to 'pass' as white for Muslims since it may be trumped by physical markers of their faith (i.e. Muslim women's veils, men's beards), which make them particularly vulnerable to discrimination.

As their claims to social, and sometimes even legal, citizenship are increasingly undermined, Muslim Americans often naturalize these racial and national exclusions by invoking race in order to talk about religious discrimination. Drawing on the language of race rather than ethnicity or religion in no way fixes Arab and Desi constructions of difference in relation to whiteness because of the inherent instability of race. Matthew Jacobsen defines race as a 'tablet whose most recent inscriptions only imperfectly cover those that had come before, and whose inscriptions can never be regarded as final' (1998, p. 142). The analogy of a tablet seems especially fitting for Muslim Americans whose definitions of race correspond to shifting social and political circumstances, yet these 'systems of "difference" can coexist and compete with one another at a given moment' (ibid., p. 140). Although religion is never constructed as biological, Muslim subjects' invocation of race does not necessarily reflect sloppiness or imprecision; rather, such contradictions may reveal their acute consciousness of the process of constructing difference (ibid., p. 170). Janet, a white American convert constructs her racial identity differently after becoming (visibly) Muslim.

Of course I know I'm still white and [Muslims] think of me as white but in my head I really identify myself as a minority now. ... [Because of my scarf] other white Americans don't see me as white. They are always trying to figure out this imaginary accent and before this *hijab* [scarf] nobody used to ask me where I was born. ... When I [say] Detroit, they [are] confused. A lot of white people see me as a traitor. ... so that makes me identify much more as a Muslim than as white. I have to worry about discrimination like any other minority; I stick out in crowds. ... How am I any whiter than a Syrian girl with blue eyes?

For Janet her 'cultural apostasy'[11] and the ensuing sense of alienation from other whites has led her to construct her racial identity differently after converting and wearing *hijab*. Although religious symbols are not racial markers, they may take on a racial cast. White converts continue to identify as white but they note that when confronting anti-Muslim prejudice their religious identity becomes more salient. In a study on white British women who veil, Myfanwy Franks argues that the discrimination they receive for betraying the invisibility of their whiteness 'demonstrates the shifting boundary not so much of "race" but of racism which can arc across boundaries by a process of uniformed association' with racially marked Muslim immigrants (2000, p. 926). Muslim Americans grapple with the expansions and contractions of racism, whiteness and social citizenship and their shifting and conflicted relationships to the dominant white majority are reflected not only in how they define themselves in relation to them, but also in the shifting internal ideologies of colour within their communities.

## Intra-racism and spouse selection

Matrimonials advertising 'fair' skin are ubiquitous in the 'lonely hearts' sections of Muslim American publications and websites.[12]

Sunni Parents of Indian origin seeking suitable match for their two daughters:
(1) Pharmacist, 24 years old, prefer someone in medical field. (2) Degree holder, 31 years old, employed in computer field. Both are US citizens, slim and *fair color*. (*Islamic Horizons 2003*, emphasis added)

Although some studies have examined the role matrimonial ads play in facilitating the matchmaking process for Muslim Americans (Hermansen 1991; Haddad and Smith 1996) my interest is on the significance of skin colour[13] and the ways it intersects with gender and class. Research on black Americans shows that the politics of skin colour still governs the most intimate of relationships (Russell, Wilson and Hall 1992, pp. 107–8). Just as the skin colour of a spouse becomes a statement about social mobility and prestige among black Americans, the same phenomenon emerges in the overlooked cases of Arabs and Desis in the US.

Although constructions of difference may be transformed as Muslim immigrants assimilate the racial discourse in the US, race is hardly new to them. As post-colonial peoples, they have an intimate history with regimes of white supremacy, which is reflected not only in the ways they construct racial difference in relation to others, but also in the ways they link privilege and colour among themselves. Intra-racism is a term describing the phenomenon of a racialized group that internalizes white supremacy and redirects it at its own members. Since each group contains a wide spectrum of individual skin colours, people are stratified along this colour line. Those individuals at the lighter end of the spectrum are considered more attractive, and are therefore privileged. This privilege is embedded in ways that are not readily apparent, and the benefits, elisions and racial myths that accompany it are re-inscribed in everyday social interactions. Dark skin is stigmatized in parallel, often imperceptible, ways.

I argue that contemporary ideologies of colour in the post-colonial Muslim world are racial, although they are categorically different from western racism since they are fundamentally reactionary, derivative discourses. Partha Chatterjee's (1986) nuanced treatment of Indian anti-colonialist nationalism reveals the ways it was trapped in a framework of false essentialisms that necessarily reproduced exclusions among Indians because it was derived from British discursive categories. Intra-racism, I would argue, is similarly a derivative discourse, the reflection of self-hatred, the internalization of notions of inferiority and defect, perhaps the most tragic scar left by systematic racism. Constructions of difference and beauty are certainly not static or unchanging in South Asia or in the Middle East, just as they are not in the US;[14] intra-racism, however, corresponds to the rhetoric of white supremacy in suggestive ways. While race should not be reduced to colour, dismissing the fetishization of fair skin as a random or benign aesthetic preference among post-colonial peoples neglects the power and continuing vitality of the rhetoric of white supremacy throughout the world.

The intra-racist ideologies of many Arabs and Desis emigrate with them and are reinforced and sometimes transformed by the racial climate in the US. Sultana, an immigrant from India, explains how ideologies of colour are reformulated in a society with a white majority. 'Most [Desis] are *samla,* neither dark nor fair. So what is fair over there might be *samla* over here. Like, in India, you would be very fair, but here you won't because of the white Americans. So it depends on the comparison.' Sultana explicitly refers to white Americans as the standard to be measured against. Interestingly, although most Muslim immigrants in these communities construct whites as racially different from them, whites remain the point of reference. For others, such as Abdullah, the ability to 'pass' informs their colour preferences.

I think [whiteness] is the ultimate beauty standard. "She's so pretty, she's white-skinned." That's always the line [in Franklin and] in Syria. ... My mother is very white and people are always surprised she's Arab. And she wants me to marry someone who looks like us.

The stigma of dark skin and the preference for light skin are coded racially as immigrants assess their status as minorities in the US and the benefits of 'passing' as whites.[15] The significance of skin colour is linked to the broader racial climate of the US, where Muslim minorities from the Middle East and South Asia regularly experience discrimination. Additionally, the intersections with class are important since immigrants internalize the racialized 'American dream' and connect climbing the economic ladder with distancing themselves from racial minorities in order to obtain the benefits of whiteness.[16] In other words, intra-racism is simultaneously a self-destructive internalization of white supremacy and also a strategy for operating within a raced class hierarchy.

Scholars of colonial history have demonstrated the ways marriage and mating were used to reproduce racial and class hierarchies and to police race, class and national borders (Stoler 1991). The derivative discourses of colour are also deeply gendered in these communities and marriage serves to regulate and reproduce the internal hierarchies of colour and class. In interviews, subjects explain how they evaluate potential mates, as well as what criteria they feel their communities hold them to. The Desis and Arabs largely have similar responses, with a few differences. More Desi men and women claim they find lighter skin more attractive and more Desi women express frustration over intra-racism than the Arab women interviewed. Since Desis, in general, consider themselves darker, they note that their definitions of what constitutes 'light' or 'fair' are more 'generous' than those of their Arab counterparts. As in most cases of male socioeconomic dominance, men tend to be evaluated on their success rather than their looks, and, not surprisingly, female subjects express much more anxiety about skin colour and beauty standards than male subjects, although men are certainly not immune to intra-racism. The popular Indian skin-bleaching cream Fair and Lovely, found in ethnic grocers throughout the US and Europe, recently began to share the shelves with the male counterpart, Fair and Handsome. Interestingly, the ad campaign launching the cream featured Bollywood heart-throb Sharukh Khan and inspired a critical, race-conscious backlash among Desi youth in diaspora (Puri 2007).

If women are evaluated physically more than men are, then they suffer intra-racism more as well. Female subjects insist that darker skin makes it harder for women to marry in their communities. Khadija describes an on-going conflict with her Egyptian mother.

My mother is always after me to stay out of the sun [because] she thinks I get too dark. She's got green eyes and everything and she gets really mad when people think I'm black. She thinks it's cause I get so *samra* (dark) and cause I have what I guess you would call curly or kinky hair like *suwd* (blacks). She always says (in accent) "You're hair used to be so nice when you were a baby. I don't know what happened." Especially when the marriage topic comes up.

Khadija refers not only to the stigma of being darker-skinned but also to other features that are racialized in the US (and in the Middle East), such as kinky hair. As they become familiar with the ways race is coded in the US, those racial signs become more deeply ingrained in their own derivative racial discourses. Muslim immigrants often talk about race and colour in surprisingly explicit ways. This reveals their unfamiliarity with the taboos of the racial discourse in the US in contrast to their children and not necessarily more virulent racist streaks. In other words, Muslim immigrants are often unfamiliar with the ways Americans talk *around* race. Therefore, the explicit and unselfconscious ways that they talk about race and colour are often reflective of their lack of mastery of the linguistic taboos associated with race in the US. Many young Muslim Americans both challenge and re-inscribe the immigrants' racial ideologies, sometimes in the same breath.

Aunties, in general, make you feel less pretty if you're too dark. I mean, I guess I'm medium-dark. I know people bleach [their skin] and get coloured contacts. ... and it looks good and you think about it. But it's fake and I hate that fake stuff. This is what God gave you. *Astaghfarallah.* [God forgive me.] (Sahar)

Sahar is conflicted about her complexion. She admits to being tempted to alter her appearance but, interestingly, her religious convictions prevent her.

The stigma attached to dark colour intersects with broader racial discourses in the US and sometimes echoes a biological racial logic. Sahar bemoans the plight of the single woman deemed unattractive. 'If a girl has a major flaw, she's just stuck. It's sad. ... In society, if [a girl is] very, very dark complected, these are all physical things, just physical abnormalities.' Like Sahar, Sultana, a Desi mother of three adult daughters, explicitly refers to dark colouring as a physical abnormality and deficiency.

Well, in [South] Asian communities, because there are so many shades, most everyone prefers light skin. ... And it is much, much worse here than in India and Pakistan because over there if you are ugly ... then at least you can make it up with money. "OK my daughter's not beautiful, but I can give you a house." But here ... they all have money and so they can't compensate deficiency with money. See, we parents are afraid [of our children marrying dark-skinned mates] because, if not for this generation, then ... our grandchildren. Because dark colour is dominant over light colour ... and the children will carry the dark colour [because it] is a dominating feature [that] stays over the generations.

It is clear in her explanation that being dark is perceived as a defect, a genetic deviation that should be feared. Sultana invokes an arguably American racist logic that includes biological dimensions of race, racial degeneracy and fears of miscegenation.

The systems of gender, class and race mutually construct and interpenetrate one another. Many immigrants argue that things that are perceived as defects (such as unattractiveness) can be compensated for relatively easily in their home countries. For example, Sultana refers to the practice in the subcontinent of marrying a daughter off with a larger dowry to attract more potential mates.[17] Interestingly, she notes that this practice does not work in her US community.[18] Since suburban communities are generally homogeneous in terms of wealth, a larger dowry is not as attractive as it might have been overseas. In these cases, families may choose to bring over a spouse from their country of origin. Thus, class, like gender, also intersects with intra-racism. As intra-racist ideologies are re-formed in the US, they may gain a potency that they may not have overseas because they are conflated with socio-economic endogamy. Asma expresses her frustration with the ways colour and class are linked. 'I know people see me as dark, and I know people don't [propose] because of that. And I want to marry a professional person, so it's hard.' Just as in the black American case, financially successful men are perceived as being more eligible and, therefore, able to get the preferred lighter-skinned wives. In these communities, fair skin may be a vehicle of upward class mobility or maintaining upper-middle-class endogamy. Russell, Wilson and Hall document that colour is related to upward mobility for black Americans, so that light-skinned women 'have the best chance of trading in on their color to flee the [ghetto], leaving the predominantly darker-skinned women behind' (1992, p. 116). Scholars must investigate whether similar patterns exist in Muslim immigrant communities.

Increasingly, young Muslim Americans in these communities draw on Islam to contest intra-racism. They often cast the fetishization of fair colour as a kind of racism, which they see as a symptom of colonialism and an eastern, 'cultural' corruption of 'pure' or 'true' Islam, revealing one of the ways post-colonial histories are reproduced in diaspora. Murtaza explains how that history haunts his community. 'I don't think being lighter makes you better looking. ... It comes from colonialism; the British are right there in your face everyday and so it gets in your head, that you are dark, bad, bad-looking. ... It has nothing to do with Islam.' Like Murtaza, Omar dismisses the beauty ideal that permeates but hardly represents his community by locating its roots in pre-Islamic history. 'My grandmother would make jokes about me getting a blond blue-eyed [Arab] wife and I'm like, "We're Arabs. What are you talking about? We hardly even know any Arabs like that!" It's a kind of *jahiliya* [pre-Islamic ignorance].' Many young people dismiss intra-racism as a form of ignorance that predates Islam or as 'culture' infecting people's views. 'Indo-Paks ... are just infatuated with ... who is white, whiter, whitest? ... It has a lot to do with who you marry, the way the community perceives you and it's sad because that is just cultural garbage' (Ahoo). Interestingly, Ahoo refers to intra-racism as 'cultural garbage', distinguishing it from religion. These critiques of intra-racism often invoke a new, deterritorialized and 'purified' understanding of Islam characteristic of the revivalist discourse (Roy 2004).

Muslim American youth contrast Islam with 'culture', which is human, constructed and polluted, but this usage usually applies only to the stigmatized elements of the immigrants' cultures. Yasmin invokes the culture/religion opposition.

> Every culture is into ... white skin. ... I don't care what they think. Why should I change what Allah gave me? Just because of what some stupid society thinks? So, no, I'm not going to dye my hair or get contacts or any of that stupid stuff. That's wrong. You should do what's Islamic, not what's cultural and it's sad that people feel pressured into that. They should get stronger *iman* [faith].

Yasmin criticizes the faith and strength of character of both those who propagate this intra-racism, as well as those who attempt to accommodate it by altering their physical appearance. These young Muslims draw on Islam as a discursive resource as they resist the ideologies of colour within and beyond their communities. They point out that intra-racism cannot be reconciled with Islam and criticize those who conform to this intra-racist beauty ideal because it is based on characteristics that are prized by culture, a human construction, and not Islam, their divine standard.

One of the risks of doing a focused analysis on a cultural phenomenon such as intra-racism is that of exaggerating its prominence. Although discussing marriage abstractly allows interviewees to map out their criteria, what people say or think about marriage does not always directly correspond with whom they marry. It may be that the correlation between skin colour and marriage patterns is very low, especially when compared to other criteria named by the subjects in their spouse selection process, such as personality compatibility, religiosity, family reputation and career prestige. My aim here is not to suggest that colour preferences are more significant in spouse selection than other factors. Rather I isolate this phenomenon in order to examine the ways ideologies of colour intersect with gender, class and religion. I argue that Islam serves as a tool for undermining the system of intra-racism that privileges and affirms light skin in numerous, imperceptible ways in mosque-based communities and it translates across the generation gap in ways that secular anti-racist rhetoric may not. Religious references lace the debates about inter-racial marriage in parallel ways.

## Interracial Muslim marriages

Although Muslims in the communities examined here believe Islam penalizes racism, they often accept race as a 'natural' category. For example, they absorb the language of race to distinguish Arab, Desi, white and black Muslims from one another. The subjects express with conviction that in Islam one's worth is determined only by the degree of righteousness and faith in God and they often criticize their communities' failure to implement the creed of Islamic egalitarianism. 'Last Friday I took a Jewish [friend] to *juma'* [services]. ... You got Malaysians, blacks, Arabs everyone all next to each other [in prayer]. No cliques, so he was very impressed. But in marriage who knows' (Abdullah). Abdullah echoes the racially egalitarian ethos that characterizes the religious discourse in these communities. However, he concedes that the Islamic principles of tolerance and unity may not be implemented in spouse selection. Interracial marriage between Muslims poses a 'boundary dilemma' that forces them to consider the meaning and consequences of 'marrying out' and to 'confront questions about the definition, meaning and significance of the boundaries that mark their identity' (Kibria 1997, p. 524). Marriage, then, may become the ultimate litmus test of an individual's views on race.

Immigrants are often confronted by children whose much broader vision of acceptable potential mates is shaped by the diversity of Muslims in the US and the often more expansive and diverse Muslim social networks the second generation has access to through university groups, professional associations, religious conferences and internet matchmaking and social networking sites. Additionally, children of immigrants often feel they have more in common with Muslim Americans of other race groups than with new immigrants from their parents' countries. Interracial marriage is a solution to the perceived problem of a limited pool of eligible mates. 'Even my parents are cool with [me] marrying a girl that's not necessarily Arab. They've even [suggested] girls to me that aren't' (Ibrahim). Although Ibrahim's parents are open to interracial marriage, for many immigrants it is a startling trend and sometimes a point of generational conflict (Haddad and Smith 1996, p. 25).

Overwhelmingly, the most common pattern among subjects is one where they prefer their own racial group among Muslims but are open-minded about interracial marriage and would consider it. One reason for the preference for endogamy is that many in the second generation want to preserve their culture in future generations, indicating that the negative connotation their parents' culture sometimes assumes is contextual. Stressing the importance of cultural, as opposed to racial, endogamy could be a thinly disguised racism, or, equally, a pragmatic approach to creating a successful partnership, or simply a reflection of a genuine attachment to one's heritage.

> I think marrying out of [your] race is fine when other people do it ... but I never could because I'm way too cultural. ... I want my culture to be carried on to the future generations and ... both parents have to have the same culture for ... [your] kids to be pure Desi. (Sahar)

Although most subjects emphasize that religion is much more important to them than their cultural heritage, for some in the second generation preserving the 'purity' of culture is just as important as preserving Islam. 'Marrying out' may be seen as compromising their culture and making it more susceptible to disappearing over genera-tions. For a number of Muslims in these communities, however, race plays no role in their choice of spouse. 'Only God knows [who I will marry]. I don't mind if they're not Desi at all as long as they're Muslim and they have a sincere heart and a good sense of humor and they can be honest with themselves, with me, with God' (Rafia). When subjects list religiosity among the most important criteria, all potential Muslim mates are on equal footing.

My findings suggest that the general sentiment in the mosque communities examined here reflects relative openness to the idea of interracial marriage, but for some the common faith does not necessarily make an individual outside of their race any more eligible. 'Islamically, you can't say no [in marriage] or discriminate on race ... because religiously Muslims are obligated not to be racist. Culturally, you can't help it. Many first and second generation Muslim immigrants consider blacks the least desirable' (Abdullah). 'I think I can marry an Arab woman and I think my parents would be pretty happy about it as well. But to be brutally honest, with a black Muslim, I could see my parents having a fit. That's wrong but that's how they are' (Murtaza). Black Muslims often perceive the first generation as more intolerant than the second generation. Hajra, a young black woman, feels that the immigrants in her mosque harbour more prejudice than their children. 'You don't see prejudice much from people my age. But you do with [their] parents....It's a colonialism thing...Their image of black people overseas is really low because they think ... we're the last rung on the totem pole.' Hajra alludes to the immigrants' insecurities about the racial hierarchy in the US and their histories of colonial subjugation, revealing the ways black Americans also participate in the production of post-colonial histories in diaspora. Black women such as Hajra not only suffer the racism of the white majority but also the racism internalized and refracted back at them by other people of colour. As immigrant communities assimilate American racial sensibilities, the black woman becomes the least acceptable daughter-in-law (Swanson 1996, p. 149). Farida explains how black women like her are disadvantaged relative to black men in mosque communities. 'There's no prestige or status in marrying a black woman. ... For a black man all his options are open because, generally, the white converts to Islam ... would consider him. For the black woman, she's not desirable to other races.'

In the context of contact with Muslims of other races in religious settings, Muslim immigrants in the US are often confronted on their racial prejudice (Hermansen 1991, p. 198). The intimate contact between different races in diverse American mosques often brings issues of prejudice and discrimination within communities to the fore.

Immigrants in these communities are often much more strongly opposed to interracial marriage than their American-born children. Interestingly, they sometimes frame their opposition in religious terms.

I tell my daughters that I think it's easier to marry within similar backgrounds. And I can't quote you a *hadith* [Prophetic tradition] but I know there is one that says try to marry within similar backgrounds, just to avoid conflict because, as [it] is, there are too many differences in the marriage. This is why we parents say stay in your own race background. (Sultana)

Although the vast majority of Muslims hold that interracial marriages are acceptable in Islam, others, such as Sultana, believe that Islam discourages interracial marriage, although they did not produce scriptural evidence in the interviews. Another Desi mother concedes that interracial marriage is sanctioned by Islamic law but insists it should be a last resort.

The young people ... think that, well, it's not *haram* [forbidden, sinful] to marry out, so what's the big deal? But the Prophet didn't say that. I mean, you have to start in and then go out. Nowadays, girls just say no [to suitors] without a good reason and that's *haram*. First you have to consider your cousins. If they are not good, then you look at other Indian boys. If you still can't, then Pakistanis. Arabs and other Muslims should be last. But the first thing some of these girls do is look outside even though they have very good cousins. They say nobody marries cousins in America but that's our tradition. (Amina)

In line with Sultana, Amina passionately defends her position on endogamy in vague religious terms. This demonstrates the extent to which arguments couched in sacred law may undermine eastern traditions and parental authority. Although the first generation recognizes the authority of revelation or lessons taught in their local mosque by religious leaders, their children often draw on those common sources of Islam to subvert their parents' vision. Clearly, Amina's vision of appropriate potential mates is much more limited (cousin marriages being optimal) than the second generation's. The young women Amina debates defend interracial marriage on religious grounds and dismiss familial endogamy by invoking Islamic law as well as cultural norms in the US. Of course, young Muslims raised in the US have also internalized the secular, anti-racist rhetoric that permeates American media and school curricula as well as the cultural norms couched in medical terms that stigmatize practices such as cousin marriages. Their multiple layers of discursive mastery may privilege them *vis-à-vis* their parents. Young Muslims often challenge their parents' values by framing their critique in strictly religious terms since Islam is a moral common ground across the generations in a way that American anti-racist discourses or American constructions of incest may not be.

Second-generation Muslims invoke religious purity in order to critique their parents' cultural practices, prejudices and attitudes that they feel cannot be justified or reconciled with Islam. As young

Muslims find the process of looking for spouses difficult due to small pools of eligible mates, interracial marriages within these communities become plausible and logically defensible on religious grounds.

> If a Muslim has any questions about our marriage, he's already gonna be blasted because that's not Islam. You cannot be a Muslim and be racist because the [Prophet] said that a white does not have any superiority over a black, a black does not have any superiority over a white. ... The only thing that divides Africa and Asia is the Suez Canal that was built in 1947 (*sic*). The Prophet encourages us to marry out. ... That's how [civilizations and] communities are built. (Rashid)

Often, even if they are opposed to interracial marriage in principle, parents may find themselves unable to protest because their children are able to defend interracial marriage in Islamic terms. 'I would consider black or Arab guys but ... my parents would, of course, ask, "Why not a good Desi boy?" But if we were happy together, then they would have to say yes because it's Islamic' (Iman). As communities engage their religious tradition in the US, old patterns of behaviour and reasoning need to be reconciled with new understandings of religion and culture. Increasingly, the first generation grants this religious authority to their American children. Momin admits that his 24-year-old son teaches him about Islam.

> We were not [as] religious back in Iraq as he is here in America ... And he argues with me and then I have to go back and read the religion. He tells me things I never thought of about Islam. ... I read the whole Quran because of him. To fight with him [laughs].

As the generational conflict plays out in Muslim American families, Islam serves as a common discursive resource in constructing arguments both for and against interracial marriage. The tug-of-war between 'cultural' Muslim parents and their 'religious' children seems to favour the younger generation, armed with religious sources that their parents recognize as authoritative.

Not surprisingly, interracial marriages among second-generation Muslims are becoming increasingly common in Muslim American communities (Hermansen 1991, p. 198). Yusuf and Nora are among the high-profile Desi-Arab couples in these communities. Nora recounts that she never accepted the idea that she had to marry an Arab.

> It's so hard to marry [someone] of your same race. We're in America, we go to school with ... different people our entire lives. And then

parents ... say ... "I don't care if you've been friends with white, black, red, whatever, brown [Muslims]. Those are not people that you can fall in love with." (Nora)

Nora's father was adamantly opposed to her marrying Yusuf because he was Desi. She spent years begging him to reconsider while rejecting other suitors until her father relented. Nora and Yusuf's marriage shocked many and sparked debate in their communities.

It was racist. Most [Syrians] didn't think Yusuf was ... enough of a catch for you to cross the [racial] barrier and marry him, anyway. I don't think they found him to be attractive enough. Well, *astaghfarallah* [God forgive me] ... he's dark-skinned. [If he] was at least a doctor. [To] break that taboo you have to be extraordinary. (Abdullah)

Even though [interracial marriage] may be an option for some, for me ... I don't really understand how an Arab could marry an Indo-Pak or a black and I never could. ... That's how I was raised. (Nayef)

Intra-racist, racial, national and class references permeate the opposition to Nora and Yusuf's marriage. Some claim interracial marriages are justified only if the person in question is exceptional compared to the potential mates within the group. The fact that Nora had proposals from eligible Arab American bachelors and yet chose to marry outside her race continues to puzzle and alarm many.

Other young people admire interracial couples because they perceive them as defying the restrictive expectations of 'cultural' parents and embodying the more expansive possibilities of life in America offered by living according to 'pure' Islam.

I don't care what people say [about my marriage]. Some [girls] were happy that I sort of broke the barrier. ... So, if you have a crush and you're secretly talking to this Pakistani guy [it's] like ... [if] she did it, I can too. If you have *iman* [faith]. (Nora)

Like Nora's, Rashid's account of how his fiancée Shirin came into his life has a strong spiritual dimension.

I just did *hajj* and no one made that call. It's the *real* million man-woman march. It brings tears to your eyes. And when I was in Mecca all the brothers were talking about their wives ... and I was just like, dang, I need to get married! So, you know, I prayed at hajj. ... In December, boom! It happened. ... I've never felt this way ... I love her. I told my parents that I'm going to marry her and they always wanted me to marry a Pakistani and Shirin is black.

Rashid's impassioned account is laced with spiritual and political references. Rashid invokes Islam in ways that undermine cultural endogamy, parental authority and even secular politics. He describes Shirin as the answer to a fervent prayer, and he also locates that prayer at the hajj in Mecca, perhaps the most symbolically charged ritual embodiment of Muslim unity, tolerance and diversity.

Increasingly, voices like Rashid's command the attention of the first generation. Many community members continue to watch interracial couples such as Rashid and Shirin and Nora and Yusuf with fear and wonder. They are curious to see how they will make their marriages work, and how (or whether) they will be able to preserve their respective cultures. The second generation, armed with a scripture-based moral authority, is increasingly defiant of its parents and its critics.

My only criteria is righteousness. They've always stressed the Pakistani thing but I'm like, "See Mom, righteousness, and Shirin wants to practise [Islam]." Shirin said, "Rashid, it don't bother me that you're so-called Pakistani." She uses that word just like I do. "You're Muslim and I love you for your Islam and your right-eousness. You're a hell of a good person." So I was like, "Ditto. Same to me about you, because of your righteousness." (Rashid)

In response to the scrutiny and criticism, interracial couples often stress that only Islam must be preserved in future generations and that it is their primary criterion. Those in the second generation who identify more strongly as Muslims than with a racial or cultural identity will be more willing to 'marry out' (Al-Johar 2005). As these communities grow more racially diverse, interracial marriage will become increasingly commonplace. For most, parental consent is essential and, sometimes, a point of conflict. In these cases, young Muslims often draw on Islam as they engage in intergenerational debates about marriage.

## Conclusion

In this study, marriage serves as a point of entry into broader issues of race and identity construction in four immigrant mosque-based communities. Many young Muslim Americans in these communities identify themselves as 'Muslim first'. They employ Islam to subvert certain racial values and what they perceive as the restrictive expectations of their 'cultural' parents, demonstrating how culture and religion can come to operate in a discursive opposition. As they test the boundaries of what constitutes an eligible spouse, they draw on religious sources that their parents recognize as authoritative in part because Islam serves as a common moral ground between generations that came of age in different cultures, creating a space for negotiating conflicting visions. Long after religion has faded as the cornerstone of social protest against racism in the US, Muslim youth in American mosques are reviving it in debates about race and colour.

## Acknowledgements

I would like to thank Ruth Behar and Erik Mueggler, who served as advisers for the original research project on which this article is based, for their time, guidance and thoughtful comments. Sherine Hamdy, Sherman Jackson, Daniel Moerman and Nadine Naber generously read earlier versions and offered helpful suggestions. I also benefited enormously from the comments of the anonymous reviewers. The Honors Program at the University of Michigan provided funding to cover the costs of my research.

## Notes

1.    Pseudonyms are used throughout the article.

2.    This 'post '65 wave' of immigrants was sparked by the Lyndon Johnson administration's repeal of the National Origins Act, which had restricted immigration almost entirely to northern and western Europeans. The demographic picture of Muslim Americans differs from that of their co-religionists in Europe. Muslim immigrants in Europe are predominantly working class and, in contrast to the black American case, there have not been significant communal conversions of Europeans.

3.    There is a vast and growing literature that documents the varied forms revivalist or reform Islam takes in Muslim societies as well as in the west. Most academic works focus on the militant transnational movements, which are often wrongly taken to represent the revival as a whole. The overwhelming majority of Muslims in the west and in Muslim societies who participate in the Islamic revival are peaceful, though certain purely cosmetic features of their calls for religious reform are shared with the militants, such as the emphasis on universalism and a global Muslim community that transcends any particular territory or society.

4.    Although it would be a misnomer to talk about a Muslim diaspora since Islam, like Christianity, is a universal tradition and is not restricted to a place, the immigrants in these communities are part of ethnic diasporas. The social challenges they face in the US as diasporic peoples inform their understanding of themselves and shape the way they construct and mediate their relationships in their mosque communities.

5.    Other studies document how young Muslim American women invoke a religious logic when negotiating their rights to education, marital choice and divorce (see Naber 2005; also, for a British case, Dwyer 1999); however, in the communities examined here these middle-class norms are usually taken for granted.

6.    This is in sharp contrast to the exaggerated amounts of attention western critics devote to gender inequalities in Muslim communities. Since September 11, debates about gender in American mosques have become more prominent as a direct result of the increased external scrutiny (including the national media) (Grewal 2004).

7.    There is great dispute among academics about the numbers of Muslims in the US, with estimates ranging from as low as Pew's recent estimate of 2.35 million to as high as the oft-cited 2005 Hartford Seminary study's figure of 7 million. Since the US census does not collect information on religion, experts agree that all figures are only 'educated approximations' (Pew 2007, p. 9). There is a corresponding scholarly dispute about the sizes of the ethnic-racial Muslim sub-groups relative to one another, as well.

8.    This study seeks primarily to offer directions for further analysis. There are other, proximate mosque communities in the greater Detroit area that are working or lower middle class, for example, Arab communities in Dearborn or the 'down-river' Desi communities in the neighbouring suburbs. I was unable to include them in this study partly because I found mosque membership to be less fluid over these class lines in contrast to the overlapping membership of the four mosques examined. This limits my scope in interpreting the findings related to class and deserves further study.

9.    See Naber (2000) for a discussion of how 'non-practising' Arabs are often linked to religion in ways that do not represent their beliefs or their sense of identity. Little scholarly attention has been devoted to 'secular' or 'non-practising' Muslims. An important angle for future research would be to compare the attitudes of 'mosqued' and 'non-practising' Muslim Americans towards race, colour and interracial marriage.

10.    The majority of these interviews were conducted in these communities in 1997–8. A smaller set of follow-up interviews was carried out in 2002. Although the topic requires deeper analysis, I did not find significant differences in the attitudes of my informants on issues related to colour, race and marriage within their mosque communities since the tragedy of September 11. Despite the seeming continuities in their attitudes on these intra-community issues, subjects stress that 9/11 and the intensification of Islamaphobia has heightened their sense of being a racially marked and politically vulnerable religious minority in the US.

11.    I borrow this term from Sherman Jackson. For an elaboration on the ways that conversion to Islam is constructed as a rejection of American cultural identity or as an expression of black authenticity, see Jackson (2005).

12.    Similar intra-racist language is commonly found in the matrimonial advertisements in the immigrants' countries of origin.

13.    Although I use this ad to illustrate intra-racist constructions of beauty, a closer reading reveals the ways racial, national and class endogamies are reproduced as well.

14.    Reading pre-modern skin-colour preferences as race in Indian or Middle Eastern history risks simply projecting contemporary, western signs of race backwards onto another time and place. Physical anthropologists have tried to determine whether racial markings, like narrow noses or light skin, were determinant factors in the caste system; however, the numbers of high-caste individuals with dark skin or flat noses in the anthropological record and the intra-caste variation in skin colour throughout Indian history suggests that, even if these factors were the original basis of caste in India, they did not remain so (Sanjek 1994, p. 3). Similarly, historians have amply documented the fluidity of the category of Arabness ('aruba) throughout Islamic history, a boundary penetrated by dark Africans well into the modern period (Jackson 2005).

15.    Whether and to what extent transformations of constructions of difference are rooted in processes overseas or in the integration of Muslim immigrants in the US remains unclear and, to my knowledge, unstudied.

16.    In *Islam and the Blackamerican* (2005), Sherman Jackson explores the evolution of the post-'65 immigrants' racial politics and of their relationship to their black co-religionists. He argues that immigrants' anti-western sentiments remained distinct from black opposition to white supremacy, which engendered an immigrant dominance of blacks within mosque communities. This incongruence may have prevented immigrants from identifying with a positive black identity, in contrast to earlier Muslim immigrants to the US (particularly the Ahmadiya) and Europe.

17. In examining these types of case, scholars must be careful not to conflate class and income level, since parents may seek out poorer individuals from high-status families.
18. The dowry enhancement Sultana references is specific to the subcontinent and should not be confused with the *mahr* in Islamic law, the material gift offered by the groom to the bride.

# References

AL-JOHAR, DENISE 2005 'Muslim marriages in America: reflecting new identities', *The Muslim World*, vol. 95, pp. 557–74

ASAD, MUHAMMAD 1980 *The Message of the Qur'an*, Gibraltar: Dar Al-Andalus

CHATTERJEE, PARTHA 1986 *Nationalist Thought and the Colonial World: A Derivative Discourse?* London: Zed Books

COUNCIL ON AMERICAN-ISLAMIC RELATIONS (CAIR) 2003 *Guilt by Association: The Status of Muslim Civil Rights in the United States*, Washington, DC: CAIR Research Center

DWYER, CLAIRE 1999 'Veiled meanings: young British Muslim women and the negotiation of differences', *Gender, Place and Culture*, vol. 6, no. 1, pp. 5–26

FRANKS, MYFANWY 2000 'Crossing the borders of whiteness? White Muslim women who wear the *hijab* in Britain today', *Ethnic and Racial Studies*, vol. 23, no. 5, pp. 917–29

GLYNN, SARAH 2002 'Bengali Muslims: the new east end radicals?', *Ethnic and Racial Studies*, vol. 25, no. 6, pp. 969–88

GREWAL, ZAREENA 2004 *Imagined Cartographies: Crisis, Displacement, and Islam in America*, Ann Arbor, MI: UMI Dissertations

HADDAD, YVONNE and SMITH, JANE I. 1996 'Islamic values among American Muslims', in Barbara C. Aswad and Barbara Bilge (eds), *Family and Gender among American Muslims*, Philadelphia, PA: Temple University Press, pp. 19–40

HERMANSEN, MARCIA K. 1991 'Two-way acculturation: between individual choice (liminality) and community affiliation (communitas)', in Yvonne Haddad (ed.), *Muslims of America*, New York: Oxford University Press, pp. 188–201

*ISLAMIC HORIZONS* 2003 'Matrimonial ads', Plainfield, IL: Islamic Society of North America (ISNA)

JACKSON, SHERMAN A. 2005. *Islam and the Blackamerican: Looking Toward the Third Resurrection*, New York: Oxford University Press

JACOBSEN, MATTHEW FRYE 1998 *Whiteness of a Different Color*, New Brunswick, NJ: Rutgers University Press

JENSEN, JOAN M. 1988 *Passage from India: Asian Immigrants in North America*, New Haven, CT: Yale University Press

KIBRIA, NAZLI 1997 'The construction of "Asian American": reflections on intermarriage and ethnic identity among second-generation Chinese and Korean Americans', *Ethnic and Racial Studies*, vol. 20, no. 3, pp. 523–44

LOPEZ, IAN F. HANEY 1996 *White by Law: The Legal Construction of Race*, New York: New York University Press

NABER, NADINE 2000 'Ambiguous insiders: an investigation of Arab American invisibility', *Ethnic and Racial Studies*, vol. 23, no. 1, pp. 37–61

—— 2005 'Muslim first, Arab second: a strategic politics of race and gender', *The Muslim World*, vol. 95, pp. 479–95

OMI, MICHAEL and WINANT, HOWARD 1994 *Racial Formation in the United States: From the 1960s to the 1990s*, New York: Routledge

PEW 2007 *Muslim Americans: Middle Class and Mostly Mainstream*, Washington, DC: Pew Research Center

PURI, NARESH 2007 'Beyond the pale?', BBC News, http://news.bbc.co.uk/2/hi/uk_news/magazine/7010885.stm

ROEDIGER, DAVID R. 1994 *Towards the Abolition of Whiteness,* New York: Verso
ROY, OLIVIER 2004 *Globalized Islam: The Search for a New Ummah,* New York: Columbia University Press
RUSSELL, KATHY, WILSON, MIDGE and HALL, RONALD 1992 *The Color Complex: The Politics of Skin Color among African Americans,* New York: Harcourt Brace Jovanovich
SANJEK, ROGER 1994 'The enduring inequalities of race', in Roger Sanjek and Stephen Gregory (eds), *Race,* New Brunswick, NJ: Rutgers University Press, pp. 1–17
SCHMIDT, GARBI 2002 'Dialectics of authenticity: examples of ethnification of Islam among young Muslims in the United States and Denmark', *Muslim World,* vol. 1–2, pp. 1–17
STOLER, ANN 1991 'Carnal knowledge and imperial power', in Micaela di Leonardo (ed.), *Gender at the Crossroads of Knowledge,* Berkeley, CA: University of California Press, pp. 51–101
SWANSON, JON C. 1996 'Ethnicity, marriage and role conflict: the dilemma of a second generation Arab American', in Barbara C. Aswad and Barbara Bilge (eds), *Family and Gender among American Muslims,* Philadelphia, PA: Temple University Press, pp. 241–9
VOLPP, LETI 2003 'The citizen and the terrorist', in Mary Dudziak (ed.), *September 11 in History: A Watershed Moment?* Durham, NC: Duke University Press

# Why do bilingual boys get better grades in English-only America? The impacts of gender, language and family interaction on academic achievement of Latino/a children of immigrants

Amy Lutz and Stephanie Crist

**Abstract**

In the United States, children of immigrants face strong pressures to shift to English. We examine how the retention of Spanish-language skills affects the academic achievement of English-proficient Latino/a children of immigrants and how this varies by gender. Further, we examine the role that family interaction may play in mediating the impact of gender and language on achievement. We find that biliterate boys significantly outperform boys who have little Spanish proficiency. However, for girls there is no significant advantage or disadvantage to biliteracy in terms of GPA (grade point average). Our results suggest that, for Latino boys, the academic advantage of biliteracy is explained by strong family social cohesion. Our results also suggest that, while within-family social capital provides a scholastic benefit from family social cohesion in the case of biliterate boys, strong family ties can also have academic disadvantages.

## Introduction

In the United States, immigrants, and particularly their children, face strong pressures to shift to English. Many immigrant groups in the past, upon arrival in the United States, have begun the process of language shift, transforming their successors into English monolinguals within a few generations (Gordon 1964). Even in recent years, both US policy-makers and publics have increasingly sought to remove bilingualism from schools, government offices and ballots. Research on contemporary children of immigrants in the United States also finds that these children not only learn English, but rapidly shift to English as a usual language (López 1978; Portes and Schauffler 1994; Portes and Rumbaut 1996; Espiritu and Wolf 2001; Alba *et al.* 2002).

Ironically, while children of immigrants rapidly shift to English, research has increasingly indicated that students who maintain high-level proficiency in their parents' mother tongue and speak English well have academic advantages over their peers who shift to English only (Fernandez and Nielson 1986; Lutz 2004; Portes and Schauffler 1994; Portes and McLeod 1996; Portes and Rumbaut 1996, 2001; Rumburger and Larson 1998; Zhou and Bankston 1998; White and Glick 2000). Little research, however, has looked systematically at how the intersections of gender and bilingual proficiency affect achievement for the children of immigrants. Likewise, little research has empirically investigated the impact of parental involvement, another trend of growing importance in the educational arena, as a mediating factor for bilingual advantage in educational achievement. In this paper we examine how gender and Spanish language skills together impact the academic achievement of English-proficient Latino/a children of immigrants in San Diego and Miami. Further, we examine the role that various types of family interaction may play in mediating the effects of gender and language on achievement.

## Bilingualism and academic achievement: family interaction as a potential mediating factor in the enhanced achievement of bilingual students

Research in the ethnicity literature suggests that the impact of language skills on achievement may be mediated by different aspects of within-family social capital (i.e. strong ties and relationships between parents and children). Much of the work on social capital focuses on issues related to social networks or communities. Coleman and Hoffer (1987), however, discussed the concept of social capital in the context of relationships between parents and children (see also an elaboration of this work on within-family social capital in Coleman (1988)). They noted that in contemporary families intergenerational transmission of human capital occurs only when there are strong ties between parents and children.

Linguistic acculturation is an important aspect of family ties and relations in immigrant families. Suárez-Orozco and Suárez-Orozco define acculturation as 'the process of learning new cultural rules and interpersonal expectations' (2001, p. 73). Portes and Rumbaut's (2001) work stresses that the success and psychological well-being of children of immigrants in the United States is linked to the similarity of the

pace of acculturation between parents and children (see also Portes and Hao 2002). They suggest that parents and children with similar linguistic skills will be better off than those whose differential language skills prevent effective communication. Achieving similar levels of linguistic acculturation is difficult because children often have greater exposure to English and tend to learn English more quickly than their parents (Suárez-Orozco and Suárez-Orozco 2001). Suárez-Orozco and Suárez-Orozco have noted that, as children of immigrants learn English, fluency in their native tongue 'is likely to atrophy over time' (2001,
p. 74). In contrast, their parents usually continue to be more comfortable using their mother tongue than English (ibid. 2001).

Linguistic acculturation and within-family social capital are also tied to the second generation's incorporation into the larger society. The segmented assimilation perspective theorizes that there are three potential routes of incorporation for children of immigrants: assimilation to the mainstream, maintenance of an ethnic identity and downward assimilation to a multicultural underclass (Portes and Zhou 1993; Portes and Rumbaut 2001). Downward assimilation is associated with acculturation to the oppositional cultural norms of a native-born underclass (ibid.). Maintaining family ties through an ethnic mother tongue is theorized to play a role in the incorporation of the children of immigrants and to enhance their well-being. In the segmented assimilation perspective bilingualism is a key mechanism for maintaining strong within-family social capital, preventing children's participation in oppositional culture that is associated with downward social mobility (ibid.). The segmented assimilation perspective theorizes that bilingualism among children of immigrants facilitates the social control over these children by parents and community elders *vis-à-vis* social capital in ways that keep children focused on education and away from negative peer influences (Portes and Zhou 1993; Fernandez-Kelly 1995; Portes 1995; Zhou 1997; Portes and Rumbaut 2001). Research in the segmented assimilation perspective suggests that this type of social control, familism and social cohesion within families maintained through immigrant languages to some extent shields children of immigrants from participation in negative aspects of American inner-city youth culture (Zhou and Bankston 1996, 1998; Portes and Rumbaut 2001).

Research from other perspectives also makes a link between language and family relationships. Mouw and Xie (1999) find that the achievement advantage related to bilingualism among Asian youth disappears when parents' knowledge of English is taken into account. Thus, Mouw and Xie argue that bilingualism provides a short-term advantage to children of immigrants whose parents do not speak English, but, once the parents' language skills in English catch up with those of their children, bilingualism no longer offers an advantage. Lutz (2004) suggests that, because biliterate children in the United States are learning mother-tongue skills including literacy in contexts outside the school, biliteracy may be indicative of unusually high levels of parental involvement. Given that a number of studies have found parental involvement to be associated with greater levels of achievement (see, for example, Milne *et al.* 1986; Fehrmann, Keith and Reimers 1987; Astone and McLanahan 1991; Keith *et al.* 1993; Singh *et al.* 1995; Sui-Chu Ho and Willms 1996), parental involvement may explain greater achievement among biliterate students.

To what extent, though, do the impacts of bilingualism and within-family social capital potentially vary by the gender of the child? Waldinger and Feliciano (2004), in their critique of segmented assimilation theory, note that the emphasis on oppositional culture in the theoretical perspective seems more targeted on outcomes of boys, while it may be a less salient explanation for educational outcomes of girls. In this sense, perhaps parental interaction with and social control of boys is more important in deterring an adversarial outlook than it is for girls. Given that both linguistic and family interactions are structured along gendered lines, the question remains as to whether family interaction mediates the relationship between bilingualism and achievement differently for girls and boys.

## Gendered experiences with language, education and family

A significant amount of research has suggested that girls are more likely to maintain bilingual proficiency than boys (Veltman 1981; Stevens 1986; Portes and Hao 2002; Lutz 2006), and that girls outperform boys in various measures of academic achievement and attainment – particularly among children of immigrants (Portes and Rumbaut 2001; Lopez 2000, 2003a, 2003b). The race-gender experience theory suggests that these differences may be related to home and school experiences that vary across intersecting gender and race boundaries (Lopez 2003a, 2003b). Lopez's research suggests that children of immigrants experience gender and race in ways that are 'overlapping, intertwined, and inseparable' (Lopez 2003a, p. 175; see also Omi and Winant 1994). She further notes that '*[e]xperiential differences* (emphasis in original) with race(ing) and gender(ing) processes have important implications for how men and women view the role of education in their lives' (Lopez 2003b, p. 6). Gendered experiences at home and in school may therefore have an effect on students' perceptions of and performance in school.

Previous research has focused on the ways that social control in the home is related to the gender of the child (Dasgupta 1998; Espiritu 2001; Williams, Alvarez and Hauck 2002). Along these lines, Espiritu finds that immigrant parents' restriction of the activities of their Filipina-American daughters is rooted in their authority to decide if their children are '"authentic" members of their racial-ethnic community' (2001, p. 434). Portes and Rumbaut (2001) argue that girls and boys in immigrant families are socialized differently across gender and encouraged to pursue different paths in life, although they do not examine this phenomenon empirically. A particular way that the experiences of boys and girls are structured differently includes the amount of domestic work done in the home. Suárez-Orozco and Suárez-Orozco find that 'immigrant girls have far more responsibilities at home than do their brothers' (2001, p. 79). Orellana found that, among Mexican and Central American children of immigrants, girls discussed 'with helping at home' more than boys, helping at home including work such as cleaning and caring for siblings (2001, p. 382). Similarly, ethnographic research by Thorne *et al.* finds that 'across ethnic groups, girls, like women, do a disproportionate share of housework' (2003, p. 252; see also Goodnow 1988) and are more 'spatially confined than boys' (ibid., p. 258; see also Kibria 1993; Olsen 1997; Zhou and Bankston 1998).

Further research suggests that home-life experiences among Latino/ a immigrants and their children are structured along gendered lines in ways that may impact on bilingual proficiencies (Urciuoli 1991; Hondagneu-Sotelo 1994; Confresí 1999; Toro-Morn and Alicea 2003). Lutz (2006) finds Spanish oral proficiency among Latino/a youth to vary significantly across both race and gender divides, giving support to the notion that linguistic differences may be structured across race/gender experiences both in the home and in other linguistic contexts. Along these lines, Williams, Alvarez and Hauck (2002) find that boys are more commonly encouraged to work outside the home than girls, giving boys more opportunities to use English. Additional research has found that girls translate and interpret for their families more often than boys; this work is structured along gendered lines and varies depending on the context (Valenzuela Jr. 1999; Orellana 2001; Dorner and Pulido 2003). For example, Valenzuela Jr. examined the specific settings where children served as translators and 'advocates' for their families (1999, p. 729). He determined that girls undertook primary roles in acting as translators or advocates in financial, employment, legal and political settings while there was no gender pattern evident in health services settings or in filling the role of 'surrogate parent' to younger siblings (ibid.). Possible explanations for these differences include the likelihood that girls may work in these roles to gain more independence and credibility in the home, giving them access to more power and privileges than they might have otherwise been able to access (Valenzuela Jr. 1999, p. 739). Translation work may also increase the likelihood of bilingualism among girls.

Gendered experiences at home and in the school environment may also affect educational outcomes. Gans' (1982) research indicates that children of Italian immigrants found school to be a feminized environment. Waldinger and Feliciano suggest that this perception persists today, noting that 'the mix of working class boys taught by female, middle-class teachers proves particularly combustible' (2004, p. 381). In contrast, they suggest that girls find school to be a more accepting environment. Waldinger and Feliciano note:

> Young immigrant women of working-class background, however, face a rather different match between communal expectations and broader, societal possibilities. Insofar as both schools and work-places present a more "feminine" environment, expectations are more confirming than conflicting. (Waldinger and Feliciano 2004, p. 382)

Similarly, Patella and Kuvlesky (1973) suggest that girls may have higher achievement levels because of the ways that they are socialized to be obedient, whereas boys are socialized to be more independent. They note that teachers might activate a self-fulfilling prophecy when engaging with young boys whom they expect to misbehave in ways that may negatively affect boys' learning.[1] Valenzuela finds that within 'subtractive schooling' environments – that is, schooling that divests students of cultural resources such as language (1999, p. 30) – 'females deviate less visibly because they respond to the same stimuli within an uncaring environment in a gender-appropriate and therefore less physically threatening manner' (ibid., p. 78). That boys are more likely than girls to react to school in ways that are seen as 'oppositional' may negatively affect their achievement. Brandon (1991), in a study of the educational attainment of Asian-American youth, suggested that boys' lower levels of attainment might be tied to expectations that males work outside the home sooner and work for longer hours. Suárez-Orozco and Suárez-Orozco suggest that, because immigrant parents tend to monitor girls highly (but not boys) at home, girls may view school as a place of 'relative freedom' and this attitude may contribute to greater achievement among girls at school (2001, p. 80). Such monitoring may also preserve mother tongue skills and prevent involvement in 'oppositional' activities.

Gender-segregated networks and gendered experiences in the home and school appear to play an important role in both language maintenance and academic performance. Given this body of research, a question remains as to whether gendered linguistic differences account for differences in academic performance between girls and boys. Further, if gendered linguistic differences are related to gendered differences in academic performance, to what degree is this rooted in differential experiences of family interaction across gendered lines?

## Data and methods

### Data

We use data from the Children of Immigrants Longitudinal Survey (CILS) to investigate differences in achievement across gender, bilingual proficiency and family interaction. Both foreign-born and US-born children of immigrants were included in the study. CILS was collected in two waves in San Diego, California, and Miami/Fort Lauderdale, Florida. The cities were originally selected because 'they represent two of the areas most heavily affected by the new immigration and because they serve as entry points for significantly different groups' (Portes and Rumbaut 2001, p. 23). As a border city, San Diego is a primary site of immigration from Mexico while Miami is a primary host city for Cubans as well as Central and South Americans and Caribbean migrants (ibid.). Thus the ethnic make-up of the sample varies by city.

The original survey was conducted in the 1992–3 school year when students were in the eighth and ninth grades. Students were re-interviewed in 1995–6 during their senior year of high school. The original sample included 5,262 students from families of seventy-seven different national origins. The second wave also includes a parent component, in which 50 per cent of the parents of the original sample were randomly selected for participation.

Our sample is comprised of youth who persisted through the second wave and who can be matched to parent data. Because we are interested in the impact of dual-language skills on academic achievement net of gender and family interaction variables we select only Latino/a children of immigrants whose overall English proficiency is reported as 'well' or above 'well' (N = 1010) to examine the impact of the maintenance of Spanish in addition to English on academic achievement.[2] While Latino/a children of immigrants are a diverse group we believe that what they share is the potential to maintain or lose Spanish. Thus, the process of language loss and maintenance is the point of commonality within this ethnically diverse group.

### Variables

Table 1 presents the descriptive statistics for all the variables used in this analysis.

**Table 1.** *Descriptive statistics for variables used in the regression equations (source: children of immigrants longitudinal study, N = 1010)*

| Variable name | Mean | Standard deviation |
|---|---|---|
| 1995 grade point average | 2.3760 | .88494 |
| Biliterate | .6604 | .47381 |
| Oral bilingual | .2356 | .42461 |
| Limited Spanish | .1010 | .30146 |
| Male limited Spanish | .0535 | .22507 |
| Female limited Spanish | .0475 | .21286 |
| Male biliterate | .3208 | .46701 |
| Female biliterate | .3396 | .47381 |
| Female oral bilingual | .0950 | .29343 |
| Male oral bilingual | .1406 | .34777 |
| Female | .4822 | .49993 |
| First generation | .4554 | .49826 |
| Mexican | .2772 | .44785 |
| Cuban | .3257 | .46888 |
| South American | .1515 | .35870 |
| Central American | .0406 | .19745 |
| Other Latino/a | .2050 | .40387 |
| Married or lives w/ partner | .7921 | .40602 |
| Number of siblings that live w/ respondent | 1.4842 | 1.19888 |
| Parent SES index | −.0358 | .75582 |
| Attend urban school | .3465 | .47610 |
| Family cohesion index | 3.7356 | .98305 |
| Familism index | 1.8106 | .58524 |
| Parental involvement | 3.4030 | .53892 |
| Parent knowledge of English | 2.8282 | .88991 |

*Dependent variable: grade point average*

*Grade point average (GPA)* is the average GPA for high school grades 11 and 12 taken from school records weighted for advanced placement (AP) and other honours classes.

*Independent variables*

*Female* is a dummy variable indicating whether the student is female or male (female = 1/male = 0).

*Dual-language proficiency* was created using a combination of six questions from the 1992 student survey. Students were asked a screening question: 'Do you know a language other than English?' If they answered 'yes' to the screening question, students were then asked: 'What language is that?' They were then asked four subsequent follow-up questions about their language proficiency in that language: 1) How well do you speak that language? 2) How well do you understand that language? 3) How well do you read that language? and

4) How well do you write that language?[3] Because we have selected only students who are proficient in English in the sample, the dual-language dummy variable indicates the youth's level of Spanish proficiency *in addition to* English.[4] We use the following typology based on a similar one used by Lutz (2004):

- *Biliterate* refers to an individual who has high proficiency in English and is also highly literate in Spanish.
- *Oral bilingual* refers to an individual who has high proficiency in English and high oral proficiency in Spanish, but limited reading and writing abilities in Spanish.
- *Limited Spanish* refers to an individual who has high proficiency in English, limited oral proficiency in Spanish and no Spanish literacy.

This typology offers an advantage over the measures of overall language proficiency used in much of the research (Fernandez and Nielson 1986; Mouw and Xie 1999; Portes and Rumbaut 2001) because it distinguishes between different kinds of language skills, namely oral proficiency and literacy, a distinction that has been found to be important in terms of language processing and development (see, for example, Kecskes 1998; Kecskes and Papp 2000).

We additionally use a series of dummy variables with categories indicating both gender and language proficiency. They include: *female biliterate, male biliterate, female oral bilingual, male oral bilingual, female limited Spanish, male limited Spanish*.

### Control variables

Because Latinos are a diverse group we control for national origin. *National origin* is a series of dummy variables that reflect the country of origin of the youth's family. If parents were from different countries, the national origin reflects the mother's country of origin (see Portes and Rumbaut 2001). The categories include Mexican, Cuban, Central American, South American and Other Latino. Mexican is the reference category.

*First generation* is a dummy variable indicating that the child was born outside the US (first generation = 1/US born = 0)

*Parents are married* indicates whether the student's parents are married or in a marriage-like relationship or unmarried (never married, divorced or widowed) (married = 1/not married = 0).

*Number of siblings* indicates the student's reported number of siblings in 1992.

*Family socioeconomic status* is a composite variable created from 1992 survey responses regarding parents' highest level of education, parents' occupational prestige and parents' home ownership.

*Urban school* is a dummy variable indicating whether the youth attends an urban or suburban school (urban = 1/suburban = 0).

### Intervening variables: family interaction

Four family interaction variables are included in the model: family cohesion, familism, parental involvement in homework and parent's knowledge of English.

*The family cohesion index* is comprised of the youth's level of agreement to the following three questions: 1) the family likes to spend time together; 2) family members feel close; and 3) family togetherness is important. There are four possible responses: agree a lot, agree a little, disagree a little and disagree a lot.

*The familism index* is comprised of the youth's level of agreement to the following three statements: 1) if someone has the chance to help a person get a job, it is always better to choose a relative rather than a friend; 2) when someone has a serious problem, only relatives can help; 3) when looking for a job a person should find a job near his/her parents even if it means losing a better job somewhere else. There are four possible responses: agree a lot, agree a little, disagree a little and disagree a lot.

*The parental involvement index* is a composite variable based on the parent's responses regarding the frequency of the following items: 1) how often the parent respondent or spouse/partner talks with the child about school; 2) how often the parent respondent or spouse/partner talks with child about future education; and 3) how often the parent or spouse/partner helps the child with homework.

*Parent knows English* is a composite variable of the parent's overall proficiency in English based on the parent's self-report of understanding, speaking, reading and writing in English.

### Methods

First we present descriptive data from the CILS data on the language and academic characteristics of Latino/a children of immigrants. Then we estimate a series of ordinary least squares regression models to examine the impact of language skills, gender and family interaction on academic achievement. We present the results of a series of regression models indicating the effect of language skills and family interaction on grade point average net of gender and a vector of control variables. Then we look at the combined impact of gender and language proficiency on grade point average and examine whether the effects are attenuated by the inclusion of family interaction variables. Finally, we present a series of regression results that examine whether within-gender linguistic differences significantly affect students' grade point averages and whether these differences are attenuated by the inclusion of family interaction variables.

## Results

Among Latinos/as with high English proficiency girls appear to maintain greater levels of Spanish proficiency than boys. Figure 1 shows language proficiency by gender. Almost 69 per cent of girls are biliterate, while almost 63 per cent of boys are biliterate. Over 26 per cent of girls are oral bilinguals, while 20 per cent of boys are oral bilinguals. A greater percentage of boys, about 11 per cent, have limited Spanish skills compared to girls (about 10 per cent). There are also marked gender differences in grade point average. The mean GPA for English-proficient girls is 2.51, while the mean GPA for English-proficient boys is 2.25 (see Figure 2).

Our results indicate that on average, biliterate students outperform those with limited Spanish proficiency and girls outperform boys. We do not find, however, that these effects can be 'explained away' by family interaction variables. Table 2 presents the results of a series of OLS regressions looking at the impact of language skills, gender, aspects of family interaction and the control variables on grade point average. In the bivariate equations we see that, compared to the reference category, limited Spanish proficiency, biliterate students have significantly greater grade point averages. Females also have significantly higher GPAs than males. Parental socioeconomic status is associated with a higher GPA, as is parental involvement, while familism is associated with a significantly lower GPA. Model 1 includes the primary independent variables and a vector of controls and models 2–5 build on the baseline model by including each of the intervening family interaction variables one at a time. Model 6 includes

**Figure 1.** *Bilingual proficiency among English proficient Latino/a children of immigrants Source:* CILS, N = 1022

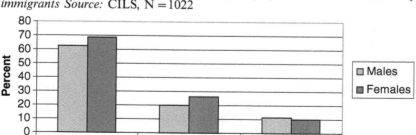

**Figure 2.** *Mean GPA for English-speaking Latino/a boys and girls in their senior year of high school Source:* CILS, N = 1022

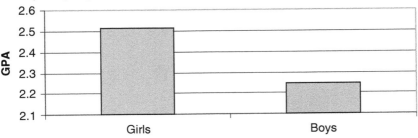

the baseline model and all the intervening variables together. We see that, net of the effects of the controls and the intervening variables, the effects of both biliteracy and female gender on GPA remain positive and significant.[5] Model 3 indicates that familism continues to have a significant negative effect on GPA net of the controls. Although not shown here, an interaction term between female and familism was added to Model 3 to determine whether familism may affect boys' GPAs differently than on girls'. However, the interaction term was not significant. While in the bivariate equation parental involvement had a positive and significant impact on GPA, in model 4, net of the independent variables and controls, it is no longer significant.

Given the impacts of both gender and language skills on students' academic performance, we build on the previous model by examining the combined effect of language and gender on grade point average net of a vector of controls (see Table 3). As in the previous table, model 1 is the baseline model and models 2 through 5 add the intervening variables individually to the baseline, while model 6 includes all the variables. In the baseline model, model 1, we see that females who are biliterate or orally bilingual significantly outperform males with limited Spanish proficiency. Biliterate males have significantly higher grade point averages than their peers with limited Spanish. Females with limited Spanish are not significantly different. However, when we add the social cohesion index as in model 2, the coefficient for male biliterate is no longer significant. This suggests that for English-proficient Latino boys, the positive impact of Spanish literacy is rooted in strong family cohesion. Models 3 through 5 indicate that no other family interaction variables 'explain away' the combined impact of gender and language on grade point average. However, models 2 and 6 indicate that familism has a significant depressive effect on academic performance.

The results presented in Table 4 build on those presented in the previous tables by examining the impact of dual-language skills within rather than across gender categories. Table 4 presents the results of a

**Table 2.** *OLS regression: the impact of language, gender and family interaction on GPA*

| Variable name | Bivariate | Model 1 | Model 2 | Model 3 | Model 4 | Model 5 | Model 6 |
|---|---|---|---|---|---|---|---|
| Biliterate | .252** (.091) | .224* (.092) | .210* (.093) | .235* (.092) | .223* (.092) | .227* (.092) | .222* (.092) |
| Oral bilingual | .088 (.102) | .081 (.102) | .078 (.102) | .086 (.102) | .081 (.102) | .082 (.102) | .084 (.102) |
| Female | .260*** (.054) | .255*** (.055) | .257*** (.055) | .244*** (.055) | .255*** (.055) | .255*** (.055) | .244*** (.055) |
| First generation | .068 (.055) | .081 (.061) | .073 (.061) | .083 (.061) | .085 (.061) | .092 (.064) | .085 (.064) |
| Cuban | −.005 (.071) | −.175* (.084) | −.171* (.084) | −.161 (.083) | −.193* (.085) | −.175* (.084) | −.172* (.085) |
| South American | .072 (.088) | −.142 (.098) | −.131 (.098) | −.143 (.097) | −.165 (.100) | −.141 (.098) | −.150 (.100) |
| Central American | −.285 (.147) | −.435** (.148) | −.417** (.149) | −.446** (.148) | −.459** (.150) | −.436** (.148) | −.449** (.150) |
| Other Latino/a | −.014 (.081) | −.230* (.093) | −.227* (.093) | −.223* (.093) | −.244** (.094) | −.227* (.094) | −.231* (.094) |
| Married or lives w/ partner | .087 (.068) | .044 (.069) | .044 (.069) | .058 (.069) | .045 (.069) | .047 (.069) | .062 (.069) |
| Number of siblings that live w/ respondent | .006 (.023) | −.005 (.024) | −.005 (.024) | −.003 (.024) | −.004 (.024) | −.004 (.024) | −.003 (.024) |
| Parent SES ondex | .176*** (.036) | .233*** (.045) | .228*** (.045) | .227*** (.045) | .223*** (.046) | .220*** (.050) | .200*** (.050) |
| Attend urban school | −.110 (.058) | −.021 (.065) | −.021 (.065) | −.006 (.065) | −.023 (.065) | −.018 (.065) | −.003 (.065) |
| Family cohesion index | .070* (.028) | | .041 (.028) | | | | .048 (.028) |
| Familism index | −.163*** (.046) | | | −.147** (.047) | | | −.154*** (.047) |
| Parental involvement | .104* (.052) | | | | .064 (.055) | | |
| Parent knowledge of English | .061* (.031) | | | | | .024 (.038) | .058 (.055) |
| | | | | | | | .019 (.038) |
| Constant | | 2.180 | 2.035 | 2.418 | 1.973 | 2.098 | 2.010 |
| Adjusted R² | | .058 | .059 | .066 | .058 | .057 | .068 |

*Source:* CILS, N =1010

*Note* *p ≤.05; **p ≤.01; ***p ≤.001.

**Table 3.** OLS regression: the combined impact of language/gender and family interaction on GPA

| Variable name | Model 1 | Model 2 | Model 3 | Model 4 | Model 5 | Model 6 |
|---|---|---|---|---|---|---|
| Female Limited Spanish | .244 (.168) | .241 (.168) | .221 (.168) | .245 (.168) | .244 (.168) | .219 (.168) |
| Male biliterate | .248* (.124) | .231 (.125) | .255* (.124) | .248* (.124) | .251* (.124) | .239 (.124) |
| Female biliterate | .441*** (.125) | .428*** (.125) | .435*** (.124) | .441*** (.125) | .444*** (.125) | .423*** (.124) |
| Female oral bilingual | .440** (.144) | .434** (.144) | .434** (.144) | .439** (.144) | .439** (.144) | .425** (.144) |
| Male oral bilingual | −.002 (.136) | −.005 (.136) | −.005 (.135) | .000 (.136) | .000 (.136) | −.004 (.135) |
| First generation | .087 (.061) | .079 (.061) | .090 (.061) | .091 (.061) | .098 (.064) | .091 (.064) |
| Cuban | −.178* (.084) | −.174* (.084) | −.164* (.083) | −.195* (.085) | −.179* (.084) | −.175* (.085) |
| South American | −.144 (.098) | −.134 (.098) | −.145 (.097) | −.166 (.100) | −.143 (.098) | −.152 (.100) |
| Central American | −.441** (.148) | −.423** (.149) | −.453*** (.148) | −.464** (.150) | −.442** (.148) | −.455** (.149) |
| Other Latino/a | −.235* (.093) | −.233* (.093) | −.228* (.093) | −.249** (.094) | −.233* (.094) | −.236* (.094) |
| Married or lives w/ partner | .053 (.069) | .052 (.069) | .067 (.069) | .054 (.069) | .055 (.069) | .071 (.069) |
| Number of siblings | −.007 (.024) | −.008 (.024) | −.005 (.024) | −.006 (.024) | −.007 (.024) | −.005 (.024) |
| Parent SES index | .230*** (.045) | .224*** (.045) | .223*** (.045) | .220*** (.046) | .218*** (.050) | .198*** (.050) |
| Attend urban school | −.025 (.065) | −.024 (.065) | −.009 (.065) | −.026 (.065) | −.021 (.065) | −.007 (.065) |
| Family cohesion index | | .040 (.028) | | | | .046 (.028) |
| Familism index | | | −.150*** (.047) | | | −.156*** (.047) |
| Parental involvement | | | | .061 (.055) | | .056 (.055) |
| Parent knowledge of English | | | | | .022 (.038) | .017 (.038) |
| Constant | 2.185 | 2.048 | 2.432 | 1.986 | 2.110 | 2.045 |
| Adjusted R$^2$ | .059 | .060 | .068 | .060 | .059 | .069 |

*Source:* CILS, N =1010
*Note* *$p \leq$ .05; **$p \leq$ .01; ***$p \leq$ .001.

**Table 4.** *OLS regressions: language and family on GPA by gender*

| Variable name | Boys (N = 523) | | | | | | Girls (N = 487) | | | | | |
|---|---|---|---|---|---|---|---|---|---|---|---|---|
| | Model 1 | Model 2 | Model 3 | Model 4 | Model 5 | Model 6 | Model 1 | Model 2 | Model 3 | Model 4 | Model 5 | Model 6 |
| Biliterate | .270* | .264* | .282* | .273* | .257* | .264* | .166 | .149 | .174 | .165 | .178 | .168 |
| | (.130) | (.131) | (.128) | (.130) | (.130) | (.130) | (.131) | (.131) | (.131) | (.131) | (.130) | (.131) |
| Oral bilingual | .020 | .020 | .017 | .026 | .012 | .013 | .198 | .193 | .206 | .197 | .188 | .191 |
| | (.142) | (.142) | (.414) | (.142) | (.142) | (.141) | (.148) | (.147) | (.148) | (.148) | (.147) | (.147) |
| First generation | -.015 | -.018 | -.011 | -.015 | -.038 | -.040 | .197* | .183* | .197* | .199* | .274** | .258** |
| | (.091) | (.092) | (.090) | (.091) | (.093) | (.093) | (.082) | (.083) | (.082) | (.083) | (.087) | (.088) |
| Cuban | -.103 | -.101 | -.097 | -.136 | -.113 | -.138 | -.254* | -.251* | -.242 | -.260* | -.286* | -.269* |
| | (.116) | (.116) | (.115) | (.119) | (.116) | (.118) | (.124) | (.124) | (.124) | (.125) | (.124) | (.125) |
| South American | -.005 | .000 | -.013 | -.037 | -.013 | -.046 | -.266 | -.258 | -.264 | -.277* | -.273* | -.263 |
| | (.141) | (.142) | (.140) | (.143) | (.141) | (.143) | (.137) | (.137) | (.137) | (.141) | (.136) | (.140) |
| Central American | -.510* | -.499* | -.535** | -.531* | -.520* | -.554** | -.329 | -.326 | -.333 | -.345 | -.371 | -.372 |
| | (.207) | (.209) | (.205) | (.207) | (.207) | (.208) | (.214) | (.214) | (.214) | (.219) | (.214) | (.218) |
| Other Latino/a | -.124 | -.123 | -.123 | -.144 | -.133 | -.153 | -.340** | -.337** | -.334** | -.347** | -.336** | -.327** |
| | (.145) | (.145) | (.144) | (.146) | (.145) | (.145) | (.122) | (.122) | (.122) | (.123) | (.121) | (.123) |
| Married or lives w/ partner | -.013 | -.014 | .002 | -.016 | -.016 | -.006 | .119 | .124 | .129 | .122 | .145 | .159 |
| | (.102) | (.102) | (.101) | (.102) | (.102) | (.101) | (.093) | (.093) | (.093) | (.093) | (.093) | (.094) |
| Number of siblings that live w/ respondent | .011 | .011 | .009 | .009 | .009 | .005 | -.026 | -.030 | -.024 | -.025 | -.025 | -.027 |
| | (.035) | (.035) | (.035) | (.035) | (.035) | (.035) | (.033) | (.033) | (.033) | (.033) | (.033) | (.033) |

**Table 4** (*Continued*)

| Variable name | Boys (N = 523) | | | | | | Girls (N = 487) | | | | | |
|---|---|---|---|---|---|---|---|---|---|---|---|---|
| | Model 1 | Model 2 | Model 3 | Model 4 | Model 5 | Model 6 | Model 1 | Model 2 | Model 3 | Model 4 | Model 5 | Model 6 |
| Parent SES index | .279*** (.064) | .276*** (.064) | .265*** (.063) | .263*** (.065) | .316*** (.071) | .285*** (.072) | .177** (.066) | .170** (.066) | .174** (.066) | .172** (.067) | .110 (.070) | .102 (.071) |
| Attend urban school | .034 (.097) | .034 (.097) | .051 (.096) | .034 (.097) | .023 (.097) | .040 (.097) | −.081 (.088) | −.079 (.087) | −.072 (.088) | −.082 (.088) | −.059 (.087) | −.049 (.088) |
| Family cohesion index | | .014 (.042) | | | | .018 (.042) | | .062 (.038) | | | | .066 (.038) |
| Familism index | | | −.216 (.067) | | | −.220*** (.067) | | | −.073 (.065) | | | −.077 (.065) |
| Parental involvement | | | | −.097 (.081) | | −.102 (.080) | | | | .027 (.076) | | .000 (.076) |
| Parent knowledge of English | | | | | −.066 (.055) | −.072 (.054) | | | | | .134* (.053) | .130* (.053) |
| Constant | 2.152 | 2.102 | 2.528 | 1.843 | 2.378 | 2.388 | 2.452 | 2.237 | 2.555 | 2.364 | 2.008 | 1.901 |
| Adjusted $R^2$ | .052 | .051 | .069 | .053 | .053 | .070 | .023 | .027 | .024 | .021 | .034 | .036 |

*Source:* CILS

*Note* *$p \leq .05$; **$p \leq .01$; ***$p \leq .00$.

series of OLS regressions examining again the impact of language, intervening family interaction variables and controls on grade point average. The left side presents results for boys and the right side presents results for girls. The results for boys suggest that biliterate boys significantly outperform boys with limited Spanish while those with oral proficiency in Spanish are not significantly different from those with limited Spanish proficiency. Unlike in the previous case, when girls were included in the model, family social cohesion does not explain away the biliterate advantage. Among girls, Spanish proficiency does not appear to provide a significant positive or negative impact on scholastic achievement.

We also see that in models 3 and 6 familism has a significant negative impact on boys' achievement, but it is not a significant predictor of girls' achievement. In the case of girls, unlike boys, parental knowledge of English has a positive and significant effect on academic achievement (model 5).

## Discussion and conclusion

This research suggests that, among English-proficient Latino/a children of immigrants in Miami and San Diego, biliterate students, on average, have significantly higher achievement than those who have little to no skill in Spanish while students with high oral proficiency in Spanish (but not literacy) are not significantly different from those who have little to no skills in Spanish. However, we find that the impact of language skills in Spanish on achievement is significantly structured by gender. Net of a vector of controls girls who are biliterate and orally bilingual and boys who are biliterate have greater achievement than boys who have limited Spanish proficiency. When we examine sex-specific impacts of language skills on grade point average we find that, for boys, biliteracy is associated with significantly higher grade point averages. Among girls, however, there are no significant differences in grade point average across dual-language proficiency categories.

Family social cohesion appears, to some extent, to explain the positive impact of biliteracy among Latino boys. We also find, however, that familism plays a role in depressing student achievement. These results indicate that the impact of strong family ties may depend on the nature of the relationship and the type of familial expectations of students. That students with a greater degree of familism had significantly lower GPAs underscores the notion that social capital is not always beneficial (Ream 2003). Researchers who have pointed to negative aspects of social capital often focus on negative elements of peer culture (Fernandez-Kelly 1995), although Pattillo-McCoy's (1999) work highlights how family connections can, in some respects, have a negative impact. Our research finds that within-family social capital can have negative consequences on academic outcomes. Students with a strong sense of familism may be more likely to be drawn away from schoolwork by family commitments.

This research tells us that strong family ties are important for students' educational outcomes, particularly for boys. However the nature of those ties is just as important as their existence. There is a key difference between supportive and competing family ties in their impact on school outcomes. Supportive family ties provide students with a sense of well-being as well as emotional and psychological support in ways that facilitate students' progress at school. Competing family ties may burden students with a strong sense of family obligation that potentially takes time away from schoolwork. Supportive family ties, such as social cohesion, may bolster a student's progress in school while a competing family tie, such as familism, may impede that progress.

The nature of family relations and their academic impacts also vary by gender and language. Strong supportive social capital is particularly important for facilitating boys' educational success. Our results indicate that strong social cohesion is the key way in which biliterate boys gain academic advantages. This research suggests that biliterate boys are able to maintain strong social cohesion within the family that boys, with lesser skills in Spanish cannot. Thus, for boys linguistic acculturation impedes the maintenance of strong social cohesion within the family relationship with negative implications for boys' scholastic achievement. Because boys typically spend less time and face less monitoring in the home, boys' language skills may be more important in maintaining strong family ties than is the case for girls. As a result of greater responsibilities at home and greater monitoring, girls may have closer or stronger ties to parents irrespective of language skills. Strong mother tongue skills may be necessary to allow boys to have the type or strength of family relationship that girls may maintain regardless of language skills.

These results also have implications for segmented assimilation theory. The segmented assimilation theory posits that bilingualism is key in preventing youth's participation in oppositional culture because it allows for greater social control over youth by parents and other immigrant adults. Waldinger and Feliciano (2004) have argued that this explanation is based more on boys' experiences than those of girls. Our findings support Waldinger and Feliciano's critique as we find that 1) bilingualism is more important in shaping the academic outcomes of boys than those of girls and that 2) family social cohesion helps to explain bilingual advantage only in the case of boys. This stronger family cohesion seems to explain why biliterate boys get better grades than those who maintain lesser skills in Spanish. As is anticipated by the segmented assimilation theory, perhaps the stronger family cohesion maintained through Spanish allows parents to maintain greater social control over boys and encourage boys to excel in school. Likewise, boys' maintenance of strong Spanish skills may allow for greater parental social control that may deter boys' participation in what schools may view as 'oppositional' or 'adversarial' activities, which may in turn enhance achievement at school and ultimately prevent downward assimilation. As is suggested by the race-gender experience theory, these findings underscore the need to pay greater attention to gendered contexts and patterns of acculturation of children of immigrants. Based on this research we might argue that the educational outcomes of children of immigrants are significantly 'segmented' by gender.

Further research is warranted on this topic. Such research might examine the nature of within-family social capital further to look at the mechanisms by which strong family interaction can have positive and negative impacts on scholastic achievement. Such research might also examine the characteristics of family life in a context where family plays a supportive versus a competing role in youths' academic lives. Further research might also look to see whether social cohesion, as a form of supportive family tie, actually prevents participation in oppositional culture which in turn leads to academic success. Finally, other research might also look at whether these results are found in other cities with different immigrant settlement patterns and in nationally representative data.

## Acknowledgements

We thank Roger Waldinger for inspiring this research. We also thank Dalia Abdelhady for comments on a previous version of this article.

## Notes

1.   However, from a different perspective, Williams, Alvarez and Andrade (2002) suggested that stereotypes and gender expectations associated with young, female, Mexican immigrants hinder the achievement of these young women because they experience more negative interactions with teachers and less access to career and graduation counselling.

2.   The number of cases of students whose overall English skills are less than 'well' is too small to include students with limited English as a separate category. Among the parent-matched sample of Latino children less than 2 per cent of the children reported overall English skills that are less than 'well'.

3.   Fishman and Terry have found that self-reported language skills have high levels of validity. In their research, they compared self-reports based on questions that are very similar to those used in CILS to proficiency measures used in linguistic and psychological research on language and find the validity of the self-reports 'tends to be rather substantial and consistent' (1969, p. 643; see also Fishman 1969).

4.   In a very small number of cases this variable refers to a language other than Spanish.

5.    Although not primary to our analysis, we also note significant differences in GPA across ethnic groups, particularly as controls are included in the model. Net of a vector of controls, including socioeconomic status, GPAs for Cubans, Central Americans and Other Latinos are significantly lower than those of Mexicans. This is interesting particularly because, prior to controls, mean GPAs for English-speaking Cubans (2.3869), Mexicans (2.3711) and Other Latinos (2.3685) are strikingly similar, while mean GPAs for South Americans are notably higher (2.4502) and those of Central Americans (2.0673) are notably lower.

# References

ALBA, RICHARD, LOGAN, JOHN R., LUTZ, AMY and STULTS, BRIAN J. 2002 'Only English by the third generation? Loss and preservation of the mother tongue among the grandchildren of contemporary immigrants', *Demography*, vol. 39, pp. 467–84

ASTONE, NAN MARIE and MCLANAHAN, SARA S. 1991 'Family structure, parental practices and high school completion', *American Sociological Review*, vol. 56, pp. 309–20

BRANDON, PAUL 1991 'Gender Differences in Young Asian Americans' Educational Attainments', *Sex Roles*, vol. 25, pp. 45–61

COLEMAN, JAMES 1988 'Social capital in the creation of human capital', *American Journal of Sociology*, vol. 94, pp. S95–S120

COLEMAN, JAMES and HOFFER, THOMAS 1987 *Public and Private High Schools: The Impact of Communities*, New York: Basic Books

CONFRESÍ, NORMA 1999 'Gender roles in transition among professional Puerto Rican Women', *Frontiers*, vol. 20, no. 1, pp. 161–78

DASGUPTA, SHAMITA DAS 1998 'Gender roles and cultural continuity in the Asian Indian immigrant community in the U.S.', *Sex Roles*, vol. 38, no. 11–12, pp. 953–74

DORNER, LISA and PULIDO, LUCILA 2003 'Accessing assets: immigrant youth's work as family translators or "para-phrasers"', *Social Problems*, vol. 50, no. 4, pp. 505–24

ESPIRITU, YEN LE 2001 '"We don't sleep around like white girls do": family, culture, and gender in Filipina American lives', *Signs*, vol. 26, no. 2, pp. 415–40

ESPIRITU, YEN LE and WOLF, DIANE L. 2001 'The paradox of assimilation: children of Filipino immigrants in San Diego', in Alejandro Portes and Ruben G. Rumbaut (eds), *Ethnicities: Children of Immigrants in America*, Berkeley, CA: University of California Press, pp. 157–86

FEHRMANN, P. G., KEITH, T. Z. and REIMERS, T. 1987 'Home influence on school learning: direct and indirect effects of parental involvement on high school grades', *Journal of Education Research*, vol. 806, pp. 330–37

FERNANDEZ, ROBERTO and NIELSON, FRANCOIS 1986 'Bilingualism and Hispanic scholastic achievement: some baseline results', *Social Science Research*, vol. 15, pp. 43–70

FERNANDEZ-KELLY, M. PATRICIA 1995 'Social and cultural capital in the urban ghetto: implications for the economics of sociology of immigration', in Alejandro Portes (ed.), *The Economics of Sociology of Immigrant: Essays in Networks, Ethnicity and Entrepreneurship*, New York: Russell Sage Foundation, pp. 213–47

FISHMAN, JOSHUA 1969 'A sociolinguistic census of a bilingual neighborhood', *American Journal of Sociology*, vol. 75, pp. 323–39

FISHMAN, JOSUA and TERRY, CHARLES 1969 'The Contrastive Validity of Census data on bilingualism in a Puerto Rican neighborhood', *American Sociological Review*, vol. 34, pp. 636–50

GANS, HERBERT 1982 *The Urban Villagers: Group and Class in the Life of Italian Americans*, New York: The Free Press

GOODNOW, JACQUELINE 1988 'Children's Household work: its nature and function', *Psychological Bulletin*, vol. 103, pp. 5–26

GORDON, MILTON 1964. *Assimilation in American Life: The Role of Race, Religion and National Origins*, New York: Oxford University Press

HONDAGNEU-SOTELO, PIERRETTE 1994 *Gendered Transitions: Mexican Experiences of Immigration*, Berkeley, CA: University of California Press

KECSKES, ISTVAN 1998 'The state of L1 knowledge in foreign language learners', *WORD*, vol. 49, no. 3, pp. 320–40

KECSKES, ISTVAN and PAPP, TÜNDE 2000 *Foreign Language and Mother Tongue*, Mahwah, NJ: Lawrence Erlbaum

KEITH, Z. T., KEITH, P. B., TROUTMAN, G. C., BICKLEY, P. G., TRIVETTE, P. S. and SINGH, K. 1993 'Does parental involvement affect eighth-grade student achievement? Structural analysis of national data', *School Psychology Review*, vol. 22, pp. 474–96

KIBRIA, NAZLI 1993 *Family Tightrope: The Changing Lives of Vietnamese Americans*, Princeton, NJ: Princeton University Press

LOPEZ, DAVID 1978 'Chicano language loyalty in an urban setting', *Sociology and Social Research*, vol. 62, no. 2, pp. 267–78

LOPEZ, NANCY 2000 'Race-gender matters: schooling among second-generation Dominicans, West Indians and Haitians in New York City', *Dissertation Abstracts International, A: The Humanities and Social Sciences*, vol. 60, no. 9, pp. 3315-A–3316-A

—— 2003a 'Disentangling race-gender work experiences: second generation Caribbean young adults in New York City', in Pierrette Hondagneu-Sotelo (ed.), *Gender and U.S. Immigration: Contemporary Trends*, Berkeley, CA: University of California Press, pp. 174–93

—— 2003b *Hopeful Girls, Troubled Boys: Race and Gender Disparity in Urban Education*, New York: Routledge

LUTZ, AMY 2004 'Dual language proficiency and the educational attainment of Latinos', *Migraciones Internacionales*, vol. 2, no. 4, pp. 95–122

—— 2006 'Spanish maintenance among English–speaking Latino youth: the role of individual and social characteristics', *Social Forces*, vol. 84, no. 3, pp. 1417–33

MILNE, ANN, MYERS, DAVID, ROSENTHAL, ALVIN and GINSBURG, ALAN 1986 'Single parents, working mothers, and the educational achievement of school children', *Sociology of Education*, vol. 59, pp. 125–39

MOUW, TED and XIE, YU 1999 'Bilingualism and the academic achievement of first- and second-generation Asian Americans: accommodation with or without assimilation?', *American Sociological Review*, vol. 64, no. 2, pp. 232–52

OLSEN, LAURIE 1997 *Made in America: Immigrant Students in Our Public Schools*, New York: New Press

OMI, MICHAEL and WINANT, HOWARD 1994 *Racial Formation in the United States: From 1960s to 1990s*, New York: Routledge

ORELLANA, MARJORIE FAULSTICH 2001 'The work kids do: Mexican and Central American immigrant children's contributions to households and schools in California', *Harvard Educational Review*, vol. 71, no. 3, pp. 366–89

PATELLA, VICTORIA and KUVLESKY, WILLIAM P. 1973 'Situational variation in language patterns of Mexican American boys and girls', *Social Science Quarterly*, vol. 53, no. 4, pp. 855–64

PATTILLO-MCCOY, MARY 1999 *Black Picket Fences: Privilege and Peril among the Black Middle Class*, Chicago, IL: University of Chicago Press

PORTES, ALEJANDRO 1995 'Children of immigrants: segmented assimilation and its determinants', in Alejandro Portes (ed.), *The Economic Sociology of Immigration: Essays on Networks, Ethnicity, and Entrepreneurship*, New York: Russell Sage Foundation, pp. 248–80

PORTES, ALEJANDRO and HAO, LINGXIN 2002 'The price of uniformity: language, family and personality adjustment in the immigrant second generation', *Ethnic and Racial Studies*, vol. 25, no. 6, pp. 889–912

PORTES, ALEJANDRO and MCLEOD, DAG 1996 'Educational progress of children of immigrants: the roles of class, ethnicity, and school context', *Sociology of Education*, vol. 69, pp. 255–75

PORTES, ALEJANDRO and RUMBAUT, RUBEN G. 1996 *Immigrant America: A Portrait*, 2nd edn, Berkeley, CA: University of California Press
—— 2001 *Legacies: The Story of the Immigrant Second Generation*, Berkeley, CA: University of California Press/Russell Sage Foundation
PORTES, ALEJANDRO and SCHAUFFLER, RICHARD 1994 'Language and the second generation: bilingualism yesterday and today', *International Migration Review*, vol. 28, pp. 640–61
PORTES, ALEJANDRO and ZHOU, MIN 1993 'The new second generation: segmented assimilation and its variants', *The Annals*, vol. 503, pp. 74–96
REAM, ROBERT 2003 'Counterfeit social capital and Mexican-American underachievement', *Education Evaluation and Policy Analysis*, vol. 25, no. 3, pp. 237–62
RUMBURGER, RUSSELL and LARSON, KATHERINE 1998 'Toward explaining differences in educational achievement among Mexican American language-minority students', *Sociology of Education*, vol. 71, pp. 69–93
SINGH, K., BICKLEY, P. G., TRIVETTE, P. S., KIETH, T. Z., KEITH, P. B. and ANDERSON, E. 1995 'The effects of four components of parental involvement on eighth grade student achievement: structural analysis of NELS-88 data', *School Psychology Review*, vol. 24, pp. 99–317
STEVENS, GILLIAN 1986 'Sex differences in language shift in the United States', *SSR*, vol. 71, pp. 31–6
SUAREZ-OROZCO, CAROLA and SUAREZ-OROZCO, MARCELO 2001 *Children of Immigration*, Cambridge, MA: Harvard University Press
SUI-CHU HO, E. and WILLMS, J. D. 1996 'Effects of parental involvement on eighth grade achievement', *Sociology of Education*, vol. 69, pp. 126–41
THORNE, BARRIE, ORELLANA, MARJORIE FUALSTICH, LAM, WAN SHUN EVA and CHEE, ANNA 2003 'Raising children, and growing up, across national borders: comparative perspectives on age, gender, and migration', in Pierrette Hondagneu-Sotelo (ed.), *Gender and U.S. Immigration: Contemporary Trends*, Berkeley, CA: University of California Press, pp. 241–62
TORO-MORN, MAURA I and ALICEA, MARIXSA 2003 'Gendered geographies of home: mapping second- and third-generation Puerto Rican's sense of home', in Pierrette Hondagneu-Sotelo (ed.), *Gender and U.S. Immigration: Contemporary Trends*, Berkeley, CA: University of California Press
URCIUOLI, BONNIE 1991 'The political topography of Spanish and English: the view from a New York Puerto Rican neighborhood', *American Ethnologist*, vol. 18, no. 2, pp. 295–310
VALENZUELA, ANGELA 1999 *Subtractive Schooling: U.S.-Mexican Youth and the Politics of Caring*, Albany, NY: State University of New York Press
VALENZUELA JR., ABEL 1999 'Gender roles and settlement activities among children and their immigrant families', *American Behavioral Scientist*, vol. 42, no. 4, pp. 720–42
VELTMAN, CALVIN 1981 'Anglicization in the United States: the importance of parental nativity and language practice', *International Journal of the Sociology of Language*, vol. 32, pp. 65–84
WALDINGER, ROGER and FELICIANO, CYNTHIA 2004 'Will the new second generation experience "downward assimilation"? Segmented assimilation re-assessed', *Ethnic and Racial Studies*, vol. 27, no. 3, pp. 376–402
WHITE, MICHAEL J. and GLICK, JENNIFER E. 2000 'Generation status, social capital, and the routes out of high school', *Sociological Forum*, vol. 15, no. 4, pp. 671–92
WILLIAMS, L. SUSAN, ALVAREZ, SANDRA D. and HAUCK, KEVIN S. ANDRADE 2002 'My name is not Maria: young Latinas seeking home in the heartland', *Social Problems*, vol. 49, no. 4, pp. 563–84
ZHOU, MIN 1997 'Segmented assimilation: issues, controversies, and recent research on the new second generation', *International Migration Review*, vol. 31, no. 4, pp. 975–1008

ZHOU, MIN and BANKSTON, CARL L. 1996 'Social capital and the adaptation of the second generation: the case of Vietnamese in New Orleans', in Alejandro Portes (ed.), *The New Second Generation*, New York: Russell Sage Foundation
—— 1998 *Growing up American: How Vietnamese Children Adapt to Life in the United States*, New York: Russell Sage Foundation

# What is the meaning of 'black'? Researching 'black' respondents

Uvanney Maylor

## Abstract

'Black'[1] is a contested term. Its usage has attracted much academic debate. Issues of terminology are important as they produce real consequences for the lives of those using and/or who are subsumed within particular definitions. A study designed to explore the experiences of 'black' staff in further education provides the impetus for examining the impact of using generic terms such as 'black' on the data collection process and its significance for those subsumed under the category. The paper explores the implications of employing collective terminology in arriving at shared meanings and understandings. It highlights the ways in which the funders of the study and a group of prospective research institutions and participants constructed and in some instances resisted the term 'black'. This is also a reflexive account of some of the challenges and ethical conflicts encountered during the research process.

## 'Black' as a political signifier

'Black' as a political signifier has at times been used to identify those who experience structural and institutional discrimination because of their skin colour; namely peoples of African, African-Caribbean and South Asian origin. Mirza describes 'black' as being:

> About a state of 'becoming' (racialised); a process of consciousness, when colour becomes the defining factor about who you are. Located through your 'otherness' a 'conscious coalition' emerges: a self-consciously constructed space where identity is not inscribed by a natural identification but a political kinship. (Mirza 1997, p. 3)

Mercer (2000) and Solomos and Back (2000) support this notion of 'political kinship'. For Mercer political definitions of 'blackness' are reflective of 'a form of symbolic unity' which arose 'out of the signifiers of racial difference' (2000, p. 210) and similarities in experience of racial oppression and history (e.g. colonialism). Such 'symbolic unity' and a commitment to being 'black' prevailed between the 1960s and 1980s in Britain. During this time, a common identification with a 'black' identity was used positively by coalitions of African, African-Caribbean and South Asian organizations in their struggles against racial discrimination and quest for racial justice (Phoenix 1998; Sudbury 2001; Alexander 2002). Modood (1997, p. 337) contends that these 'antiracist solidarities' were formed as a response to the 'sense of rejection' and 'insecurity' these communities felt at the hands of the white majority. Arguably, the effectiveness of the coalitions among these ethnically diverse groups was based on the fact that they placed greater emphasis on their similarities than on their 'differences' (Sarup 1991).

## 'Black' as an inclusive research category

The use of the term 'black' in research has engendered much discussion about its meaning, appropriateness and the consequences of its usage. Aspinall, for example, claims that the category 'black', while having a precise meaning when used by individuals as a 'self-identifier', becomes 'imprecise' when 'used as a collective term for groups perceived to share some common ethnic attributes' (2002, p. 810). He maintains that when 'black' is employed 'as a term of self-identity' it 'sets it apart from the collective meaning of the term to encompass all minority ethnic groups' (ibid.). This is illustrated for instance, by the selection of the category 'Black British' (introduced in the 2001 Census) by individuals born in Britain and the 'reclaiming' of 'black' by African and African-Caribbean groups (Aspinall 2002) with 'the splintering of the black consensus' (Alexander 2002, p. 553) in the 1990s. According to Parekh 'blackness' became an 'essential part' of African-Caribbean self-definition in Britain following their 'rediscovery of an African...past' (2000, p. 29). Ethnic group self-selection is considered 'a pre-eminent necessity' (Cole 2003, p. 963). However, in trying to comprehend how the category 'black' is used by those subsumed within it, Aspinall (2002, p. 811) notes that '[e]stablishing which terms – overarching or specific – are salient or acceptable to the different ethnic groups is problematic because the choice of terminology is strongly context- or situationally dependent and some people have allegiances to more than one identity'. Aspinall's (2002) contention is exemplified by the following quote:

> I would view myself as a member of the following communities, depending on the context and in no particular order: black, Asian,

Azad Kashmiri, Kashmiri, Mirpuri, Jat, Maril'ail, Kungriwalay, Pakistani, English, British, Yorkshireman, Bradfordian ... Any attempt to define me as only one of these would be meaningless. (Bradford Commission 1996, p. 92)

As the quote above indicates, individual identities are not only complex, but are always in a state of becoming (Hall 1996, 2000). Like individual identities, 'black' identities are 'constantly [being] redefined in the light of shifting public discourse and political necessities' (Sudbury 2001, p. 44).

Nazroo and Karlsen argue that collective terminologies 'are of limited use if we seek to understand the processes that actually produce a sense of [an individual's] and others' ethnic affiliation' (2003, p. 902). When 'black' is used in ethnic monitoring as a broad or headline category it is deemed less useful in reflecting the diversity of the groups it purports to refer to (Aspinall 2002), and can hide important differences (and similarities) between and within peoples encompassed within the term (Solomos and Back 2000). Modood (1994a, 1994b) opines that the lack of recognition of South Asian diversity (e.g. language, religion) in the category 'black' has contributed to cultural differences within South Asian communities being obscured, and as such it 'harms' 'Asians' as it marginalizes/silences their experiences (see also Phillips 2007). As well as negating South Asian experiences, the political definition 'black' fails to elucidate the specificity of the everyday experiences and/or identities of the groups concerned and the ways in which collective identities are differentiated (by ethnicity, class, gender) and/or experience racisms. It ignores also the exclusionary effects of inclusive terminology (Solomos and Back 1996; Werbner and Modood 1997; Anthias 2001).

Phoenix suggests that the reason for 'black' being a contested term is that 'some of those included in it, and some of those excluded from it, seek to change its usage in attempts to redress power imbalances' (1998, p. 863). One of the consequences of groups trying to redress perceived power imbalances is that, rather than acting collectively, they focus on their 'differences' and, by so doing, they work against each other as they act separately and/or in competition with each other. This can be potentially harmful as the power imbalances remain, with 'differences' over-emphasized and further divisions created between these respective groups (Sarup 1991). Brah (2000, pp. 433–4) similarly contends that the generic term 'black' can 'fail to address the relationship between 'difference' and the social relations of power in which it may be inscribed'.

The fragmentation of the 'black' accord witnessed during the 1990s together with the increasing emphasis in recent years on 'difference', particularly between African-Caribbean and South Asian groups, led

Alexander to argue for a discourse that goes 'beyond black' (2002, p. 552), one in which the 'colour/culture divide' is re-thought. Phillips however, asserts that, rather than the death of 'black' as a political category occurring, it has been 'resurrected in the early twenty-first century to challenge racism' (2007, p. 377), but that its usage 'displays all the familiar hallmarks and tensions of inclusion/exclusion' (ibid, p. 392) that existed before. The 're-emergence' of 'black' as a political signifier as evidenced by Phillips (2007) has brought with it the need to review its meaning and relevance for those incorporated within the category. This article attempts to add to this on-going debate by exploring the impact of the inclusive term 'black' on the data collection process. It aims to demonstrate how potential respondents can be excluded, on one level, by the definition of 'black' employed and, on another, choose to exclude themselves from the research process owing to misgivings as to what constitutes 'black'. The article argues for more critical reflection on the effects of using inclusive terms in collecting data.

**The study**

The study, funded by the Commission for Black Staff in Further Education, was conducted between 2001 and 2002. It sought to develop an understanding of the numbers and experiences of 'black' staff (lecturers/support) working in further education [FE]. 'Black' staff were defined by the funders as 'members of African, African-Caribbean, Asian and other visible minority ethnic communities who are oppressed by racism'. An integral element of the research was therefore to identify institutional racism within the sector and the processes through which discrimination and racism operate.

The study consisted of a national survey of all 412 FE and sixth form colleges in England. The survey assessed 'black' staff numbers, their employment position and roles, the curriculum areas that lecturing staff teach in, how 'black' staff are developed, promoted and retained and the type of contracts they are employed on. Recruitment and selection processes were explored together with employment policies. In order to compare and contrast employment positions and experiences of 'black' and 'white' staff, similar data were collected on white staff working in the sector.

Additionally, quantitative and qualitative data were obtained from eight case-study colleges located in ethnically and geographically diverse areas across England, six of which had a proportion of 'black' staff ranging from 10 to 35 per cent[2] and two of which were classified as predominantly white. A questionnaire distributed to all staff produced statistical data on staff numbers, employment positions and their perspectives/experiences of equality procedures and practices at their respective colleges. Interviews were undertaken with 'black' and white lecturers/support staff and managers with responsibility for staffing, staff development and equal opportunities. The intention was also to hold focus group discussions with two groups of 'black' and two groups of white staff in teaching and support positions in each institution. A target of eight respondents was set for each focus group. In two institutions, the 'black' staff attendance exceeded this number three-fold.

The case studies, participants and colleges were given pseudonyms and respondents were assured confidentiality and anonymity. Equality policies were gathered during both the national and case-study research.

## Defining/monitoring 'black' staff

As stated earlier, the inclusive term 'black' was used in this study to refer to members of 'African, African-Caribbean, Asian and other visible minority ethnic communities who are oppressed by racism'. This definition was prominent on the survey questionnaire and the accompanying letters that were sent to each FE institution requesting statistical information. An initial pilot of the questionnaire utilized in the national survey had suggested that the definition of 'black' to be adopted was amenable to the FE sector as no objections were raised. During the national survey it was noticeable that not all of the responding colleges agreed with the definition of 'black' applied as a few noted their disapproval and declined to comply with the survey. Two colleges while having reservations about the definition nevertheless completed the questionnaire, with one submitting the following response:

> I was uncomfortable about completing the survey given the definition of 'black' by the Commission, as I find this very offensive. To state that 'black' means 'members of African, African-Caribbean, Asian and other visible minority ethnic communities who are oppressed by racism' seems to me to be making huge assumptions about the perceptions of any staff from ethnic minority backgrounds as to whether or not they consider themselves to be 'oppressed by racism', and also to be implying that we as their employers are so oppressing them. I hope that, as employers, colleges are not expected to ask their 'black' staff for their views as to whether this definition applies to them, as I do not feel that this would be either appropriate or constructive. (HR manager)

This college found the definition 'very offensive', but arguably they were more concerned that the survey would encourage 'black' staff to question if they experienced racism and/or other inequalities in their working environment. Notwithstanding, objections such as these may have accounted for some colleges with significant numbers of 'black' staff not responding to the survey.

It is not unusual for research to use terms that are not amenable to the institutions or groups being studied. In Carter, Fenton and Modood's (1999) study participants objected to the use of 'ethnic minority' in reference to themselves as the term 'minority' can be misleading (Brah 1996; Parekh 2000; Aspinall 2002). The pigeonholing of diverse groups into inappropriate ethnic categories is likely to have a negative impact on the process of ethnic monitoring (Bonnett and Carrington 2001) and overall data collection. This was evident in the national survey and was further illustrated by staff who declined to be involved in the institutional case study survey:

I think that the definition given of black staff is too vague and unsuitable to a multicultural society.

I do not consider myself 'black' or any other shade for that matter. As far as I am concerned we are all created equal and are equal. I find such surveys, schemes etc. extremely divisive and unconstructive. As such I wish to play no part in this survey.

The importance of self-identification also posed difficulties for colleges when trying to produce accurate survey returns of the numbers of their 'black' staff:

Whilst the survey only identifies one black employee it is not entirely representative. The college has five permanent employees who in terms of their complexion would be regarded by many people as being black. However, only one of these employees has formally identified themselves as black. On questionnaires they have returned to the college they have either chosen not to answer the question or have chosen white. Clearly, the question of ethnic origin is subjective, which leads to a situation where two people from the same ethnic background can legitimately regard themselves as having different ethnic origins. (HR manager)

Hall encourages us to question the 'negative consequences of ... positionality' (2000, p. 152). It seems that the research was not only positioning prospective respondents as 'black', but also asking them to conform to an identity which was viewed by some as false and non-specific and/or 'uncomfortable'. The above comment by a human resources manager suggests that some 'black' employees are fearful of being identified and/or labelled 'black' because they are unsure what the ethnic monitoring information is going to be used for. Such concerns are not unfounded as it has been shown that ethnic monitoring 'can reproduce racism by entrenching racial categories' (Bhavnani, Mirza and Meetoo 2005, p. 1). Anxieties about ethnic monitoring were apparent in one case-study college where 17 per cent of the staff surveyed did not comply with the ethnicity question. It is not known how many of these staff were 'black' or how the 'black' non-questionnaire respondents wanted to be defined, but it is notable that, just as some 'black' staff objected to the definition of 'black' applied, a few white staff also found the ethnic monitoring process problematic: 'It is high time the terms black and white were omitted from ethicity surveys. They are outmoded and useless. (NB: I have mixed race children).'

## 'Black' engagement/non-engagement with the research

The case-study element of the research posed particular challenges in terms of engaging 'black' staff in focus group discussions. The greatest difficulties were encountered in a college with a low proportion of 'black' staff.

Although the case-study research was asking 'black' staff to share employment experiences of a sensitive nature, there was an implicit assumption (on the part of the research team) that the staff being sought for the focus groups would participate because they regarded themselves as 'black', and had opinions on their college's equality practices and their work experiences in relation to this. This assumption was supported by the individual case-study staff questionnaire responses received which had indicated that there were a range of experiences that some staff wished to highlight (albeit anonymously). However, this perception was disrupted in one college when only three 'black' respondents turned up for one focus group and one individual for another. Candid discussions with the sole focus group participant and an individual interviewee revealed a level of uncertainty among 'black' staff at the college about the purpose of the research, and at the same time uneasiness about the meaning of the term 'black':

> When we received emails about you coming to do this, we within ourselves had quite a reaction and some staff felt that it was divisive and some staff felt that we should not be looking at ourselves as black or white staff. Some staff sent an email back in a very clear and positive way, saying, "no, this is why this is happening, we need to address this, the word black means this, this and this".

Staff concerns about the concept 'black' and participating in research with 'black' as a central focus need to be seen in the context in which the case-study research was undertaken. First, it was about people's workplace experiences of equality and, second, the study was conducted in their workplace with senior management staff in some respects acting as gatekeepers. Prior to the commencement of the case-study research, the research team visited each institution and sought the assistance of these gatekeepers in publicizing the research, distributing and collecting the individual staff questionnaires and eliciting respondents for the focus groups. During the case-study visits posters designed by the research team were put in prominent positions in each college as a means of informing staff about the study and attracting focus group volunteers. A letter attached to the staff questionnaire further informed staff about the study. Third, there was an expectation (by the research team) that focus group respondents would be self-selecting and in choosing to attend one of the groups would have their confidentiality and anonymity respected. Despite the research team's best efforts to ensure that senior management staff understood the salience of staff self-selection and anonymity, at one particular institution, some 'black' staff, rather than self-selecting for the focus groups, were insensitively identified by senior management. The quote above referred to staff at this college being informed about the research via college emails. The email request for people to join focus groups was, however, sent only to a list of 'black' staff names selected by HR/management. The email asked that those wishing to attend a focus group inform the personnel department of their availability. This initial request for focus group volunteers led to a series of email exchanges among a group of designated 'black' staff. This exchange continued during the case-study visit. Some of the emails[3] from 'black' staff questioned the selection process for the focus groups, in particular the basis on which a 'black' staff list had been compiled and the definition of 'black' that had been used in doing this:

> I want to know how this list was prepared. Was any foreign sounding name automatically assumed to be 'black'? Such blanket application does not work. For instance, how many people of Chinese origin would consider themselves as black? The Jews are regarded as white, does this mean they all have fair skins? Consider the term 'Caucasian' that refers to an area that has peoples of varying skin colours and shades, and yet 'Caucasian white' is another blanket term used. If I had time I could go on and on.

The personnel department at the institution concerned had sought to identify 'black' staff for the groups through data submitted by individual staff as part of the college's own ethnic monitoring process, requests made to union representatives and management appeals (via email) to designated 'black' staff. Informal discussions with union representatives indicated that, although they were approached by senior management for named suggestions of 'black' staff for the focus groups, they did not offer any, as they did not want to break staff confidences. Arguably, it was not difficult for some 'black' staff to be designated as 'black' by the college, as the numbers were small (as determined by the national survey) and some were known by name because of the positions they occupied; two for example held management positions. Nonetheless, the use of institutional ethnic monitoring and soliciting union representatives to identify potential respondents raises questions of institutional power and confidentiality, and whether or not data that are given for one purpose can be legitimately used for another without further consent being sought. The mechanisms adopted by the senior management staff in question for getting 'black' staff for the focus groups is reflective of institutional racism (Macpherson 1999).

The email exchanges among this group of 'black' non-respondents offer an insight into why institutional (and researchers) efforts to recruit 'black' staff to the focus groups proved fruitless. Some were unsure whether they considered themselves 'black' and what the defining features were. In trying to define the term 'black' one of the email writers went to great lengths (four emails) to outline the historical common struggles that had contributed to the development of 'black' as a political category in Britain. The staff reactions were indicative of some staff not being 'politically aware' (Sarup 1991) with regard to being 'black'. Staff comments suggest that some found the term 'black' ambiguous, seeing it as a colour signifier as opposed to a historical, political and cultural category (Hall 1996, 2000) or even a unifier. A few considered it 'old hat' and irrelevant in the twenty-first century. In disagreeing with its irrelevance, the main email writer made reference to structural inequality in society and the need to 'address existing inequalities'. It was intimated that 'oppressed' groups should be prepared to raise issues of inequality and use the policy process to fight the 'common cause' and to influence and effect change. It was advocated that the 'big bullies' who are 'exercising [their institutional] powers unfairly on the defenceless and the vulnerable' and who are requiring 'black' people to 'prove' themselves should be challenged. In effect 'black' staff were being encouraged to assert their identity as 'black' people and engage in the research as a way of challenging the status quo and bringing about institutional change, but none seem prepared to take the next step and participate in the focus groups. This lack of engagement encourages one to question if it is simply a-political not to claim 'blackness' or acknowledge institutional racism. While the collective 'call to arms' failed, the stance adopted by most of this email group could be viewed as political (albeit with a small 'p') and not just an inability or unwillingness by some to identify with a political definition of 'black'. Notwithstanding, for the non-politicized (i.e. those who 'had not been through the debates around being/not being black' as one interviewee argued) the term was insignificant. This is reminiscent of Bulmer and Solomos's concerns about political definitions of 'black' and identity politics discussions that occur as part of this. They contend that such discussions are 'underpinned by the presumption that one's identity necessarily defines one's politics' and that what is needed is an understanding of 'the way in which [collective] identit[ies] grow out of and [are] transformed by action and struggle' (1998, p. 826).

In an attempt to get a group together to highlight their employment experiences and equality concerns I sent an email to all the 'black' staff on the circulation list that I had received. The email also sought to address staff concerns by explaining how the definition of 'black' had been arrived at and by pointing out that:

> The case study questionnaire, which was sent to all staff, makes it clear that the research team are interested in hearing (via the questionnaire and focus groups) about the employment experiences of *'black'* and *'white'* staff who work in FE. The intention is to use staff contributions to inform policy and practice which is aimed at improving equality for *all* staff nationally in the FE sector.

Shortly after, the following response was received:

> I note the comments from [name of researcher] particularly in relation to this staff circulation list. However, it appears that the discrimination continues, as the circulation has not been revised. I would suggest that this group does not reflect [name of researcher's] intention.

These staff were aggrieved that, by the institutional circulation of 'black' staff only, the process had served to discriminate against 'black' staff. The apparent lack of understanding as to the focus of the research and the intended contributors is worth exploring further. Staff emails suggest that, despite being informed about the nature of the research (as outlined earlier), some 'black' staff had failed to comprehend that the research, while emphasizing 'black' staff experiences, was also seeking the experiences of white staff (and that they too had been similarly targeted). It is likely that this lack of understanding, combined with overriding concerns about being identified as 'black', punctuated reasons for most of this college's 'black' staff lack of engagement with the focus groups. The issue of the 'black'/white dichotomy in this study is particularly problematic as it seemed to have undermined both the inclusion and salience of 'black' and white staff experiences. It is also possible that negative perceptions about research directed at 'black' people accounted for the limited individual 'black' questionnaire completion at this institution: 'When you put it down on black staff, I think most ... just read the headline and they don't go through all the forms, they just see the top line and if it's anything to do with black people it will end up in the bin.'

Phoenix observed that issues of 'race' and racism tend to generate 'ideological' reasons for 'black' non-engagement such as 'what research has done to black people' (1994, p. 53; see also Moodley 2003). Without asking the non-respondents why they refused to take part one can only speculate as to their reasoning. It is possible (as Phoenix concluded in her own study) that some of those who refused to participate may have considered the research 'damaging, rather than beneficial to them' (ibid.), especially as staff questioned if colleges are 'going to treat one better if they consider one black'. Clearly, some 'black' staff saw the research as dangerous because, instead of completing the individual staff questionnaire, an article entitled 'Errors of the Afrocentrists' (by Wortham 1995) was put in envelopes provided for individual questionnaire returns to highlight strength of feeling on the issue. Notwithstanding, this lack of compliance and angst could have been more reflective of disquiet with institutional equality practices as, prior to the agreement as to the involvement of the college as a case study, the college management inferred that 'negative experiences' (presumably encountered in the college) could affect 'black' staff responses.

An unintended, but nevertheless positive consequence of this study is that the college request for focus group volunteers stimulated staff discussion (via the emails) about being 'black' and the relevance of participating in research on such a basis. The study also contributed to a few people thinking about the positions 'black' and white staff occupied within the institution, the reason for this and the fact that such issues needed to be debated more openly: 'We need some kind of platform, black staff to be able to address our own place, where we are ourselves, all of us from lecturers out there to cleaners, all of us need to readdress and redefine where we're at ... higher positions are held by non-black people and why is it?'

One interviewee was hopeful that the research would 'make a significant difference for all staff regardless of ethnicity'. There were, however, no other focus group meetings or email contributions from 'black' staff at this college. Given the sensitivity of the area of focus, this is hardly surprising. It was noticeable from the individual 'black' staff interviews conducted that some of the experiences shared would not have been forthcoming in a group context because of concerns about others knowing about their negative experiences. Some were fearful of being identified through quotes and were keen to ensure they were not misinterpreted; some questionnaire respondents deleted questionnaire identification numbers in order to prevent being further identified. This suggests that more detailed considerations might be required when trying to engage the participation of 'black' staff in research.

## Other research challenges

Finlay argues that exploring challenges within the research process can be valuable, but cautions that 'confessing to methodological inadequacies can be uncomfortable' (2002, p. 212). As well as having a political definition of 'black', a decision was made by the funders to have the research (in particular the case-study fieldwork) conducted by 'black' researchers. This strategy was adopted as a means of aiding the data-collection process because, as Madriz states, 'A facilitator of the same race/ethnicity as participants usually enhances rapport and increases the willingness of participants to respond. A facilitator of the same racial or ethnic background contributes to participants' feeling that the facilitator shares with them common experiences' (2003, p. 380).

However, as was demonstrated in this study and as reported elsewhere (e.g. Phoenix 1994; Bhopal 1995; Song and Parker 1995; Johnson-Bailey 1999) simply 'matching' researchers with the research sample is insufficient to ensure the participation and/or engagement of potential participants from the same prescribed ethnic group(s). Moreover, at some of the colleges involved in this study perceived interviewee/interviewer compatibility did not result in the greater participation of 'black' staff, or 'black' staff being any more willing to share their experiences with the 'black' researchers. This was evidenced where the individual 'black' staff member being recruited or interviewed was the only 'black' person in that position. In these instances there were no assumptions (on the part of respondents) of empathetic shared experiences and understandings with those of the researchers. Furthermore, while the 'black' researchers in this study may have, on one level, apparently shared an ethnic identification with some of those researched, on another, they may not have shared gender, social class or other identity attributes and experiences. As such I concur with Howarth who argues that '[s]uggestions that we can study only those similar to ourselves may bolster essentialistic assumptions that we fit into particular categories of others with the same intrinsic traits and concrete experiences' (2002, p. 22; see also Francis 2001).

*Self-recriminations*

Prior to undertaking this study I understood that being 'black' might mean different things not only to those we seek to research through this category, but also to those conducting the research who consider themselves 'black'. I was experienced enough to comprehend that being a 'black' researcher was no guarantee of encouraging 'black' staff to participate in the research. Nonetheless, I naively assumed that my appeals to individual 'black' staff at one institution would engender their engagement, but these requests were in vain. Regretfully, I internalized these 'black' staff rejections of the study as a rejection of me as a 'black' person. This led me to question whether or not I had presented myself as sufficiently 'black' (whatever this means in practice) to those I had interacted with and/or as someone who was able to connect with others of the same racial background. I queried what else I could have done to appeal to these staff sensibilities of being 'black'. I worried that I was somehow viewed and positioned as part of the college (white) establishment rather than as someone from an independent institution who shared experiences of racism.

Colleagues tried to reassure me that I was not to blame for the lack of recruitment of 'black' staff at the college in question, but it took a considerable amount of time to recover from these feelings of uncertainty. What was absent from these periods of self-doubt was, first, an acknowledgement that respondents 'have the ultimate power to refuse to be involved in a study' (Phoenix 1994, p. 55). Second, that, as active agents, the forms of agency exhibited by the non-respondents could have been as a result of them being relatively 'powerless' in their college (and possibly other areas of their life). Third, the act of non-participation does not constitute the sudden taking of power from the researcher or indicate that researchers are powerless in the research process (see Ali 2006). Indeed I retained power by emailing the non-responders and encouraging them to reflect on and respond to my comments, which they did (see James 2007). Despite this, the difficulties encountered illustrate the complex ways in which power is constructed, negotiated and experienced in researcher/researched power relationships, and supports post-structuralist arguments (e.g. Francis 2001) about power being, at least in part, locally and individually constructed and exercised.

## Discussion

As a political category the term 'black' is open to challenge, as people's identities are not fixed or immutable. Furthermore, individuals have the right to choose how they wish to be identified. The ability of individuals to self-define (and the power derived from this) was demonstrated by a group of 'black' staff who refused to fit into the imposed category and participate in this study. Interestingly, most of the concerns expressed about the meaning of 'black' used in the research and how a list of 'black' staff had been composed at one institution came from South Asian members of staff; this assertion is based on the names that accompanied the various email responses. From this it seems fair to suggest that the staff who had the greatest difficulty identifying with the inclusive term 'black' were South Asian. This would seem to support Modood's (1994a, 1994b) contention and that of other research (e.g. Brah 1992, 2000; Modood *et al.* 1997; Egharevba 2001; Aspinall 2002) that few people of South Asian heritage would define themselves as 'black' or accept the term as referring to themselves. Where South Asian respondents have defined themselves as 'black' this has been done with some difficulty (Sudbury 2001) because of its association with peoples of African and Caribbean heritage.

Phillips (2007, pp. 382–3) reported that a historical practice within the probation service of using the ethnic monitoring categories of 'White/Black/Other' to the exclusion of 'Asian' was responsible for some of her South Asian interviewees rejecting the term 'black'. It is unclear whether, if a separation between 'black' and 'Asian' had been made, this would have been more conducive to the designated 'black' staff in this study participating in the focus groups. Notwithstanding, individual interviews with participants who referred to themselves as both 'Asian' and 'black' suggests that, unlike the South Asian contributors to the email discussion, many had an affinity with the term 'black' or saw it in 'pragmatic' terms (Phillips 2007, p. 385). Thus they did not object to being referred to as such. Moreover, it is possible that these South Asian staff had a heightened sense of awareness of being 'black' (and not just being culturally different – Modood *et al.* 1997) because of the time during which the data was being collected; shortly after September 11 2001, a time when the South Asian community was experiencing considerable backlash.

Arguably, an all-encompassing 'black' category is useful for exploring 'black' staff employment experiences as the 'black' experience is 'fantastically different from the white experience' (Chahal 1999, p. 3). However, it would seem that the study's appeal to 'visible minorities' and those 'oppressed by racism' had little resonance for some 'black' staff as they did not consider themselves 'visible minorities' or necessarily 'oppressed by racism'. Yet colour-based racisms are embedded at an institutional level in contemporary Britain (e.g. Osler 1997; Macpherson 1999; Parekh 2000; Maylor *et al.* 2002; Shields and Wheatley Price 2002). Nonetheless, it is evident that some 'black' people do not acknowledge the existence of institutional racism, as doing so would 'damage their sense of being' (Carter, Fenton and

Modood 1999, p. 55), or regard their experiences as being 'shaped' (Modood *et al.* 1997) or conditioned by racism (Essed 1991). Smith, in exploring such lack of acknowledgement among African-American students, argues that, while being constructed as 'black' provides those constituted as such 'with a 'third eye', that is 'a split consciousness on the meaning of their racial identity', this 'third eye' 'does not guarantee vision of racial discrimination'(2005, p. 446). Rather than a lack of vision, Chahal (1999, p. 3) argues that experiences of racism are 'managed as part of the lived ['*black*'] experience' (emphasis added). Therefore such experiences are seemingly not given any greater credence than other experiences. It is salient that the 'black' staff in Carter, Fenton and Modood's study saw 'racism as a problem for the[ir] institution not just ethnic minority staff'(1999, p. 58), which may go some way towards explaining why some 'black' staff in this research were reluctant to enter into a debate about experiences of institutional racism. Furthermore, although 'black' people may experience racism, their understandings and experiences of oppression are differentiated by several variables, not just ethnicity. Within education 'black' staff experiences are differentiated additionally by their status, role, contract type, promotional opportunities, institutional and geographical location. Experiences, like identities and affiliations (which may or may not be based upon identity), are complexly composed and would need to be taken into consideration when examining the conditions/constraints/challenges under which potential respondents might 'choose' to participate (or not) in a study.

Clearly, the definition of 'black' applied in this study was inappropriate for some of the colleges and staff we wished to research. But, what remains unanswered is what would lead some 'black' staff to complete a questionnaire (operating the same definition) about their employment experiences and, at the same time, discourage others from participating in focus group discussions. Previous research suggests that 'black' staff would have been more inclined to engage in focus groups rather than completing questionnaires. For example, Carter, Fenton and Modood found that minority ethnic staff were suspicious of 'quantitative methodologies as they only scratched the surface of experience and therefore systematically understated the phenomenon of racism' (1999, p. 57) in their institution. Similarly, Dyke and Gunaratnam contend that qualitative data are more effective in capturing 'the effects of racism and wider structural inequalities' (2000, p. 326). Sudbury (2001) reported the term 'black' as being a useful concept for provoking discussion and facilitating shared understandings of oppression. This would seem to indicate the suitability of focus groups (as well as individual interviews) for unlocking 'black' staff experiences of racism and other inequalities. Unfortunately, the email discussants and some other staff did not share any of these viewpoints. This suggests further research is needed which explores reasons for participating/not engaging in 'race'-related research predicated upon collective terms. Additionally, closer scrutiny would need to be given to the factors that might influence some groups to perceive themselves as 'black' in one context, but not in others. Without such an understanding the implications for data collection are likely to be immense.

## Conclusion

This paper has shown that the political category 'black' remains problematic. In this study the term was insufficient to capture the experiences of all those incorporated within the category. The tensions evident in the email discourse and the questionnaire responses (national and case studies) epitomized 'insecurities of meaning' (Gunaratnam 2003) individually and collectively around the term 'black'. The experiences encountered illustrate the need for the use of appropriate ethnic categories that facilitate respondent self-definition and individual research participation. They also underline calls by Bonnett and Carrington for the 'diversity of identities within "black" communities to be recognised' (2001, p. 491) in research.

This research has underlined the complexity of the different discourses associated with being 'black' and the need to problematize 'catch all' categories. Without greater clarity it will be difficult to conduct research that has 'black' communities as a key concern. This study has raised queries about data collection that should be of concern to all researchers, namely how the opting for particular terminologies (without engendering a shared understanding) can negatively impact on the data collection and analytical process. If researchers are to gain access to diverse communities and secure their involvement in the research process, it will be important to use terms that are considered appropriate and acceptable by the communities we seek to investigate. Recognition rather than misrepresentation of diverse groups will facilitate constructive dialogue and lead to an enhanced research process both for participants and researchers.

## Acknowledgements

I would like to thank Professor Carole Leathwood and this journal's anonymous reviewers for their helpful comments and suggestions for this article.

# Notes

1. 'Black' is used throughout in inverted commas to highlight the contested nature of the term.
2. Institutions with large numbers of 'black' staff (as identified from the national survey) were targeted for the case-study research.
3. As researchers we are expected to work to the highest ethical standards by obtaining informed consent when conducting research, but at the time the emails were not construed as data and therefore no attempt was made to obtain consent to use the emails. As such making reference to the content of the emails poses an ethical dilemma. However, the fact that the emails were forwarded to me by an interviewee and I had replied to an earlier email that contained messages sent by the group and their names, and they in turn responded to my email, suggests they were not concerned that I was privy to their thoughts or names. While the ethical dilemma remains, the emails are worthy of consideration as they provide an insight into how the concept of 'black' is viewed.

# References

ALEXANDER, C. 2002 'Beyond black: re-thinking the colour/culture divide', *Ethnic and Racial Studies*, vol. 25, no. 4, pp. 552–71

ALI, S. 2006 'Racializing research: managing power and politics?', *Ethnic and Racial Studies*, vol. 29, no. 3, pp. 471–86

ANTHIAS, F. 2001 'New hybridities, old concepts: the limits of "culture"', *Ethnic and Racial Studies*, vol. 24, no. 4, pp. 619–41

ASPINALL, P. 2002 'Collective terminology to describe the minority ethnic population: the persistence of confusion and ambiguity in usage', *Sociology*, vol. 36, no. 4, pp. 803–16

BHAVNANI, R., MIRZA, H. S. and MEETOO, V. 2005 *Tackling the Roots of Racism: Lessons for Success*, Bristol: Policy Press

BHOPAL, K. 1995 'Women and feminism as subjects of black study: the difficulties and dilemmas of carrying out research', *Journal of Gender Studies*, vol. 4, pp. 153–68

BONNETT, A. and CARRINGTON, B. 2001 'Fitting into the categories or falling between them? Rethinking ethnic classification', *British Journal of Sociology of Education*, vol. 21, no. 4, pp. 487–500

THE BRADFORD COMMISSION REPORT 1996 *The Report of an Inquiry in the Wider Implications of Public Disorders in Bradford which occurred on 9, 10 and 11 June 1995*, London: The Stationery Office.

BRAH, A. 1992 'Difference, diversity and differentiation', in J. Donald and A. Rattansi (eds), *Race, Culture and Difference*, London: Sage, pp. 126–45

—— 1996 *Cartographies of Diaspora: Contesting Identities*, London: Routledge

—— 2000 'Difference, diversity, differentiation: process of racialisation and gender', in L. Back and J. Solomos (eds), *Theories of Race and Racism: A Reader*, London and New York: Routledge, pp. 431–46

BULMER, M. and SOLOMOS, J. 1998 'Introduction: re-thinking ethnic and racial studies', *Ethnic and Racial Studies*, vol. 21, no. 5, pp. 819–37

CARTER, J., FENTON, S. and MODOOD, T. 1999 *Ethnicity and Employment in Higher Education*, London: Policy Studies Institute

CHAHAL, K. 1999 'The Stephen Lawrence Inquiry Report, racist harassment and racist incidents: changing definitions, clarifying meaning?', *Sociological Research Online*, vol. 4, no. 1, paras1.1–2.7 http://www.socresonline.org.uk/socresonline/4/lawrence/chahal.html

COLE, M. 2003 'Ethnicity, "status groups" and racialization: a contribution to a debate on national identity in Britain', *Ethnic and Racial Studies*, vol. 26, no. 5, pp. 962–9

DYKE, R. V. and GUNARATNAM, Y. 2000 'Ethnic monitoring in higher education: some reflections on methodology', *International Journal of Social Research Methodology*, vol. 3, no. 4, pp. 325–45

EGHAREVBA, I. 2001 'Researching an "other" minority ethnic community: reflections of a black female researcher on the intersections of race, gender and other power positions on the research process', *International Journal of Social Research Methodology*, vol. 4, no. 3, pp. 225–41

ESSED, P. 1991 *Understanding Everyday Racism: An Interdisciplinary Theory*, Newbury Park, CA, and London: Sage

FINLAY, L. 2002 'Negotiating the swamp: the opportunity and challenge of reflexivity in research practice', *Qualitative Research*, vol. 2, no. 2, pp. 209–30

FRANCIS, B. 2001 'Commonality AND difference? Attempts to escape from theoretical dualisms in emancipatory research in education', *International Studies in Sociology of Education*, vol. 11, no. 2, pp. 157–72

GUNARATNAM, Y. 2003 *Researching 'Race' and Ethnicity*, London: Sage

HALL, S. 1996 'Introduction: who needs identity?' in S. Hall and P. du Gay (eds), *Questions of Cultural Identity*, London: Sage

—— 2000 'Old and new identities, old and new ethnicities', in L. Back and J. Solomos (eds), *Theories of Race and Racism: A Reader*, London and New York: Routledge, pp. 144–53

HOWARTH, C. 2002 'Using the theory of social representations to explore difference in the research relationship', *Qualitative Research*, vol. 2, no. 1, pp. 21–34

JAMES, N. 2007 'The use of email interviewing as a qualitative method of inquiry in educational research', *British Educational Research Journal*, vol. 33, no. 6, pp. 963–76

JOHNSON-BAILEY, J. 1999 'The ties that bind and the shackles that separate: race, gender, class and color in a research process', *Qualitative Studies in Education*, vol. 12, no. 6, pp. 659–70

MACPHERSON, LORD 1999 *The Stephen Lawrence Inquiry*, Cm. 4262-1.rdr

MADRIZ, E. 2003 'Focus groups in feminist research', in N. K. Denzin and Y. S. Lincoln (eds), *Collecting and Interpreting Qualitative Materials*, 2nd edn, Thousand Oaks, CA, London and New Delhi: Sage, pp. 363–88

MAYLOR, U. *et al.* 2002 *National Survey of Black Staff in Further Education (Final Report)*, London: Institute for Policy Studies in Education, London Metropolitan University

MERCER, K. 2000 'Identity and diversity in postmodern politics', in L. Back and J. Solomos (eds), *Theories of Race and Racism: A Reader*, London and New York: Routledge, pp. 503–20

MIRZA, H. S. (ed.) 1997 *Black British Feminism*, London: Routledge

MODOOD, T. 1994a 'Political blackness and British Asians', *Sociology*, vol. 28, no. 4, pp. 859–76

—— 1994b 'The end of hegemony: the concept of "black" and British Asians', in J. R. B. Drury (ed.), *Ethnic Mobilisation in a Multicultural Europe*, Aldershot: Avebury

—— 1997 'Culture and identity', in T. Modood *et al.*, *Ethnic Minorities in Britain: Diversity and Disadvantage*, London: Policy Studies Institute

MODOOD, T. et al. 1997 *Ethnic Minorities in Britain: Diversity and Disadvantage*, London: Policy Studies Institute

MOODLEY, R. 2003 'Matrices in black and white: implications of cultural multiplicity for research in counselling and psychotherapy', *Counselling and Psychotherapy Research*, vol. 3, no. 2, pp. 115–21

NAZROO, J. and KARLSEN, S. 2003 'Patterns of identity among ethnic minority people: diversity and commonality', *Ethnic and Racial Studies*, vol. 26, no. 5, pp. 902–30

OSLER, A. 1997 *The Education and Careers of Black Teachers*, Buckingham: Open University Press

PAREKH, B. 2000 *The Future of Multi-Ethnic Britain: Report of the Commission on the Future of Multi-Ethnic Britain*, London: Profile Books

PHILLIPS, C. 2007 'The re-emergence of the "black spectre": minority professional associations in the post-Macpherson era', *Ethnic and Racial Studies*, vol. 30, no. 3, pp. 375–96

PHOENIX, A. 1994 'practising feminist research: the intersection of gender and "race" in the research process', in M. Maynard and J. Purvis (eds), *Researching Women's Lives from a Feminist Perspective*, London: Taylor & Francis, pp. 49–71

—— 1998 'Dealing with difference: the recursive and the new', *Ethnic and Racial Studies*, vol. 21, no. 5, pp. 859–80

SARUP, M. 1991 *Education and the Ideologies of Racism*, Stoke-on-Trent: Trentham Books

SHIELDS, M. and WHEATLEY PRICE, S. 2002 'The determinants of racial harassment at the workplace: evidence from the British nursing profession', *British Journal of Industrial Relations*, vol. 40, no. 1, pp. 1–21

SMITH, D. 2005 'These house-negroes still think we're cursed: struggling against racism in the classroom', *Cultural Studies*, vol. 19, no. 4, pp. 439–54

SOLOMOS, J. and BACK, L. 1996 *Racism and Society*, London: Macmillan

SONG, M. and PARKER, D. 1995 'Commonality, difference and the dynamics of disclosure in in-depth interviewing', *Sociology*, vol. 29, no. 2, pp. 241–56

—— 2000 'Introduction: theorising race and racism', in L. Back and J. Solomos (eds), *Theories of Race and Racism: A Reader*, London and New York: Routledge, pp. 1–28

SUDBURY, J. 2001 '(Re)constructing multiracial blackness: women's activism, difference and collective identity in Britain', *Ethnic and Racial Studies*, vol. 24, no. 1, pp. 29–49

WERBNER, P. and MODOOD, T. (eds) 1997 *Debating Cultural Hybridity*, London: Zed Books

WORTHAM, A. 1995 'Errors of the Afrocentrists', *Political Notes, No. 104*, Occasional publication of the Libertarian Alliance, London: Libertarian Alliance, pp. 1–7.

# Index

Page numbers in *Italics* represent tables.
Page numbers in **Bold** represent figures.

9 780415 686327